"Stella Resnick has written an invaluable and insightful book that addresses the important issues of the real relationship and that the mind, brain and body are one. Her well-written approach is positive, and the book highly detailed and well researched. She has a positive and healing vision which successfully integrates couples therapy and sex therapy. Dr. Resnick has brought back the concept of 'corrective emotional experience' and effectively weaves the current thinking about attachment theory and interpersonal neurobiology into couples and sex therapy. I highly recommend this book for anyone interested in relationships."
—**Walter E. Brackelmanns, MD,** *Professor of Psychiatry,*
Director, Couples and Sex Therapy Training Program,
David Geffen School of Medicine, UCLA

"Filled with the integrative wisdom of a seasoned relationships therapist, Stella Resnick's new book weaves together interpersonal neurobiology, somatic awareness of the mind-body connection, and attachment dynamics within the couple. Dr. Resnick's emphasis on present-centered experiential processes highlights ways that therapists can access our own body-based wisdom to help couples drop beneath their words to recognize and learn from the deeper meanings in their non-verbal, implicit communications."
—**Bonnie Goldstein, PhD,** *Lifespan Psychological Center Director,*
Sensorimotor Psychotherapy Institute, Teaching Faculty

"Stella Resnick, author of the classic *The Pleasure Zone*, has done it again! She has created a compelling case for the need to integrate mind and body, past and present, the individual and the relational in sex and couples therapies. Recommended strongly for novices and the experienced therapist."
—**Peggy J. Kleinplatz, PhD,** *Professor and Director of*
Sex and Couples Therapy, University of Ottawa; editor of
New Directions in Sex Therapy: Innovations and Alternatives

"In this new book, Stella Resnick, a highly regarded expert on human sexuality and relationships, uses a vast range of research to create her own model of dealing with sexual concerns and issues. She integrates the

Gestalt approach with those of Maslow, Reich, and even Freud. But what is most interesting is her attention to the *right brain*, describing the large, often unacknowledged role of the sensory, emotional, and kinesthetic in all relationships. At the end, it is her ability to add her wisdom, compassion, and joy to this endeavor, which makes this book so important for all therapists and practitioners."

—**Joseph Melnick, PhD,** *founding editor of Gestalt Review,*
Co-Chair of the Cape Cod Training Program,
Gestalt International Study Center

"Resnick's work on couple's sex therapy is arguably one of the most important contributions to body psychotherapy for couples in recent years. It leverages the experiential wisdom of her Gestalt orientation that is endowed by contemporary neurobiology. This book will help foster embodied intimacy through a contemporary relational approach, and invites us all to experience a greater, more playful and creative form of love."

—**Christopher Walling, PsyD, MBA,** *President,*
United States Association for Body Psychotherapy

"With a laser focus on the body/mind connection, Resnick's *Embodied Relational Sex Therapy* model is an integrated system directing therapists to work with the couple as a living, breathing entity, instead of a problem to be solved. Incorporating cutting-edge neuroscience with Resnick's years of experience and wisdom, this multi-faceted approach situates dyadic regulation where it belongs – between the couple—to create deep empathy and change. This book is a 'must read' for the modern couple/sex therapist!"

—**Alexandra Katehakis, PhD,** *founder of Center for Healthy Sex,*
author of Mirror of Intimacy: Daily Meditations on
Emotional and Erotic Intelligence

"Finally, a professional book has arrived that details the primacy of sexual issues to emotional intimacy! Stella Resnick's latest book, *Body-to-Body Intimacy*, provides couples and sex therapists with everything they need to know about sex but either have been afraid to ask or not known where to get answers. Just as the body is inseparable from the mind, so too is couples therapy inseparable from sex therapy."

—**Terry Marks-Tarlow, PhD,** *author of* Clinical Intuition in
Psychotherapy; Awakening Clinical Intuition;
Truly Mindful Coloring; *and* Psyche's Veil

"This is an important book. Dr. Resnick brings a wealth of knowledge of individual and couples therapy, neuroscience and developmental theory, and brings all of these to her work with couples experiencing difficulties in their sexual relating. The most important aspect of her work is that she does not separate out couples therapy and sex therapy, seeing them as inextricably linked."

—**Peter Phillipson, MSc,** *author of* The Emergent Self: An Existential-Gestalt Approach, *Gestalt Institute of Manchester, UK*

"This brilliant book by Dr. Stella Resnick is a 'must read' for all who are interested in the intersection of sex therapy with couple counseling. Dr. Resnick uses pieces of her personal story and illuminating clinical examples to illustrate her holistic approach to relational healing—an approach which combines the latest findings in the neurobiology of attachment, with positive psychology, sex therapy, and Gestalt therapy."

—**Elinor Greenberg, PhD, CGP,** *Gestalt Therapy Institute of New York trainer, author of* Borderline, Narcissistic, and Schizoid Adaptations: The Pursuit of Love, Admiration, and Safety

"In this well-written, engrossing, and trailblazing book, Dr. Stella Resnick integrates a wealth of data from diverse fields of science into her decades of experience as a therapist to expand upon our understanding of the transformative power of pleasure in achieving sensual intimacy. It is destined to become a classic in the study of sexual and relational dynamics and in the practice of couples and sex therapy across multiple disciplines."

—**Carol Cassell, PhD,** *former health scientist with the Centers for Disease Control and Prevention and author of* Put Passion First: Why Sexual Chemistry is the Key to Lasting Love

"Stella Resnick is a dedicated genius of collaborative exploration. Her new book, *Body-to-Body Intimacy*, creatively integrates neuroscience, Gestalt psychology, life experience, couples and sex therapy. It instructs those seeking relationship to resist the trigger, ignore the knee jerk, live for moments of presence. Dr. Resnick shows how to ride the wave of right brain to right brain communion. She is a pleasure activist who convinces us pleasure can make us better."

—**Susan E. Stiritz, MBA, PhD, MSW,** *President-elect, American Association of Sexuality Educators, Counselors and Therapists, (AASECT), Associate Professor of Practice Chair, The Brown School Washington University in St. Louis*

"Stella Resnick has broken new ground with her alchemical integration of the seminal ingredients that will help our clients to repair the damage from their sexual wounds and seize the opportunity for sexual healing and pleasure fulfillment. Professionals of all backgrounds will find this a readable, thought-provoking, evidence-steeped paradigm shift, worthy of acclaim."

—**Patti Britton, PhD,** *co-author of* Designing and Leading a Successful SAR *and co-founder of SexCoachU.com*

"Stella Resnick presents an integrated, comprehensive, and neurobiologically informed fresh approach to therapy, distilling a brilliant career as a Gestalt couples and sex therapist. Finally, we can stop separating the emotional, sexual, and relational when we practice therapy—transferring people from one provider to another. This is the book the field has been waiting for. Every therapist needs to read this book!"

—**Tina Schermer Sellers, PhD,** *author of* Sex, God and the
Conservative Church: Erasing Shame from Sexual Intimacy

"Sexuality is ubiquitous but it's astounding how little we know about the intertwining of relational intimacy and sexual expression. Shame, insufficient personal exploration, and inadequate training in this vital realm of treatment restrict the therapist in the quest to help others. Dr. Resnick's personal wisdom journey through the deepest realms of the heart, the spirit, the psyche and human sexuality make this a riveting book."

—**Susan Warren Warshow, LCSW,** *Founder, DEFT Institute*

"Stella Resnick's new book, *Body-to-Body Intimacy* gives therapists a powerful theoretical, and skills training model; one that will positively enhance working with clients in couples and sex therapy. Her work deserves serious time for consideration, digestion, discussion, and application. This is a remarkably important work and a reflection of a lifetime journey of discovery."

—**Melvyn S. Kimura Bucholtz, MA,** *Invited Lecturer on Psychology,
Harvard University Medical School; Boston University
School of Biobehavioral Medicine*

"Dr. Resnick's latest book, *Body-to-Body Intimacy*, delineates her approach to couples and sex therapy. She skillfully utilizes research from interpersonal neurobiology, sexology, positive psychology, and Gestalt therapy, to demonstrate how pleasure and body-to-body intimacy can lead to a closer and more dynamic relationship. *Body-to-Body Intimacy* will be a valuable resource for any therapist engaging in couples and sex therapy."

—**Herb Samuels, PhD,** *Past President, The Society for
the Scientific Study of Sexuality (SSSS)*

Body-to-Body Intimacy

This book presents an integrative, growth-oriented approach to therapy with couples that demonstrates the dynamic interplay between partners' emotional issues and their sexual difficulties. It offers a model for relational and sexual enhancement that focuses as much on partners' present, nonverbal body-to-body communications as on their words. Dr. Stella Resnick draws on research from interpersonal neurobiology, sexology, positive psychology, and Gestalt therapy, and shares a rich assortment of therapy vignettes to demonstrate the transformative power of pleasure and how a focus on body-to-body intimacy can heal emotional wounds from the past and encourage greater presence, empathy, authenticity, playfulness, and sexual pleasure between intimate partners.

The therapeutic process is explored in four related spectrums: the Problem-Transformation Spectrum, the Attachment-Sexuality Spectrum, the Pain-Pleasure Spectrum, and the Cognitive-Somatic-Experiential-Behavioral Spectrum. Part I lays the theoretical foundation for the work. Part II examines the early attachment bond between parent and child and its effects on adult capacity for emotional closeness and sexual pleasure. Part III offers methods for resolving painful emotional issues underlying many sexual difficulties. Finally, Part IV describes the procedure for moving from a cognitive reframing of the problem to a somatic focus on the body and tracking present-moment emotional interactions to the repair of relational injuries that nurture transformational change. Also included is a series of process-oriented exercises and a handout that therapists can use in their own practice.

Body-to-Body Intimacy will enable couples and sex therapists to expand their practices and enrich their clients' sexual and relational dynamics. This book also contains valuable information that will be appreciated by anyone interested in a greater understanding of a growth-oriented therapeutic process for couples and what can be achieved together by gaining a deeply loving and sexually fulfilling intimate love relationship.

Stella Resnick, PhD, is a clinical psychologist specializing in couples and sex therapy in Beverly Hills, California. She is an AASECT-certified sex therapist and supervisor who trains therapists and leads couples retreats at Esalen Institute and other centers around this country and abroad.

Body-to-Body Intimacy

Transformation Through Love, Sex, and Neurobiology

Stella Resnick

Routledge
Taylor & Francis Group

NEW YORK AND LONDON

First published 2019
by Routledge
711 Third Avenue, New York, NY 10017

and by Routledge
2 Park Square, Milton Park, Abingdon, Oxon, OX14 4RN

Routledge is an imprint of the Taylor & Francis Group, an informa business

Library of Congress Cataloging-in-Publication Data
Names: Resnick, Stella, 1939– author.
Title: Body-to-body intimacy : transformation through love, sex, and neurobiology/Stella Resnick.
Description: New York, NY : Routledge, 2019. | Includes bibliographical references.
Identifiers: LCCN 2018013901| ISBN 9781138123892 (hardcover : alk. paper) |
    ISBN 9781138123908 (pbk. : alk. paper) | ISBN 9781315648552 (e-book)
Subjects: LCSH: Sex therapy. | Couples psychotherapy. | Couples—Sexual behavior. | Intimacy
    (Psychology)
Classification: LCC RC557. R47 2019 | DDC 616.89/1562—dc23
LC record available at https://lccn.loc.gov/2018013901

ISBN: 978-1-138-12389-2 (hbk)
ISBN: 978-1-138-12390-8 (pbk)
ISBN: 978-1-315-64855-2 (ebk)

Typeset in Minion
by Apex CoVantage, LLC

Visit the eResources site: www.routledge.com/9781138123908

For Alan
My body-to-body healing soul mate whose love has taught
me more about loving than all my research.

For Fritz and Laura
I am forever grateful for their presence in my life and for the timeless
beauty of Gestalt therapy that has inspired so much of my own
growth and creativity

Contents

Part IV
The Cognitive-Somatic-Experiential-Behavioral Spectrum

Acknowledgments

This book has been a unique experience for me in that I have attempted to write something very different from anything I have written before. I decided to research and integrate data from four different fields— neurobiology, Gestalt therapy, sex therapy, and positive psychology— to expand the foundation of the couples and sex therapy that I have been practicing for over four decades. It has been an illuminating experience.

I am particularly grateful for the inspiration I continually enjoy from Allan Schore and being a part of our bimonthly peer study group. The papers we read and our stimulating discussions have broadened my perspective on the power of therapy to change people's lives. I'm especially grateful to fellow group members Wendy Cherry for her support on obtaining research for me and to Susan Warshow for her warmth and friendship.

I have benefited greatly from the able assistance of Raquel Ross who has slogged through an enormous assortment of references and Inara de Luna who runs my newsletters and keeps me on track when I disappear for intense periods of writing.

I am grateful to Nina Guttapalle, the Senior Editorial Assistant for Mental Health at Routledge/Taylor & Francis, for her kind spirit, warmth, and tremendous support during the process of bringing this book to publication.

I also want to thank my close friends and talented artists, Margie and Bob Moskowitz, for their help in selecting the beautiful cover of this book from several excellent designs offered by the Routledge art department.

Some of my closest friends are also colleagues. Carol Cassell and Patti Britton are dear friends and never-ending resources for me in many ways. When I don't know something I need to know they will always steer me in the right direction.

My clients, trainees, and supervisees are truly my greatest teachers. I am grateful for their appreciation and dedication to this process. I have taken the liberty of utilizing some of our memorable experiences together to elucidate this practice. Of course, I have carefully disguised their identities and changed some descriptive details of our work.

Finally, I am eternally grateful for the love and support of my husband, Alan Kishbaugh, a fellow writer. There are days when we go into our respective studies to write and hardly emerge except in passing when we grab a sweet kiss before being off on our own again. He has been enormously patient while I have been absorbed in this book. And now it's done and I'm very ready to emerge from my cave to play.

Introduction: Body-to-Body Intimacy—The Link Between Couples and Sex Therapies

Couples therapy and sex therapy traditionally have been viewed as separate disciplines. Clients follow suit. They assess their biggest problems in the relationship based on what hurts the most, either their feelings or their sexual frustration. Then they reach out to a specialist in that area. If they feel misunderstood and frustrated with their quarreling they will look for a couple's therapist. If a man has difficulty with erection or ejaculation, or the woman with orgasm, or they are both yearning for more affectionate and spontaneous sex they will look for a sex therapist.

What happens is that this schism between couples therapy and sex therapy perpetuates a false dichotomy between emotional intimacy and sexual intimacy. Partners in couples therapy who feel misunderstood and frustrated with each other may also have a troubling sexual issue that they are embarrassed or afraid to address. On the other hand, partners in sex therapy are likely to have unresolved emotional issues related to early childhood and adolescent sexual experiences that block their ability to enjoy sexual pleasure as adults. Without looking into the emotional issues that may challenge their sexual fulfillment an important realm of relational connection is ignored.

Another issue regarding the overlooked interplay between emotional and sexual intimacy is that the distinction between the two specialties—psychotherapy and sex therapy—is often necessary.

Clinicians typically have not been sufficiently trained to talk comfortably about sex except in more formal, clinical, or anatomical terms, which could do more harm than good. Psychotherapists who have not faced their own sexual issues or confronted their own limiting beliefs or biases about sexuality in personal therapy are ill equipped to explore sexual issues with their clientele.

In addition, due to the disregard of the critical role of sexuality in human development in many educational programs for psychotherapists, clinicians may have only the most rudimentary background in clinical sexology. When clients raise sexual concerns, they would indeed be better off referred to a sex therapist.

Certified sex therapists go through an extensive program studying sexuality from many different perspectives, including with regard to their own personal sexual growth. Sex therapy trainings provide opportunities for participants to examine their biases about what is normal and what they might consider aberrant. Human sexuality classes study sexology research including demographic surveys that separate science from myth, social convention, and religious dogma.

Studying sex therapy and talking openly about the diverse nature of sex over a period of time does have a way of making people more comfortable with the topic. In some programs, having the opportunity to address one's own sexual concerns and desires in a group or workshop further lays the groundwork for being more conversant and relaxed about all kinds of sexual practices, less likely to be judgmental and especially, more informed and accepting of sexual diversity. Sexual health is more broadly defined in terms of whatever two mutually consenting adults agree on that causes no harm to either and affords both participants pleasure.

On the other hand, sexuality is more than satisfying sexual activity. Sex therapists may know more about sexual dynamics than they do about relational dynamics, particularly about the profound interplay between early attachment programming and adult sexual interactions. A substantial body of research has shown that early attachment history deeply affects emotional and physiological reactivity in adult sexual encounters and can limit the possibility for fulfilling sexual experience.

Relational dynamics are not just about what people say to each other. Much of partners' most intimate interactions are communicated body-to-body on an implicit, i.e., unconscious, level, largely through facial and bodily micro-expressions. They can look at each other with love, warm eyes, and soft smiles that linger on the partner's face, or their faces may reflect tension, tight mouths, and worried eyes that quickly turn away. Therapists working with couples need to be attuned to the subtle interactive exchanges that hint at each partner's bodily reactions to one another.

While they are talking or just looking at each other, messages are unconsciously and automatically being sent and received by partners nonverbally that can elicit a sense of safety and affection or trigger a reflexive defensive pattern antithetical to sexual responsiveness. These reactions are not just a reflection of unsettled current issues between them but likely to be filtered through the unresolved emotions from each partner's past. Our bodies are neural and physiological reservoirs of all our significant experiences starting in our prenatal past to the present.

Does a woman have a motherly tone of voice with her husband or female partner or conversely does she act like a petulant child? Does a man act like a stern father with his wife or male partner, or like a resentful or passive-aggressive son? I've seen the same family patterns play out in both opposite-sex and same-sex couples. Or do they just act out old sibling, best friends, roomies, or rivals relationships that are non-sexual or supposed to be. Those intimate relational models get laid down both in the brain and nervous systems during the first years of life and can influence our interactions with the ones we share our closest emotional ties for the rest of our lives.

This book is not an invocation to merge the fields of psychotherapy, couples therapy, and sex therapy. There is a distinct and worthwhile role each specialty plays. I do maintain, however, that each specialty, to be a genuine specialization, must broaden its foundation.

For both couples therapists and sex therapists, that means starting with oneself. The professional work is personal, and the personal is the foundation for the professional. It involves getting in touch on an *inner* level with our own body-based emotional and sexual entanglements and experiencing felt-sense methods for processing whatever is revealed.

A Holistic Approach to Sexual Concerns

Human sexuality is integral to the whole person, the brain and the holistic body, and not just localized in the pelvic region. Our sexual selves are neurobiologically intertwined with our emotional development and attachment histories, an important part of physical health and a core aspect of subjective sense of well-being. How individuals' earliest experiences of sexual pleasure are reflected back to them, implicitly and explicitly, by the significant people in their lives shapes their relational neurobiology, their social interactions of all kinds, and most fundamentally, their sense of self.

Whether a person's sexual interest at each stage of life is met with understanding or with shaming plays a significant role in the shaping of our brain/mind/bodily selves. The earliest reactions of parents, siblings, teachers, teenage crushes, and first lovers can have a profound impact on whether we expect pain or pleasure in life, especially with our most beloved intimates.

This means that our approach to sexuality also needs to be holistic. We particularly need to recognize that each person's sexuality is a reflection of his or her early family and sexual programming and their emotional wounds of the past and present. When we treat couples, the emotional, intersubjective relational dynamics between the intimates are essential aspects of their sexual dynamics.

Integrating Embodied Gestalt Therapy and Relational Neurobiology

The methods described in this book to integrate emotional and sexual healing and growth are also an integration of Gestalt and relational neurobiology. I had been a body-based Gestalt therapist with a specialty in couples and sex therapies for decades when I was first introduced to the work of Allan Schore and the theoretical foundations and research in interpersonal neurobiology. That was in 2001, and I have been absorbed in this study ever since. I have especially found this work to both support and augment the present-centered, somatic-experiential focus of Gestalt therapy.

I appreciate the emphasis on the right brain-to-right brain, body-to-body communications that take place between two people in close proximity that can trigger unresolved emotional memories below the level of conscious awareness. These intersubjective interactions are particularly potent reactivations of unsettled issues from childhood. Old wounds and early deficits of parental love and lack of effective caregiving have been long recognized as the healing arena of the growth-oriented therapist. But thanks to a burgeoning literature in the field, the subtleties of our work are now in the foreground.

Therapist Personal Growth: Implicit Communications About Sex

Research in attachment neuroscience and relational neurobiology provides scientific evidence to support the critical aspect of therapist personal growth on clinical effectiveness. This is particularly true when it comes to working with sexual issues. Since the brain and nervous system are programmed in the face-to-face, vocal tonality, and implicit body-based communications with mother or primary caretaker, it makes sense that repairing the early communications about sexuality in therapy will also take place through subtle body-to-body communications between clients and therapist.

These body-to-body communications are implicit, automatic, and not under our conscious control. That means that therapists' repair of our own early deficits and wounds about sex is critical if we are to be capable of communicating the kind of empathy and compassion that sensitive therapy requires when clients bring up sexual issues. One couple came to see me after having been in rewarding therapy with another therapist. But when they felt comfortable enough with her to reveal a lack of satisfaction with their sex life, her anxious reaction and discomfort with sex led them to terminate therapy with her. The woman said she felt guilty bringing up sex, like she had to protect the therapist about her sexual desires the same way she had to protect her mother.

Therapists working with couples' sexual issues need to be able to hear their concerns in a relaxed non-judgmental way despite the fact that clients may share very personal information with us. Listening to a couple reveal intimate details about what works or doesn't work for them in their sexual interactions requires that we have come to terms with our own sexual selves and can be open-minded, compassionate, and informed about sexual health and comfortable with sexual diversity.

Body-to-Body Communication

Whenever we come into close contact with another person, we literally pick up their "vibes." Our highly sensitive sensory receptors pick up all sorts of bodily cues unconsciously and uncontrollably emitted by the individuals we meet. This is especially true for those who enter our personal space. According to research in the science of proxemics, the study of comfortable space between people, personal space is within 1.5 to 4 feet. Intimate space is closer, considered to be from 6 to 18 inches apart.

All present interactions with another person are at some level embodied. We pick up information by how someone looks at us, in whether or not they make eye contact, in how straight or hunched the posture, the tone of the voice, the feel of the handshake or the embrace. As therapists, we're typically more aware than most people of what we're reading in other's bodily expressions. But it is also important to know that our clients are also picking up our own bodily reactions, especially through facial expression and vocal tones.

Our bodies take in a lot more than we even realize, facial microexpressions can occur in nanoseconds, faster than we can consciously recognize. It may be just a flicker of a look in the eye, and we suddenly feel anxious or suspicious. Implicit cues like this can automatically trigger emotions without there being any awareness of being triggered. Thanks to advances in brain research we now understand the significance of this communication, particularly in how it affects our most intimate relationships.

Two people emotionally committed to each other, physically intimate, and living together develop a bodily connection and dynamic between them that is the underlying affective energy sourcing their interaction. Depending on the nature of their interaction, this affective undercurrent can shift with whether or not they take out their daily stresses on one another in how they talk to each other, whether they agree or disagree, whether their interactions generate good feelings like gratitude and appreciation or unpleasant feelings like resentment or anxiety.

If they have a contentious relationship with frequent bouts of anger and fighting, that relationship likely has an energetic dynamic that is often on alert, sensitized to a possible attack. One person may subconsciously read signs of resentment in the other even without the other being in touch with the emotion. Or maybe it's not there, just expected. This is essentially the complex of biological affective reactivity in the presence of an intimate other who has a history that goes back to day one.

Body-to-Body Intimacy

The bright side to this unconscious reactivity is that, imbued with qualities of empathy and compassion, the body-to-body communications between intimate partners have the power to heal. With trust in the love and good will of the partner, the present-centered energetic undercurrent between intimate partners can repair present ruptures and childhood deficits, and build a sense of safety and relational security.

With empathy, caring radiates energetically from their bodies in subtle expressions. It can be felt internally in how they look at one another when they make eye contact. Love is communicated in the vocal tones in how they speak to one another, in the quality of their touch when they touch, and how present and focused they are on one another when they are together. Warmth and understanding is in the melody and rhythmic undertones that accompany their words. Like music, intimacy is a temporal art, it occurs in real time, moment by moment.

Good couple's work, whether initiated because of relationship or sexual dissatisfaction, has the potential to be a deeply powerful therapy, as it can do double duty. Working with a couple's very primal and bodily familiarities, the process can both enhance the current relationship and be a deeply personal developmental repair for each partner.

For the intuitive therapist, the key to uncovering and resolving the leftover emotions, expectations, and stresses from the past that sabotage current relational challenges lies in processing not just the verbal communications but also the nonverbal body-based communications. The work involves focusing on the present-moment cues passing between partners as they interact with one another during couples and sex therapy sessions.

While this book emphasizes expanding the applications of sex therapy, it is also intended to broaden the resources of the couples therapist into the somatic and sexual realms of intimate partner relationships.

Embodied Relational Sex Therapy™

I identify this work integrating couples and sex therapy as Embodied Relational Sex Therapy. It is informed by relational neurobiology, clinical sexology, and psychodynamic psychotherapy, and utilizes the profound methods of body-based, present-centered, experiential Gestalt therapy. For that reason I consider this application of Gestalt methodology to be Full-Spectrum Gestalt therapy (FSG).

This therapeutic process aims at relational fulfillment for intimate partners and occurs along four interrelated spectrums, each of which is explored in four sections. Part I examines the Problem-Transformation Spectrum; Part II the Attachment-Sexuality Spectrum; Part III the Pain-Pleasure Spectrum; Part IV integrates Cognitive-Behavioral and Somatic-Experiential approaches, viewing these methods as complementary along a Cognitive-Somatic-Experiential-Behavioral Spectrum. I think of it as a "full-spectrum approach."

In each of these four spectrums we explore the role played by the presence or absence of body-to-body intimacy in close human interactions—first between parent and child, then between lovers, spouses, and on a nonverbal intuitive, reflective, and somatic level, between therapist and clients. With the overwhelming evidence showing the healing power of body-based empathy, we particularly focus on this critical interactive factor as modeled by the therapist to support body-to-body intimacy between partners in couples therapy.

When the term spectrum is used in psychology, it is often applied to a variety of mental disturbances that occur along a continuum of severity, as in *the autistic spectrum*. In this case, I apply the term *spectrum* to mental *health*, to identify a broad range of related experiences that affect growth, both during child development and during therapy. These experiences involve past and present events in close interactions with significant others, emotions aroused, memories stored, habits formed, insights gained, and much more. All these experiential chains start at one end of a continuum and progressively transition into what is typically seen as the opposite end. Yet as research and clinical practice show, the opposites are actually interconnected—two sides of the same coin. Most importantly, the apparent opposites are developmentally interrelated both in childhood and in therapy.

Neither end of the spectrum exists without the other end, and each is an essential part of growth potential. There can be no *transformation* without the motivation of a *problem*. There is no *sexuality* unaffected by experiences of *attachment*, bonding, and affection. Our greatest emotional *pleasures* often come with overcoming the *pain* of our trials and errors—from solving puzzles to facing a fear and finding courage, to opening a heart that has been closed. In therapy, a client's new *cognitive* model of problem-as-opportunity can encourage and support a focus on the more difficult *somatic-experiential* work. And ultimately, the *behavioral* goals made manifest in the presenting problems can only be reached through the present-moment mindfulness that comes with experiential presence and practice.

Part I, on the **Problem-Transformation Spectrum** provides the theoretical foundations in three chapters of the focus of this work: body-to-body intimacy. Chapter 1, "The Problem," starts with a look at how the presenting problem is a reflection of the impasse between partners and how to assess the impasse at the level of their body-to-body interaction before we can know how to move through it. Chapter 2, "Transitional Resources," looks at how people change in therapy and some of the experiential processes we can explore. Chapter 3, "Transformation," takes a broad view on the great potential for sexuality-focused therapy to unblock arrested emotional development and reactivate a developmental growth spurt that can transform lives.

Part II on the **Attachment-Sexuality Spectrum** addresses the fact that babies are born sexual. Chapter 4, "Attachment," looks at the sensory and emotional interconnections between the development of the early attachment bond between parent and child, while at the same time the parents' reactions to their baby, as a sexual infant, child, and adolescent affects their sexual development. Chapter 5, "Sexuality," examines the effects of childhood and adolescent developmental history on adult sexual pleasure.

Part III on the **Pain-Pleasure Spectrum** starts with Chapter 6, "Pain," and explores the unresolved painful emotional issues underlying many kinds of sexual disturbances. It offers methods for getting to the core of those issues and resolving them through "corrective emotional experiences" both with a focus on the individual as well as on the couple. Chapter 7, "Pleasure," delves into the power of positive emotions to transform individuals and a couple's emotional and sexual life together. Pleasurable experience is shown to broaden the scope of personal attention, enhance mental and physical health, vitality, social resources, and a couple's spiritual connection.

In Part IV the entire step-by-step process of Embodied Relational Sex Therapy is summarized as **The Cognitive-Somatic-Experiential-Behavioral Spectrum**. Chapter 8 describes the procedure moving from a *cognitive* reframing of the problem as a developmental opportunity, to a *somatic* focus on the body and the senses, to observing and describing inner emotional reactions and tracking the couple's present-moment *experiential* interactions. The progressive therapeutic process moves toward embodying the *behavioral* and sexual goals originally sought through therapy.

Sexuality Is at the Core of the Self

This book reflects my commitment to advancing the professional recognition of sexuality as a core factor in human development in the fields of mental health and psychotherapy, and that sexual healing and education can reach into an individual's earliest programming and heal more than sex. Sexuality is a systemic and integral part of the whole person and the holistic body. Sex is not an anatomically localized and contained aspect of the self. A parent's subtle signs of displeasure at witnessing a baby joyfully touching his or her genitals, or shaming a sexually curious child, can have a lifelong influence on that individual's ability to take pleasure in everyday living as an adult and not just in sexual intimacy. In this mission, I stand with Sigmund Freud who insisted on the significant role played by infantile and childhood sexuality in the development of the human psyche. *Body-to-Body Intimacy* is my attempt to put it all together.

Getting Personal

This book is a neurobiological, sexological, embodied relational, Gestalt approach to couples and sex therapy. It is all that and more because it is a summation of my own personal and professional history, inspired by my yearning to live my life not as the woman I was programmed to be, but as the woman I wanted to be.

As a graduate student in clinical psychology at Indiana University, I knew that if I were to become a therapist, I would need to be in therapy myself. In fact, I had no doubt I could benefit from good therapy.

I had an unhappy childhood growing up in a one-bedroom apartment in the working class neighborhood of Bensonhurst in Brooklyn. My parents separated and were divorced when I was five years old. I didn't have much of a connection with my mother whom I remember mostly as screaming at my father and me. I don't recall her ever hugging me or playing with me. I adored my father who always stuck up for me when my mother yelled at me. When my mother demanded that my father pack up and leave, he came to say goodbye to me and I pleaded that he take me with him. He said he couldn't but he would always be there for me. And he was there—for or a couple of hours every other weekend. With him gone I felt terribly alone and lonely.

Three years later my mother married a man who resented that she had a child by another man. She still yelled at me, only now she complained about me and her life to my stepfather who took out his frustrations on me. He would become livid and lunge at me, tossing me against walls and slapping me hard on the head and face. I never let him see me cry. After eight years of abuse, I had enough. One Saturday afternoon as he sat on the living room sofa, I sat down beside him. I spoke slowly and softly, with venom in my throat. I said that if he ever hit me again, one night while he slept, I would get the big knife from the kitchen and drive it through his ugly heart. He never looked up as I spoke, and he never hit me again.

Many years later at a conference on child abuse, a speaker announced that a number of children who stop the abuse do so by threatening to kill the abuser. I thought I was unique in discovering that desperate solution. I found it touching to know I was merely part of a statistic.

At no time did I tell my father about the beatings. I was afraid he would challenge my stepfather, who was bigger than my father, and could be hurt. Feeling lonely and anxious and not knowing how to reach out for support made me tough and determined, and became a way of life.

At Indiana University I signed up for therapy at the counseling center and was assigned to a therapist who sat behind a desk in a stark room while I sat on a metal folding chair facing him. He asked me a lot of questions and I answered as best I could, but I just seemed to be complaining about my past. I don't remember having much of an emotional connection with him. The therapy hour often consisted of long silences between us.

Finally, I found therapy too boring for words, literally, and I dropped out. At that point, I decided to go ahead with the PhD in clinical psychology but felt that teaching and an academic life would be much more stimulating. I was accepted for an internship at the Langley Porter Neuropsychiatric Institute, at the University of California Medical Center in San Francisco, and I fell in love with California. In 1966, I started my professional career as an assistant professor of psychology at San Diego State College.

While in San Diego I began to dabble in the therapy workshops that became popular during the time. I was particularly attracted to the creativity and liveliness of Gestalt therapy. Two years later, I transferred to San Jose State College so I could live in my beloved San Francisco again, in what was then the hub of the Human Potentials Movement. I got to know the Gestalt community there, and I became particularly eager to experience Gestalt work with Fritz Perls.

When I finally got the chance to be in a weekend professional seminar with Fritz, the experience changed my life. I don't remember what I actually worked on. I only remember that I experienced being present with myself, inside my inner being, in the moment, and open to whatever I found in there. My true self had real value. My insides were of value, not something to avoid but to study. I had never experienced myself like that before. I was hooked.

I followed Fritz for a few months on his tour offering professional workshops around the country. One day as he was ending his trainings in the States, he approached me and invited me to become a trainee at his Gestalt Residential Training Center in Canada. After serious deliberation over giving up the security of being on the tenure track at San Jose State, I took a leap of faith, quit teaching at the end of the semester, and moved to Lake Cowichan on Vancouver Island. I was there with about 30 other professionals for five months to do the personal work and professional training to become a Gestalt therapist. We all left Cowichan for a winter break. A few months later, on March 14, 1970, Fritz Perls died.

In 1971, I had the opportunity to live for several months at Esalen Institute in Big Sur, California, to do Gestalt trainings for staff and the work study program. In return I was able to be a participant in groups with leading figures in the Human Potentials Movement that was flourishing at that time. Later that year I was invited to join the training faculty at the San Francisco Gestalt Institute, and my development as a Gestalt therapist continued as I taught and co-led weekly training groups with experienced Gestalt trainers. Each had his or her own style while adhering to the present-centered, body-based, whole person principles of Gestalt therapy. All our training groups were run as therapy groups with didactic interludes. This is a model I continue to follow. I consider it the most in-depth, comprehensive approach to launch new therapists with the empathy, personal integration, and professional skill-set to do imaginative growth-oriented therapy.

From those earliest experiences in Gestalt, I began to widen my personal studies and professional trainings. I felt drawn to different approaches that were driven by my desire to grapple with my own continued feelings of loneliness and anxiety. I had achieved a level of professional and financial success beyond anything I had imagined as a young teen hanging out on street corners in Bensonhurst. I had managed to get from there to accomplish a top-notch education and professional standing. Yet, more than anything I yearned for lasting love—and that seemed as elusive as ever. I kept falling in love with the wrong person and leaving every man I loved.

My professional studies continued driven by my own needs for personal growth. As an intern at Langley Porter I was living in Haight-Ashbury during the historic era that became known as the Sexual Revolution. I took advantage of the time to learn more about sex personally and professionally, and that led to my studies in human sexuality. In my practice I began to specialize in couples work and sex therapy in the context of a loving relationship, which is what I personally craved. I figured my clients and I would learn from each other.

In Gestalt groups, I learned to notice when people held their breath in pain and to encourage them to take a breath. Yet, I had my own breathing problems. Ever since I was a child, there were times when I couldn't get a deep enough breath. Those bouts of breathlessness continued to plague me as an adult. My spells of gasping for breath impelled me to study breath work and sensory awareness with Magda Proskauer and Charlotte Selver, both students of Elsa Gindler, the original pioneer in experiential breath work.

Finally, I got tired of being unhappy, alone, and lonely. I had tried to make friends with my mother before she died and again, my stepfather stood between us. I went into a deep mourning over never having a loving connection with my mother. I decided that the only way to come to terms with my aloneness was to learn to live alone. I found a cabin in the woods in Woodstock, N.Y., and went into retreat for a year. I had been studying Tibetan Buddhism and Vipassana meditation and practicing yoga for many years. Those practices, reading, writing, walking in the woods, and just daily chores filled my time.

In the simple lifestyle alone with myself, I discovered that I wasn't happy because I didn't know how to be happy. I didn't know how to be present to the easy pleasures of everyday life. In the background of all my activity, my mind was constantly churning, complaining, and bemoaning my sorry fate. But when I looked around I was in a charming little cottage in a beautiful spot in the country. From my desk where I wrote, I could look out the window and watch the birds at the feeder and catch an occasional deer at the salt lick I left on a tree stump. I could step out my back door and walk in the woods. Or I could go out my front door and ride my bike on the road, past meadows and farms with horses grazing and with the Catskill Mountains all around me. What was I feeling bad about?

That's when I began my research into pleasure, the health science of psychoneuroimmunology (PNI), why pleasure is so healthy, how so many of us have been trained to resist the core pleasures that are essential for emotional and physical well-being. Using myself as a subject I studied how I, and many of my clients, had learned to hold back from feeling as good as we can. Using the tools I had learned in all my studies, I focused in on Wilhelm Reich's notion of pleasure-resistance and how to use the breath to let go and to embrace life's joys. *The Pleasure Zone* (1997) became my first book.

My personal growth-motivated studies have worked out for me. My practice grew in a specialization I find endlessly inspiring and rewarding. And I met and married the love of my life and we've been happily together over 35 years.

I discovered neurobiology in 2001. I had just joined the faculty of Santa Barbara Graduate Institute, which was offering a four-year graduate training program and PhD in somatic psychology and body-based therapeutic approaches. One afternoon, I attended an invited lecture by Allan Schore on the Interpersonal Neurobiology of Attachment Theory.

As I sat and followed Schore's exposition about how our brains and nervous systems are programmed during our earliest relations with primary caretakers and what makes those experiences so indelible, my heart began to race with excitement. It made sense to me on so many levels, particularly as I thought about myself as a baby and young child developing out of mother's incapacity to be a mother, a devoted but limited father, a witness to violent fights between them, and then my stepfather's ominous presence.

Gestalt therapy had a profound method for treatment, and a theoretical foundation based in the wisdom of a humanistic and existential philosophy that I valued highly. Now the neuroscience of attachment filled in the developmental blanks that explained why our earliest experiences are so resistant to change. In particular, the studies showed why a body-based experiential approach like Gestalt therapy and other somatic approaches are absolutely essential in order to change those early-forming emotional and behavioral patterns and restart a developmental process. Once again I was hooked. I wrote my second book, *The Heart of Desire* (2012), on what I knew so far to integrate neurobiology, relationships, sexuality, and Gestalt.

In the years since, I have learned much more and I remain inspired by relational neurobiology especially, the groundbreaking work of Allan Schore. The body of knowledge generated by the wealth of research in relational neurobiology completely supports the pioneering work of embodied Gestalt therapy, and I am committed to a neurobiologically informed Gestalt practice.

I am also committed to shift the study of sexuality, early sexual development, and the practice of sex therapy from the sidelines in the science of psychology, mental health, and psychotherapy to the central role that sexuality truly occupies in the forming of human consciousness, the neurobiological unconscious, and the somatic self.

With our guidance as therapists, supported by our own personal growth in our capacity to sustain body-based presence and intimacy, we can help our clients broaden their relational prospects and grow beyond their expectations.

Part I
The Problem-Transformation Spectrum

1

The Problem: Distress as a Developmental Opportunity

Maybe it's because I do both couples therapy and sex therapy that I have come to see the clear connection between a couple's emotional life and their sex life. My observation is this: when a couple has relationship problems, their sex life suffers; when they have sexual distress, their relationship suffers. The two sets of issues are inextricably connected.

If clients come for therapy because of a sexual issue, at some point it certainly makes sense to ask, "How is this affecting your emotional connection?" Or if their primary concerns are about arguing or feeling out of touch with each other, it also makes sense eventually to ask, "How is this affecting your sex life?"

Their answers are diagnostic. The therapist gets a broader sense of the scope of their intimacy issues, their personal and relational challenges, and a beginning peek at their personal and relational resources.

Every course of therapy for a couple typically begins with the couple sitting shoulder-to-shoulder facing the therapist. After some friendly small talk he or she asks, "What brings you to therapy?" There is always an issue that propels the visit. The presenting problem is usually described in behavioral terms, a lack of loving contact, too much fighting, not enough affection, or disappointing sex. They may want more emotional connection and affection; they want to fight less, or they want to enjoy more satisfying lovemaking.

The Present Moment in the Presenting Problem

A therapist attuned to body-based communications between partners begins to assess their nonverbal interactions right from the start. Here's an example of a woman and man in their mid-thirties whose presenting problem is sexual.

In their first couple session, each voices dissatisfaction with their sex life together. The woman is very attractive with her long brown hair pulled back into a slick ponytail. I particularly make note of her straight posture with her head held high, like a good student. The man is thin and handsome, and he seems more casual, sitting slumped on the couch with his legs crossed, ankle resting on the opposite knee. She speaks first, and says she's hoping that they can learn some techniques for making sex better.

My mind flashes on a number of touching exercises I might offer them to experiment with at home. I resist the urge to step in prematurely, and sweeping a glance at each of them I ask, "What's not working for you?"

"That we don't have it!" the man jumps in with a smile but he doesn't look happy. Now he's sitting up, and his voice is tight and tinged with annoyance. She smiles a wry smile back and stiffens her back even more. "He doesn't seem to be able to remember how I like to be touched," she says defiantly, still smiling. "I've asked you to be gentle with me," she says turning toward him.

He leans in toward her. "It doesn't matter how I touch you. You used to be turned on to how I touched you. But now nothing I do seems to work anymore." Her shoulders and chest collapse with a sigh. She folds her arms across her chest, crosses one leg over the other, and shakes her head from side to side in a gesture of hopelessness. "He just doesn't get it," she says to me.

So, is this a sexual issue, a relational issue, or both? Clearly it's both. All their gestures, facial expressions, tones of voice and bodily movements are subtle, but they are an important part of the body-to-body nonverbal conversation that is triggering painful emotions and sabotaging their ability to hear each other. Their dilemma displays a stuck place not only in their sexual interaction but also in their ability to engage the other intimately and to lovingly work it through.

Here's another first session with a heterosexual married couple in their forties whose presenting concerns center around having grown emotionally distant. They've been together eight years, have no children, and both work and are invested in their career. They seem cordial with one another, maybe even a little formal in their tone of voice and how they look at each other. I can see that they don't seem to have much emotional connection. I ask, "How does this affect your sex life?" To my surprise, the woman says, "We usually have sex once a week and it's fine. That's not our problem." He wobbles his head in a yes-no gesture suggesting that the sex is okay but not great. Now I want to know more.

I direct my next question to him. "Is the sex not fine with you?" "Oh, it is fine," he says, "but it's routine and not very affectionate. I'd like more kissing, more playfulness. I feel like she just wants to get it over with." She smirks at his response and says nothing. Obviously, their lack of connection plays itself out in their sexual life despite the fact that they are sexually active.

In fact, which problem came first is immaterial. Our emotional, physical, and sexual energies are confluent—they flow together in the body in a shared physiological and dynamic interplay. Two biologically complex human organisms have crisscrossing personal and relational histories from infancy to the present that shape the make-up of our brains and bodily reactivity, especially in how to relate to an intimate.

For most couple clients, emotional and sexual troubles are systemic and interconnected. Disappointments, resentments, and feelings of guilt, shame, or fear are likely to bleed over into many areas of their lives together. If therapy is going to have staying power, it will not only alleviate the distress that brought them to therapy but also have a value added benefit.

Resolving their distress can open up a quality of emotional closeness and sexual pleasure that can heal wounds from childhood. Unresolved painful early experiences underlie a pattern of reflexive defensiveness in a couple. One person's emotional distance or resentment can elicit the other's neediness, anxiety, or shame, while that person's neediness can be a burden to the partner and elicit feelings of obligation and detachment. Therapy has to reach those deeper emotional patterns, the projections that give rise to familiar feelings—the fearful or furious expectations that are triggered when an emotional or sexual intimacy is under stress.

Underlying Sexual Issues in Couples Therapy

Couples who seek therapy with a couples therapist are likely to complain about deficits in how they relate emotionally to one another. They fight too much, or they feel like they are not being heard and respected. Yet that doesn't mean that their sexual relationship doesn't play some part. In fact, while it may be easier to talk about "relationship issues," sexual dissatisfaction may actually have a major role in their relational discontent.

As Johnson and Zuccarini (2010) note, "Couples therapists almost inevitably find that sexual anxieties, conflicts, and deprivation are part of relationship stress." The authors acknowledge that therapists often expect that if they focus on relationship issues and the couple gets along better the sexual issues will resolve themselves. More likely, however, those therapists may simply know that they are ill equipped to deal with the couple's sexual interactions. For those couples, picking up on their therapist's expectation, the sexual aspect of their relationship becomes cordoned off as though sex is a separate issue. This is an unfortunate message to be reinforcing in their clients.

Moreover, the authors recognize that not addressing a couple's sexual dissatisfaction may contribute to a breakdown of the strides they do make in therapy and a recurrence of the troublesome relational interactions:

> [M]any couple therapists find themselves actively helping couples to specifically address sexual difficulties as part of the process of relationship repair and relapse prevention, especially when it is clear that the relationship is contributing to partners' sexual functioning difficulties. ... The line between sex and couple therapy is becoming finer and finer.
>
> (Johnson & Zuccarini, 2010)

However, it cannot be assumed that a couples therapist who has not been trained in sex therapy is automatically capable of comfortably and knowledgeably dealing with sexual issues. A therapist who has not dealt with his or her own sexual history, authenticity, erotic predilections, sexual and/or body shame, current relational sexual satisfaction, and sexual self-acceptance cannot facilitate the deeper work on the emotional challenges with regard to sex that partners bring to one another.

One of the advantages of being trained as a sex therapist is the requirement that trainees look at their biases, beliefs, attitudes, and moral judgments toward individuals whose sexuality is different from their own. The SAR program, for example, is a requirement for all clinicians seeking certification by the American Association of Sexuality Educators, Counselors and Therapists (AASECT). SAR stands for Sexual Attitude Reassessment and is typically a weekend "sensitivity training" program that utilizes sexually explicit videos, diverse speakers, field trips, and experiential processing "to explore the landscape of human sexuality and ultimately themselves" (Britton & Dunlap, 2017).

Besides, though the couple has obvious emotional issues with one another, it may very well be that it is the quality of their sexual connection that is underlying issue. In one study, researchers found that couples in happy marriages attribute only 15% to 20% of their happiness to their satisfying sex life while unhappy partners attribute 50% to 70% of their distress to sexual problems (McCarthy & McCarthy, 2003). This suggests that contented mates view their sex life as one of many qualities they enjoy with one another but when sexual fulfillment is lacking, that deficit can have a big impact on the overall quality of a couple's connection.

Underlying Relational Issues in Sex Therapy

On the other hand, if the couple seeks a sex therapist it doesn't mean their emotional connection is not the issue. Couples may come in with a specific sexual concern like low sexual desire for one or both, or an inability for a man to sustain an erection or for a woman to orgasm. Yet a man's chronic inability to sustain an erection may reflect his expectations of disapproval from his partner, perhaps a re-surfacing of old feelings of sexual inadequacy and shame, which may be reinforced by subtle signs of frustration on his partner's face.

A woman's inability to orgasm or a condition of vaginal spasms preventing penetration may result from obliging her husband's impatience for intercourse. Vaginismus may occur when a woman consistently sacrifices her need for more sex play and loving connection in order to become aroused and lubricate. Short-circuiting warmth and affection during lovemaking may also be a pattern in their day-to-day life.

In other words, the presenting problem may be indicative of the relational disturbance that is currently most disruptive, but it could also be the concern they can both agree to concentrate on, though one of them may be more eager to tackle that issue than the other. While clients focus on symptoms, the experienced clinician is alert to signs of unacknowledged or hidden disruptive dynamics between partners or within the subjective experience of each individual that may be contributing factors.

For more than a decade, prominent sex therapist and researcher Peggy Kleinplatz has bemoaned the lack of integration of up-to-date psychotherapy research and treatment applications into the practice of sex therapy. As a result, sex therapists have been primarily focused on fixing performance problems rather than maximizing a couple's erotic potential. She notes:

> My objection here is to the implication that problems are to be understood primarily as technical difficulties, subject to treatment and cure devoid of the psychological, relational, and social contexts in which they come to be perceived as problematic. . . . In fact, to the extent we confound sexual symptoms with the underlying problems they mask, clinicians may be inclined to target the wrong problem.
>
> (Kleinplatz, 2012)

Other voices in sex therapy have also drawn attention to the myopic model of sex therapy focused on fixing performance rather than the dynamics of the relationship limiting the quality of the experience. Instead of focusing on sustaining erections and controlling ejaculation for men or achieving orgasms or preventing vaginismus for women the shift for many clinicians has been to tackle some of the deeper issues that may account for the sexual distress.

Couples therapists and sex therapists alike recognize the need for greater integration in their practice. For example, David Schnarch (1997) drew from Bowen's family systems theory to examine how the lack of differentiation between mates can dampen their sexual interest in one another. Carol Ellison's sex therapy is centered on helping the couple achieve a more fulfilling emotional connection (Ellison, 2012). Esther Perel focuses attention on intimate partners' unrealistic expectations of one another—to be best friends and lovers, where friends are supposed to be predictable and lovers are most exciting when they are spontaneous (Perel, 2006).

Integrating Couples and Sex Therapy

As a body-based Gestalt therapist, my work has always been present-centered, experiential, and interactive. But it wasn't until I came upon the relational neurobiological work of Allan Schore that I came to more fully understand the developmental neurobiological programming underlying the emotional and relational patterns in the couples I was seeing. I have found the theory and research spurred by the relational neurobiological attachment model to be consistent with and most productive in my somatic approach to working with couples.

Securely attached individuals come to an intimate relationship with an expectation that they will be treated with respect, that their needs matter, and that when there are differences between mates, they will be able to work it out. These people are most likely to enjoy sexual contact for the emotional connection and shared pleasures.

Insecurely attached partners are more likely to have the opposite expectations and depending on their backgrounds and programming anticipate that when there is conflict, they are less likely to get their needs met and they have less faith that they can work things out. Sharing a lifestyle together may involve more familiarity than intimacy.

Satisfying sex for both members of a couple involves a quality of bodily intimacy that is not easily achieved when they are stressed or in conflict. Each person needs to feel safe to relax in the presence of the other.

They want to feel loved and accepted for who they are and not for who they can pretend to be. All this can be challenging for a couple with unresolved attachment issues between them.

The ability to desire bodily contact with the partner and feel physically unrestrained and emotionally free to surrender to the pleasures of skin-to-skin intimacy requires the capacity to be present with and open to one another. Achieving this quality of emotional, physical, and sexual connection in an intimate relationship is always a process of personal as well as relational growth. Growth occurs on many levels throughout the life of the relationship. What all levels have in common is the capacity to be focused and present in the moment, in tune with one's own body, empathically attuned to the other, and welcoming pleasure. This body-to-body intimacy is the healing factor that links relational and sexual fulfillment.

Body-to-Body Intimacy

In the popular culture being intimate with someone typically has two possible meanings: either you can tell each other anything and still be friends, or you have sex. In this social schema, the one you can say anything to, you generally don't have sex with. Conversely, the one you have sex with, you may hold back your true thoughts and feelings. The first passes for emotional intimacy, the second for physical intimacy. Clearly, therapists can do better than that.

I like to refer to the original meaning of the word intimacy in the Latin root, *intimus*, inmost, and the verb, *intimare*, to press into. Following these fundamental meanings what is that inmost part shared by two people that they can press into together?

There is now a substantial science of intimate relations that tackles that question. Interpersonal or relational neurobiology is supported by a multidisciplinary group of neuroscientists, psychologists, psychiatrists, child development specialists, and sexuality scientists who are contributing to an interconnected and multidimensional body of research. They are all studying various aspects of how our brain and nervous system are shaped in the earliest days and years of life primarily between infant/child and primary parent through eye contact, subtle facial expressions, vocal tone, and touch.

These early implicit experiential exchanges of attunement, referred to as intersubjective interactions, program the young brain and nervous system, and become the foundation for the emotional patterns that drive the course of adult life in relationships with others, especially with intimates.

Research shows that this quality of body-based connection between two people in close physical proximity when driven by empathy, and communicated implicitly and spontaneously through eye contact, facial expression, and bodily gestures, has the power to heal emotional wounds of the past. A caring human presence, the therapist, can restart a developmental process in the brain and nervous system of an adult that was blocked by insufficient nurturance at earlier stages of life.

This felt-sense connection has been called implicit relational knowing and therapeutic presence when it refers to the therapeutic alliance between therapist and client (Boston Change Process Study Group, 2010).

Between lovers and intimate partners, body-to-body intimacy is no less therapeutic when the caring presence comes from your life partner, and likely even more healing. It is this quality of intimacy between partners that is often lacking or disrupted during patterns of relational distress or sexual dissatisfaction.

One person's inner subjective experience and pattern of emotional distance can evoke the other's inner subjective experience of neediness and anxiety. Then that partner's longing for closeness and reassurance can elicit feelings of obligation and push the distant partner further away. Therapy has to reach those deeper subjective emotional patterns, the programmed projections that give rise to familiar feelings—the fearful or furious expectations that are triggered when an emotional or sexual intimacy is under stress. These are the intersubjective relational interactions that are a product of the intertwining of each individual's subjective experience in the moment.

Respectfully addressing each partner's distress and how their defensive habits can trigger each other's reactions can open up a freshness of response and a quality of closeness that can go deeper to repair past injuries as well as present hurts. The most rewarding outcome of an integrated approach to couples therapy on a relational level is a more embodied, richer quality of emotional and sexual intimacy. On a personal level, repairing past injuries and learning more loving and empathic ways to be in an intimate relationship is ultimately rewarded by a more integrated and fulfilled sense of self.

The Presenting Problem

Let's see how this is translated into the therapeutic encounter beginning with the first session. The introductory session typically starts with the partners sitting shoulder-to-shoulder, facing the therapist. This is a time for the clients to get an initial impression of the therapist as well as for the therapist to greet the clients and establish a feeling of warmth and rapport.

What all therapists hear in this initial description of their problems is where each of these people feels stuck. Something important for one or both is not being satisfied and what they have tried so far hasn't helped. They are not moving forward. What each partner expresses in this first session is what they are looking for from therapy. Essentially, they want movement. They want to see change—and they especially want it in the other.

Couples therapy at its most fundamental level is intended to be a relational process that promotes change. It starts at the impasse in the couple's relationship, whether relational or sexual and more than likely both. Each partner expresses his or her dissatisfaction with some aspect of the relationship. Yet they love each other and want to stay together or they wouldn't be there.

From the initial visit, through a series of advances and inevitable regressions, therapy progresses though various stages as the therapist helps widen the clients' perspective on the deeper less obvious dynamics between them that contribute to their stuckness.

Identifying the Impasse

Before there can be movement, there needs to be an exploration of the stuck place. Here are some important questions to ask about the impasse:

- When did the problem start?
- Did the problem develop gradually or was there a precipitating factor?
- What have you tried so far? What helped? What made it worse?
- What precipitated your coming for therapy now?
- Has something occurred that makes the situation more urgent?
- How do you understand what is going on between you?
- What are your goals for therapy?

This last question particularly gets at whether each mate has the same aspirations for treatment. How they work together on answering these questions and how their answers may differ are informative. It's also important to know how each of them has attempted to make meaning out of the situation and if they agree on what the issues are between them. We want to see if they are supportive or if they blame one another;

if they listen respectfully as the other speaks or interrupt, and whether they discount one another in subtle or not so subtle nonverbal messages like rolling their eyes, shaking their head, smirking, or groaning.

If the partners are secure with one another and working in concert, the process becomes deeper faster. Each partner is less likely to feel threatened and defensive, at least at first. Feeling safe, they are more available to look within themselves to find their own contribution to the stuck place and to support growth in the other.

If the partners are at odds, they are likely to feel more threatened and to become emotionally triggered during the session. In neurobiological terms, the partners emotionally dysregulate rather than regulate each other's stress. Therapy then is likely to start at the level of threat, focusing on how their current patterns of interaction are evoking emotional pain. Even more pertinent for them to get is that each person's interactional style is a reflection of his or her past relational history. What they witnessed at home was imprinted in their brain and nervous system and is being elicited in this interaction. Whatever that was, it is not bringing out the best in them.

Working with a dysregulated couple takes nuanced skill for the therapist who has to help modulate a combustible situation enough to be productive while at the same time support each partner's need to express feelings and their right to be heard. To accomplish this feat, the attuned therapist has to be empathic with each partner equally while simultaneously self-regulating the contagion of biological stress she or he is being exposed to in the room.

The Experiential Intake: Building a Foundation for Growth

The critical factor in the efficacy of both couples therapy and couples sex therapy is for committed partners to become more capable of realizing their mutual goals through how they interact with one another, i.e., their relational process.

After each partner has expressed their feelings about the problem, and therapist and clients have established a person-to-person-to-person warmth and presence with each other, I want to get a sense of how they communicate with one another both verbally and nonverbally. I also want to establish that the real work of therapy is in their interaction with one another—present-centered, body-based, experiential, and relational—and not just talking about it to me.

The session naturally begins with the partners facing the therapist. Next I want to see how they relate to one another and how they look at each other. I tell them that therapy works by building on the strengths of the relationship as well as eliminating the distress. To establish what's good about this relationship, I ask them to turn and face each other and to take turns sharing with one another what they most love and appreciate about the other. I ask that they do it this way: first one person speaks and completes without interruption, and then the other speaks and completes without interruption. That method encourages them to focus and to listen. I tell them I will eavesdrop on what they share.

As they do this, I am watching for how they look at each other, whether they make eye contact, their tone of voice with the other, whether they are able to stick to the positives or if they can't help but bring in criticism. If they do, I may interrupt and ask that they stick to their appreciations.

Typically, this experiential exercise can be illuminating as partners often share appreciations that have not been articulated before and may be pleasantly surprising to the other. This can generate considerable good will and feelings of love and support. Couples in crisis are more likely to share a begrudging acknowledgment of some good qualities of the other.

When both partners have shared whatever positive regard they have for one another, I will then ask them to share how they would like to see the relationship change—and just to make the implicit explicit, how they would like the other to change. I encourage them to be candid and to be sure to ask for everything they want. I remind them to do so in the same way, first one speaks and completes without interruption and then the other. Again, I'm paying attention not only to what they are saying, but how they are saying it. I'm looking at their facial expressions and bodily postures, movements, gestures, and any signs of emotional reactions.

Finally, I ask each to share with the other how they recognize that they themselves may be contributing to the difficulty between them. I ask them if anything they witnessed in their own families may be influencing how they respond to their partner's distress or to not getting their needs met. These questions uncover each person's willingness to admit that they are likely to be playing a part in whatever is not working between them.

Taking a Family History and a Sexual History

I typically give couples a brief tutorial on how the brain and nervous system of each individual is programmed by what they witnessed in their family during their early childhood and the emotions activated. If this is a typical intake and a double session, I will then give each of them paper and pen and describe how to draw a diagram of their family as they were growing up. If there is no time in the first session I will aim to do that at the second session. I find it essential to have an early attachment history in order to move into the deeper work exploring their interactional roadblocks. I include several questions about early sexual development. If the couple presented in therapy with sexual concerns, I will at some point ask about their sexual history. I call this procedure for taking a family history the Family Closeness Profile, and it is further described in Chapter 8 and in complete detail in the Appendix.

Therapist Overview: Reframing the Problem as an Opportunity

The most effective therapist is a facilitator of an empathic relational process of discovery as well as an educator providing information about human functioning and sexuality. This is especially critical when we are dealing with sexual concerns.

The relational process is based on each partner experiencing the roots of their distress and feeling safe enough in the session to express their feelings, broaden their emotional and behavioral repertoires for self-expression, and discover nurturing alternatives to reactive patterns.

The educational aspect has to do with the therapist giving plain talk information from research and anecdotal evidence about what typically works and doesn't work in human relations and in a fulfilling emotional and sexual connection, It also helps to describe how therapy can help break through the logjam and inspire growth by having them interact with each other and not just with me during therapy sessions.

This opening procedure provides a foundation to do all that. We now have an understanding of the glue that holds these two people together, their expressed love for and appreciation of one another, and their internal models of relationship and sex that are reflected in their attachment and sexual histories. At the end of the first session I want to acknowledge their relational strengths and some patterns I may have noticed that raised their stress level.

I also reassure them that while they may be unconsciously triggering each other's painful expectations and emotions, the couple's relationship is the most powerful opportunity for repairing wounds and deficits from their past. Together, their relationship has the power to heal their past and to recreate with each other the quality of love and intimacy each craves.

2
Transitional Resources: Change as a Body-Based Experiential Process

Therapy is a process of change over time, progressing though various stages as the therapist's input widens the clients' perspective on the deeper, less obvious dynamics between them that contribute to their current discontent. Their stated goals for therapy keep us on track, what is often referred to as goal-directed movement. But while we are aiming for certain results the path is by no means a straight line.

There are times we don't seem to be moving forward. It may even seem we are losing ground that we had gained and are regressing—maybe even getting worse than when we started. One step forward and two steps back. But nothing is wasted. Learning progresses through trial and error, with the errors just as important as the trials. It's in the errors that we can most fully mark the blind alleys, repair and refine our actions, and sharpen our determination to move forward. We put our trust in the messy process of discovery.

In the accepting therapeutic environment, the advance toward a solution to the problem becomes so much more. Irrespective of the issues, whatever propels a couple into therapy can ultimately lead to a genuinely transformative experience for both of them. It may start with behavioral or performance goals but it can become an uncovering of an interactive pattern that triggers feelings in one or both of shame and inadequacy, unresolved grief, lingering resentments, and troubling anxieties that go all the way back to childhood. The unfinished pain of the past is present, capable of casting a gloom over a whole day or even a lifetime of dissatisfaction. Being revealed as such is the good news, because now something can be done about it.

A wider therapeutic perspective can do double duty, identifying knee-jerk triggers that sabotage best intentions and repairing current injuries and disappointments while healing emotional wounds from childhood. No matter what the issues that propelled a couple to seek help, effective therapy can help foster in each partner a new sense of one's truly lovable self and a deepening of the bond with each other.

The long and winding road of discovery can result in a more relaxed, more pleasurably loving, even a more romantic and sexually enlivened relationship that can accommodate and welcome change. Call it collateral repair or even post-traumatic healing and resilience. Good therapy can reactivate a developmental process that was put on hold a lifetime ago.

Symptom Reduction vs. Growth

In a sense, the presenting problem is the resolution imperative that prompts a therapist referral and a phone call for help. For some clients, therapy that results in alleviating the symptom is sufficient. The man is becoming more relaxed in sex, gaining control over his ejaculation, and the lovemaking with his spouse is more pleasurable for both. The woman has been able to have some orgasms, fulfilling decades of long-ing. Mates are better at catching themselves in old patterns and have fewer fights. They try to make requests instead of making demands or playing "discover-me" games, and they are learning to negotiate their dif-ferences and be generous with one another. Once achieving some level of success in their end goals, partners may elect to terminate therapy.

On the other hand, as the wider ramifications of their problems unfold, the therapeutic process may lay bare a systemic pattern that has limited more than the relationship or their sex lives. It has impeded one or both partners to personally realize their dreams in other ways, with family, friends, or in their work or profession. As often happens, the presenting problem plays the grander role of providing a transitional objective that inspires a life-changing reorientation on many levels. I call this "mutating up."

It becomes the couple's choice: "Do we stop here or do we continue?" They may elect to take a break and come back later when they reach another challenge. Or they may be animated by what has been uncov-ered so far to continue. They have seen how probing the link between their current interactions and their family history has awakened old memories and emotions buried at an earlier age when they closed down and closed off to their feelings, needs, and desires. Their thirst for self-discovery has been whetted. They want to keep exploring to realize more of their personal potential and the possibilities for greater fulfillment in their relationship.

Depending on a variety of factors, on their commitment to one another, their relational histories, their degree of early trauma, how they trigger each other's anxiety and defensiveness, and the duration and complexity of the issues they came in with, therapy will continue as long as the issues that brought them to therapy are being illuminated and processed in a new light.

What is being described here is a growth model of therapy rather than a symptom-reduction model. A symptom-reduction model aims to alleviate specific problems that prompted the clients to seek treatment. It's easy for sex therapists working with sexual difficulties to get caught up in a symptom reduction model since many of our clients present with very specific bodily issues related to performance. But focusing only on the genital concern can be counterproductive because it reinforces the notion that the difficulty is local rather than systemic, and a personal rather than a relational matter.

A growth model casts a wider net. The focus of Gestalt therapy has always been on growth and a fundamental belief in therapy as providing an opportunity for the continuing development of the individual, particularly in the context of relationship. Through present-centered experiential processing clients can become more aware of aspects of themselves that have been suppressed or disowned and that unconsciously exercise profound influence determining their actions and reactions.

Couples therapy provides a unique prospect for re-owning parts of each person that have been dissociated or neglected due to pain, punishment, trauma, and lack of support. This is particularly true for the sexual stunting endured by many of our clients as children as a result of their parents' discomfort with their curiosity about sex, social and religious prohibitions about sexual exploration, and resulting feelings of shame and inadequacy about their bodies and desires.

Working with sexual issues can be a profound opening for each partner beyond the sexual realm, into aspects of their emotional lives that have been underdeveloped. Here's an example of recognizing some aspect of the sexual difficulty as a larger reflection of a limiting life pattern.

The Symptom as Life Metaphor: Phoebe and John

One couple I worked with began to connect the dots between their sexual difficulties and each person's stuckness in other areas of their lives. Phoebe and John originally appeared for therapy because Phoebe had lost all sexual interest in John who was doing his best to revive it. Phoebe admitted that John was really a very skilled lover, that he touched her just the way she enjoyed being touched, he kissed her and told her how lovely she was, and she liked his body and found him very attractive. But nothing seemed to arouse her. Phoebe nevertheless would submit to sex because she loved John and seeing him happy made her happy.

But that wasn't good enough for John. He wanted to be wanted. He also wanted a genuine participant, one who would not just take his arousal for granted but would be sexually playful and tempt and tease him too. That just sounded like work for Phoebe and she was already working too hard at her job to be willing to work at pleasing her husband sexually. She was, however, "willing to show up as long as I don't have to put too much of myself into it."

I asked Phoebe if there was anywhere else in her life where she was just showing up and not putting too much of herself into it. And I asked John if there was anywhere else where he felt like he was knocking himself out doing quality work and yearning to be wanted, but felt like he wasn't. That was a great moment in therapy, when literally both their jaws dropped and they shared a somewhat bitter laugh!

As it turned out, that was right on the money, literally, because they were both frustrated professionally. John, because he was doing great work but not receiving the financial rewards he felt he deserved, and Phoebe, because she felt like she was stuck in a job that wasn't really utilizing her talents but which was financially lucrative.

The dynamic that was sabotaging their sex lives and other aspects of their relationship was also limiting them professionally and creatively and could be traced to their family history. The root of each person's pattern to persist despite getting less than they felt they deserved was at the heart of their frustrating sex life. To see their therapy merely as improving a sex act would have lost a valuable developmental opportunity for personal growth.

Body-to-Body Intimacy: Communicating Without Words

Relational neurobiology is also a growth model with a particular focus on nonverbal, implicit communications between individuals. Allan Schore has been a central figure in support of an integrative, brain-mind-body approach to therapy—in particular a right-brain, somatic, developmentally oriented psychotherapy. Schore identifies the nonverbal, emotionally connected right brain as the foundation for all later intimacies.

The right brain, which precedes the development of the language dominant left-brain by about 18 months, is shaped by the quality of care during the face-to-face, body-to-body interaction between primary caretaker and infant/child. These early experiences "indelibly affect and alter the developing right brain," which for the rest of life underlies the need for affiliation and intimate connection, "and thereby for emotional regulation and personal growth" (Schore, 1994, 2003, 2012, 2014; Schore & Schore, 2014).

The attachment relationship shapes the ability of the baby to communicate with, not just the mother, but ultimately with other human beings. This survival function—the capacity to communicate one's own subjective internal states to other human beings and to receive their resonant responses—is the basis of all later social relations (Schore & Schore, 2014).

Naturally, we want couples to talk about their distress, to describe their difficulties and disappointments and also to share what they love about each other. Emotions are the stock and trade of psychotherapy and the session is their opportunity to address their feelings toward one another or to say why they are afraid to do so. We want to identify their expectations, beliefs, and attitudes, any resentment they may be holding on to from years ago, and to articulate clearly what they want from one another. We can also talk about where they learned some of the patterns causing them distress and trace a couple's dynamic back to each partners' early history. It helps to understand the connection between their family history and how each has brought their past into their present relationship.

But a therapy session that is all talk, without any attention to partners' nonverbal interactions, fails to expose the programmed right brain implicit communications and the subtle body-based emotional triggers that underlie their impasse. While partners engage each other verbally in left brain-to-left brain communications they are also communicating right brain-to-right brain through their subtle cues in facial microexpressions, tones of voice, and bodily movements.

It is in identifying these often unnoticed, barely perceptible triggers and directing both individuals' attentiveness to internal visceral reactivity that I have found the most productive resources for growth in therapy. That's because noticing what has been unnoticed often causes a surprise reaction, as we saw with Phoebe and John, and illuminates what has been subtly felt but previously unseen.

Relational Couples Therapy: Co-Creating Body-to-Body Intimacy

Thanks to scientific studies observing mother-infant preverbal interactions in laboratory settings and advanced by innovations in brain imaging, the individual's sense of self and security is recognized as having developed out of body-based interactive experiences with primary caretakers, typically the mother (e.g., Trevarthen, 1993; Tronick,1989, Beebe & Lachmann, 2002).

When a mother is consistently misattuned and ineffective in meeting the child's biological and emotional needs, the child grows into an adult programmed with certain emotional deficits, expectations of interpersonal disappointment, trust issues, and limits in the capacity to self-regulate stress. These deficiencies are especially prevalent in the context of intimate love relationships.

Since the brain and nervous system is shaped through social interactive experience, the relational approach to psychotherapy focuses on the person-in-relationship, and is referred to as a "two-person relational psychology." A key factor in a relational approach is the recognition of *intersubjectivity*, that two interacting people co-create their emotional experience of one another. This is in contrast to traditional psychotherapy, now typically referred to as a "one-person psychology," where the emphasis has been on the person as an individual and the healing factor has been seen as insight into the unconscious needs, desires, fantasies, and intrapsychic struggles motivating his or her choices ((Stolorow, 2002; Beebe & Lachmann, 2002)

By asking partners to face each other and to interactively tackle their issues in the therapist's presence, the therapist can help them widen their perspective on the reciprocal nature of how they trigger each other's feelings, not only in what they say to each other, but in how their bodies are reacting, and emotionally communicating with each other without words, while their heads are doing the talking.

The notion of intersubjectivity describes how in any two-person interaction both individuals' inner subjective experiences are at the same time influencing and being influenced by each other. Even when people are in touch with their inner experience and attempting to regulate their inner state, no one can completely suppress the emotional leakage. The biological exchange happens too rapidly and subliminally, below the level of conscious awareness.

Gut feelings can cringe in a nanosecond as the speaker's eyes pick up a twitch of scorn in the listener's mouth, the widening of the eyes in disbelief, the angry tightening of the jaw, the deriding smirk, the barely perceptible negating shake of the head, the exasperated exhale, or the cold clipped voice. The right brain sees it all and sends a message of familiar pain via the nervous system directly to the viscera. Only when the left brain registers what just happened does the connection between stimulus and response make it into conscious awareness.

They may or may not be in touch with what triggered them, but while two people are engaged in left brain dialogue, exploring what they think, imagine, demand of themselves, and expect of the other, their right brains are picking up body-based cues from each other that may suddenly induce a heavy heart of despair in one, a gut grip of shame, fear, or resentment in the other.

It is also essential for couples to recognize that just as they are triggering one another's unresolved feelings from their respective pasts, they are also in a unique position to help each other heal those old wounds and develop a new sense of security and belonging.

In fact with guidance, loving intimates are potentially more powerful as interactive healers than one-on-one with a therapist. The quality of bodily proximity that life partners are likely to share in face-to-face, skin-to-skin, body-to-body interactions more closely approximates the original parent-child attachment programming when the young brain was imprinted.

Yet, if each partner comes into the relationship with a history of attachment insecurity as a result of early deficits in genuine bodily resonance and affective regulation, they will not have a well-developed repertoire of loving support. A big part of what the therapist does is to interject her empathy, compassion, and wisdom to guide that process of repair.

In some cases, the therapist is also in a position to call attention to expressions of pseudo-love, like compulsive self-sacrifice, acting out of obligation rather than generosity, offering praise with a dollop of stinging damnation, and insensitive boundary intrusions. These patterns come straight out of controlling family patterns from early childhood that diminish both partners in the process and leave an undercurrent of resentment in their wake.

The Therapist as Catalyst: The Process of Experiential Processing

A catalyst is anything that accelerates a reaction between two elements to produce a new entity without being consumed in the process.

In therapy, the couple starts out in a place of inertia, at least with regard to the issue in focus. The therapist becomes the catalyst to ignite a productive reaction, a transmutation of sorts. For the couple, the new entity is a qualitatively enhanced way of being in relationship without the therapist present. The essential shift in their physical closeness occurs when their newly minted body-to-body intimacy is transferred to their sexual connection.

In a successful therapy, the problem they came in with has been transformed from lead into gold. They have utilized their emotional baggage to tap into rich inner resources to become true partners in each other's well-being. They have more empathy for one another, are more loving and more fun to be with, and better able to deal with whatever daily irritants or serious challenges their lives may bring.

From a neurobiological standpoint, one or both partners start out by acting out internalized, emotionally pre-programmed, multifaceted though limited, inner working models of intimacy and of sexuality in a committed relationship. When wound-up emotionally, they become like wind-up toys that keep banging into the same furniture and the same walls. They are stuck in left-brain, solution-oriented struggles as one or both act out their attachment insecurities, unrepaired emotional injuries, fear, shame, and programmed expectations of how things are or should be.

The therapist becomes a catalyst by throwing her right brain into the mix. She draws on her training and her own experiential brain, nervous system, and gut feelings to creatively and intuitively hold the space to foster emotional repair for each of them through their interaction.

From a relationally embodied Gestalt perspective, the troublesome aspect of the relationship is a fixed Gestalt, typically reflecting unfinished business from the past that strives for completion. Realizing a couple's goals for therapy involves helping them to repair and resolve unfinished emotional activation from the past that they trigger in each other.

Therapy focuses on the couple's present-moment interactions while examining the emotional triggers as experienced moment-by-moment in the session. The therapist is an impartial, intuitive witness who offers keen observations of subtle bodily cues and a variety of body-based relational experiments to try out new ways of interacting and noticing whatever feelings are aroused in the process.

In a way, the couple in the beginning is stuck in a relational duality of thesis-antithesis: "This is the way it is"—"no this is the way it is." With the therapists as a third force, as a catalyst, together they can form a thesis-antithesis-synthesis experience and the relationship becomes more than the sum of its parts in a more positive, loving, and fulfilling engagement for them both.

The process is biochemical, neurobiological, and relational and becomes transformative when we move from a belief that only one person can be right to where both are right, even when they see things very differently. When bodily experience is processed to explore how they co-create stuckness, they become more capable of positively co-creating movement and a more fulfilling connection.

To explore the body-based communications that are triggering those feelings and possibly even early implicit or explicit memories underlying unresolved pain or trauma, partners need to become mindful of how they may be re-traumatizing each other by stoking old wounds and insecurities. They then have more of possibility of authentically responding to one another differently. The trick is to slow down and become alert, attentive, and aware of moment-by-moment inner subjective bodily reactiveness. For those who are highly reactive, the challenge is to become more present.

How People Change in Couples Therapy: A Three-Person Dynamic

Informed by relational psychology, much of the focus in the literature on how people change in therapy is on the relationship between therapist and client. In particular, it is the intersubjective therapeutic relationship itself that is recognized as the essential factor in promoting therapeutic change. Since the research shows that the experience-dependent brain is shaped through interactive present-moment experience, the critical therapeutic skills are seen to involve the therapist's ability to engage in a quality of emotional connection with the client *experientially* in a way that engenders a new sense of safety in the client, ultimately leading to a new sense of self. The healing factor is no longer understood to be insight but safe, self-honoring, self-affirming experience that is communicated primarily through moment-by-moment implicit, i.e., body-based, experience (Boston Change Process Study Group, 2010).

But in couples therapy the therapist is already starting with a two-person psychology in that of the couple. Here the therapist has to form a relationship with each person individually as well as intrude herself or himself into the couple dynamic to help shape a reparative interaction and restore a healing developmental process between them.

With the relational couples therapist as catalyst, the qualities of body-to-body intimacy—especially presence, authenticity, empathy, understanding, and compassion—can be transmitted in a three-way process: body-to-body-to-body, right brain-to-right brain-to right brain, from the therapist to each partner. In that way the therapist can imbue the intersubjective exchange between partners with those same healing qualities of implicit communication. That's what it takes to be a catalyst, though it may take time to get there and some emotional terrain to explore in the process.

The Experiential Present: Therapeutic Presence Is Body-to-Body Intimacy

The methodological foundation of Gestalt therapy is present-centered experiential processing, tracking the present in moment-by-moment experience. Gestalt processing involves being both awake to external events as they impinge on the senses and aware of internal bodily experience. That includes felt-sense perceptions of emotional arousal, physical sensations and tensions, images or memories that flash before the mind's eye, and urges to act and self-restraint. It also involves developing the skill to phenomenologically describe these inner phenomena as present-moment internal experiences, without judgment or explanation.

Inner experience also entails noticing shifts in attention to whatever becomes figural in the moment. These shifts in moment-to-moment attention between outer stimulation and inner reactivity is recognized as occurring along a "continuum of awareness" (Perls, F. et al., 1951; Perls, F., 1981; Perls, L., 1973; Latner, 1973; Polster & Polster, 1974; Zinker, 1977; Resnick, 1997; Yontef, 2009; Wheeler, 1997, 2015, etc.).

Presence is the *sine qua non* of experiential Gestalt work, and it begins with the therapist. The therapist cannot hide behind a façade of authority or a mask of imperviousness. The major requirement of the therapist during the session is to be present and contributing relationally and creatively to the experiential process, which may involve talk, but also experiments in movement, repetition of gestures, and in a playful activity.

"Therapeutic presence" has gained increasing attention from person-centered and neurobiologically informed psychodynamic therapies.

> Therapeutic presence involves therapists being fully in the moment on a multitude of levels, physically, emotionally, cognitively, spiritually, and relationally. The experience of therapeutic presence involves (a) being in contact with one's integrated and healthy self, while (b) being open and receptive to what is poignant in the moment and immersed in it, (c) with a larger sense of spaciousness and expansion of awareness and perception.
>
> (Geller & Greenberg, 2002)

Canadian psychologist Shari M. Geller (2013) describes therapeutic presence as a core quality in experiencing times of "relational depth" between the therapist and the client and offers research to show that this quality of connection generates a more "synergistic relationship" of "greater mutual presence" and a more "genuine," "authentic," "more open and fully immersed," and even "spiritual" relational encounter.

> As the essence of each person comes into direct encounter with each other, a larger state of transcendence emerges that is healing. This state of transcendence can also be seen as emerging from connectedness and awareness of what presents itself in the here and now.
>
> (Geller, S. M., 2013)

To the Boston Change Group (2010), these encounters, described as "moments of meeting," are experienced in what is "happening here and now between us" and are a reflection of authentic "implicit relational knowing," i.e., how to be with someone. To Allan Schore (2012), therapeutic presence describes a state of right brain receptivity of a sensitive therapist and further, that "implicit right brain-to-right brain intersubjective transactions lie at the core of the therapeutic relationship." Most importantly, "intersubjectivity is more than just an interaction of two minds, but also that of two bodies."

A corollary of being present in the moment is experiential awareness—to be awake to what is happening right now. Much of the time, people do not pay close attention to their shifting ongoing experience as they go through the motions of their daily activities. They may not hear the steady hum of the air conditioner in their ear until it stops or notice leftover feelings of a heavy heart from a disappointing exchange with a co-worker, or be aware of the stream of their own thoughts competing with hearing their mate's account of the day.

Therapy becomes a unique opportunity for couples to engage with one another and at the same time, tune into and track their inner experience. What are they picking up from their partners? What meaning do they automatically make of it? What are they sensing in themselves? Does this moment bring up any memory flashes from the past? What feelings are being aroused and where in the body are the feelings felt? What do you call these emotions? What may be unfinished from the past that is interfering with the uniqueness of this moment?

The ability to be attentive to the shifts in the "experiential now" both between partners and within each of the individuals in the therapeutic triad is the absorbing activity of present-centered processing. For the partners, it involves being able to identify their own subjective experience—the flow of sensory, motoric, emotional, visceral, and mental events within their bodies. What does each of them see, hear, and imagine about the other, and how does that feel in their own body?

The stuff of experiential processing in the moment involves the clients developing the skill to bear witness to and describe one's inner experience as it is happening in the moment. The therapist at the same time is witnessing the exchange, noticing the match between each person's subtle implicit cues and explicit response, while attending to his or her own subjective experience of gut feeling and sensitivity to what is being revealed without being said. The experienced therapist who is fully focused on the interactive exchange between partners relies on her intuitive sense of how and when to intervene in this moment to expand the experience.

Practicing Presence: The Gestalt Experiment

One of the major contributions of Gestalt theory and practice is the method of offering the client a present-centered experiment to play with, or try out a new way of doing something and to notice how it is experienced in the present moment (e.g., Polster & Polster, 1974; Zinker, 1997).

At a conference in 1973, Laura Perls described the creative process involved in devising the therapeutic experiments at the core of Gestalt work:

> The experiments are not fixed constellations of technical steps, but invented ad hoc to facilitate awareness of *what is*. Fritz Perls—with a pre-psychiatry history of interest and active involvement in the theater—would use a psychodramatic approach. Other Gestalt therapists work with art, music, poetry, philosophy, meditation, yoga and other body awareness methods . . . in an expansion in whatever direction is possible and with whatever means are available between therapist and patient in the actual therapeutic situation.
>
> (Perls, L., 1973)

A big part of the difficulty partners may have with one another is a limited relational repertoire, not only of behaviors but also of emotional expression as a result of their early family histories and their working models of relationship. For couples, the relational experiment has to be designed to tease out and try out new behaviors in a playful and exploratory framework while still accessing their inner truth and authenticity. It has to be open ended enough for clients to make it their own behaviorally and simple enough for both of them to become aware of their internal activation. Partners can trigger each other in subtle ways. Here's an example of a simple experiment based on movement.

Experimenting With a Movement: Fran and Roger

Fran wanted more physical affection with her husband and spoke sweetly to him as she asked for what she wants. Roger responded warmly saying he regretted that he was often too tired when he came home from work to be affectionate. They were being very nice to each other, but I got the impression that their superficial politeness was part of their stalemate.

As an experiment, I suggested that they take a deep breath, turn and face each other and notice how their bodies felt in the moment. Then I asked them to remain seated where they were about an arm's length apart, to join hands and to take turns slowly leaning back then toward the other in a kind of rowing motion keeping their arms straight. In other words, as one person leans back the other is drawn in and then that person leans back as the first is drawn in. I watched as they went through several cycles and I noticed that Fran leaned in more than Roger. At one point, as she got even closer to him, his chin automatically lowered and his head made a subtle motion to pull back. I saw her flinch and straighten her back.

When I asked what just happened, she said directly to him, "I just get the feeling you don't want to be close to me." When I questioned where that feeling was coming from, she said that he just doesn't look welcoming. She was picking something up from his body language but couldn't quite pinpoint what it was. But I could.

I described what I saw and asked Roger if he was aware of that subtle gesture. He said he was not, but then I asked him if he would try it out. As soon as he did, he laughed shyly and said it was indeed familiar to him. Fran too said she recognized it as a familiar reaction of his whenever she moved toward him to be close. She said his reaction to her made her feel sad and lonely.

That brief exercise opened up another look at their personal histories in how Fran was a beloved child who was hugged a good deal through her childhood. Roger, on the other hand, said he was hardly touched as a child. He claimed that he learned that he doesn't really need physical affection and that he thought women need that more than men. Yet, when he described his childhood, he said he was lonesome and cut off from his parents and younger brother.

While we were discussing their different early experiences, Roger's behavior suddenly changed. He threw his head back as his eyes briefly scanned the ceiling and then he leaned forward, and with his bent elbows propped up on his thighs he held his head in his hands. Roger sat that way for a few seconds as Fran and I watched silently, curious at his uncharacteristic behavior.

Finally, Fran spoke, "Are you okay?" she asked. He nodded but looked unsettled. "I just remembered something I haven't thought about since I was a kid. I was about nine and hanging out with a girl cousin who was two years older. My family was visiting her family and she and I were exploring an empty lot near her house that had some high grasses. We crouched down in there like we were hiding and we were laughing. But then she suddenly reached out and grabbed at my penis. I was shocked for a second and I swatted her hand off me. I got up real quick and just walked away. She ran after me and said she thought I would like it. She apologized later but I felt violated and I didn't want to have anything to do with her again."

Roger didn't know if that one incident could have had that great an impact on him, but he was coming from a place in which he had little affectionate touch and to be treated so rudely clearly had an impact. Still, Roger didn't think he needed physical contact as an adult as much as he may have wanted as a child. He certainly didn't need it as much as Fran, although he did recognize that when they hugged and kissed he enjoyed the contact.

That simple experiment highlighted the boundary issue in their impasse by uncovering an early violation that was buried in Roger's memory. The revelation paved the way for a more focused attention on Roger's personal boundaries regarding touch, physical closeness, and a history of feeling intruded upon.

During the course of therapy we also looked at how Fran's comfort with physical closeness as a sign of love and acceptance made her approach Roger with a kind of abandon that he interpreted as disrespectful. Meanwhile, she had read his reserve not as a reflection of his own personal wound but as rejection of her. These discoveries enabled us to work more sensitively utilizing breath awareness as we experimented with physical closeness and touch.

Experimenting With Emotion: Jan and Marcy

Jan and Marcy were a female couple who had come for therapy, hoping to resolve their different erotic preferences during sex. Jan preferred what they both referred to as "rough sex." She liked to grab Marcy by the wrists and pin her down when she got excited, to kiss her hard, squeeze her tight, and she enjoyed forceful, pounding pelvic movements. She also felt she had a higher libido than Marcy.

Marcy objected to being characterized as having a "low libido." While she could occasionally enjoy rough sex, mostly what she enjoyed and found erotic was slow and more affectionate lovemaking. She wanted lingering wet kisses, looking into each other's eyes, slow caresses, exploring each other's body with kisses and tongues. She felt that Jan was too controlling and aggressive sexually and that the same dynamic infused their everyday life. Jan had to have her way in everything, like on which shelf Marcy should put the leftovers in the refrigerator.

We started to work on their differences and how their family backgrounds had influenced their relational dynamics, their early sexual and erotic histories, and how to bring their breathing into sync to bring their bodies into sync. I gave them a breathing exercise called "matching breaths" to do together at home. We were moving along nicely when on the fourth session, the work shifted. The session began in the midst of bad feelings between them. Jan was livid; Marcy was contrite.

Jan was berating Marcy for not having told her that she had lunch with an ex-girlfriend. Jan was going on and on about how betrayed she felt that Marcy hadn't mentioned the lunch with Peggy, whom Jan suspected of wanting Marcy back. It was only when Jan found a book of matches from the restaurant on the kitchen table and asked Marcy about it that the lunch date was revealed.

As Jan continued to excoriate Marcy, I watched Marcy get stiffer and stiffer, and her body language looked as though she was steeling herself against Jan's attacks. Marcy just looked stunned, like she didn't know how to respond. I asked Jan what she was feeling and she said, "Pissed!" I asked Marcy what she was feeling and she said, "Guilty, regretful, and confused." She also looked very sad and self-protective. They sat there looking at each other on the couch across a gulf of painful feelings. Knowing each woman's history, I understood what was behind their limited repertoire.

Rather than stay in the place of pain and delve deeper into some of the issues from their past we had already explored, I asked if they would be willing to do a little experiment. They each nodded. I told them I was going to whisper a statement into Jan's ear and I would like her to simply try it out and repeat it to Marcy. Marcy was free to react any way she felt. They both agreed to the experiment. I walked over to Jan and whispered in her ear, "I love you and I'm scared you're still attracted to Peggy." Jan scrunched her mouth up tight and glared at me. I urged her on.

She snorted as she turned toward Marcy and indignantly with her nose up, she repeated most of the words I offered her. "I love you and I think you're still attracted to Peggy." "Say it right," I urged her quietly, "and take a breath." This time she looked at Marcy and repeated softly, "I love you and I'm scared you're still attracted to Peggy." Her face contorted in pain and, looking deeply into Marcy's eyes, she repeated the words, "I'm scared."

Suddenly a spontaneous gasp of breath came through her throat and jerked her body. The dam broke. Jan began to sob, her face in the crook of her forearm. This time Marcy reacted like she was shot from a cannon toward Jan. She wrapped her arms around Jan and began to rock her and got teary as well. Then suddenly they looked at each other and both began to laugh through their tears. Then they got teary again and then laughed again. Their laughter was infectious, a combination of embarrassment and excitement at the exposure of vulnerability. I was smiling. Finally, they shared a brief kiss.

Yet another little experiment turned out better than I expected. At the end of the session, as they sat on the couch holding hands we examined the power of expressing vulnerability instead of attacking. We saw how Jan's rage had elicited Marcy's shame and defensiveness instead of her love and her desire to soothe and reassure her. We identified the early family history in each of them that triggered their reactions and how Marcy had contributed to Jan's insecurity by purposely hiding the lunch from Jan because she was afraid of her reaction. An unexpected treat for us all was the laughter, a jolt of excitement at the vulnerability and as much a sign of release as their tears.

In subsequent sessions, we were able to take a more nuanced look at how some of their blocked emotions had contributed to their erotic impasse. In particular, we worked on how body-to-body they could sync up and blend their erotic desires to ratchet up their empathically attuned excitement.

Authentic Contact at the Boundary: Finding the Right Balance of Needs

An old shibboleth has it that when two people fall in love and get married, "two become one." In modern times, this saying could be applied simply to making a commitment to one another and moving in together. But I like to say, if two become one, which one of them have they become?

In Gestalt therapy, authentic contact between two individuals is seen to occur at the "contact boundary" between the two, where each respects the other's individuality and difference from oneself. Two major boundary issues for all couples involve balancing the contrasting needs for autonomy-interdependence and of contact-withdrawal.

Balancing Autonomy and Interdependence

This involves respecting each individual's distinctive tastes, needs, and desires while also enjoying times of togetherness and the pleasures of connection. Difficulties here may involve one or both being intrusive, continually needing reassurance and contact, or conversely, being emotionally unavailable, secretive and resisting connection.

In terms of attachment styles, the former might be described as an anxious insecure attachment style and someone who is frequently in need of attention while the latter would be seen as an avoidant attachment style and someone who needs substantial time alone. If an anxious individual is in a relationship with an avoidant individual their stress will be compounded during difficult times because each of them requires a different response from the partner. The anxious individual requires contact to be comforted while the avoidant individual needs space and time alone. Clarifying the differing needs during therapy can help each partner to provide, and make room for, each other's needs in an empathic, non-confrontational manner.

Balancing Contact and Withdrawal

Spending quality time together and also taking time apart has to do with achieving a delicate equilibrium since most individuals need both. On the one hand, two people feel loved and valued if they are able to make good contact, give each other the attention they need to feel seen and heard, and to enjoy the warmth of being in touch both emotionally and physically. Yet we also need time to be alone, for solitude and reflection.

Making good contact has to do with being fully present to the other when you are together—looking into each other's eyes when speaking, paying attention to what is being said, registering the meaning of the communication, and reflecting it back appropriately in facial expression. Attending to one another in this way is the essence of relational connection.

Authentic Sexual Contact: Body-to-Body Pleasures

Autonomy-interdependence and contact-withdrawal issues have important implications for a couple's sex life. In the first case, the greatest pleasures of sexual union involve their interdependence and catering to each individual's personal sexual tastes and desires to be able to reach the heights of melting into each other. In the second case involving connection and aloneness there are likely to be times during sexual encounters when partners may lose contact with one another. Is that person withdrawing to fully savor the intensity of the experience or because he or she has lost interest?

When one person becomes overwhelmed with sensation and withdraws deeply inward that can be an indication of the power of the sexual pleasure, particularly if that person soon reconnects passionately with the partner. Taking turns giving each other pleasure can be enjoyable for both. A less satisfying sexual pattern that couples will want to address in therapy is when one or both partners tend to disconnect during sex and stay in their own world.

Research shows that different attachment styles are also associated with different sexual patterns. Anxious individuals have been shown to be more likely than either secure or avoidant people to engage in sexual activity for reasons besides desire for sex, to be reassured of their desirability or to safeguard a relationship. Avoidant individuals report a lower sex drive than others and are more likely to have sex out of a sense of obligation to their partner rather than for love or pleasure (Mikulincer & Shaver, 2007)

As the couple develops greater empathy for one another in therapy and each becomes more securely attached, they become more comfortable with their individual differences and needs for contact and withdrawal. Tackling their sexual connection becomes part of the repair process as their developing body-based empathy can have positive transfer for their sexual interactions.

Breathing and Body-to-Body Intimacy

Breath work is a critical element in working with clients' sexual issues. Much of the difficulties people have sexually, whether it has to do with erection difficulties, delaying ejaculation, staying present, getting aroused, enjoying intercourse, or allowing orgasm, all are associated with either holding the breath or, as in the case of rapid ejaculation, breathing rapidly and feeling out of control. Hearing the clients' descriptions of what takes place when they have sexual difficulties and noticing the clients breathing rhythms during the therapy session provides direction for delving deeper into the roots of the sexual-emotional distress for each individual.

As therapists, we can learn a great deal about our clients' present state just by making note of how deeply or shallowly they are breathing in the moment. We can look for where the breath is visible in their bodies, whether it is near the collarbone reflecting mental activity, thinking, or analyzing the situation or if they appear open and relaxed, breathing more fully in the belly or chest. We can observe when they may show signs of difficulty breathing by trying to force a yawn. Or we may notice them having to lift their shoulders to take in a breath indicating that the chest is too tight for the lungs to expand and fill up with air. Both of these conditions are often indications of anxiety.

Physiologically, each inhale triggers the sympathetic nervous system and each exhale is associated with the parasympathetic system. In terms of attachment styles, the autonomic nervous system (ANS) of anxiously attached individuals is said to have a sympathetic bias, while the ANS of an avoidant or depressed individual is said to reflect a parasympathetic bias (Hill, 2015).

This is particularly important when it comes to sex. For example, sex educator Paul Joannides (2009) reports on studies that have shown that men who have difficulty delaying ejaculation tend to maintain a sympathetic bias during sex. Once they get aroused their heart rates speed up and stay elevated triggering ejaculation. On the other hand, men who can control ejaculation are able to pace themselves, taking long deep breaths out, thereby slowing down their heart rate. Their arousal becomes dominated by the parasympathetic nervous system and they relax into their excitement. When they are ready to orgasm, they may speed up their movements and breathing and the sympathetic system takes over. Clearly, when a couple has sexual difficulties, having them notice their breathing patterns and learning different breathing methods can have valuable rewards in their physical connection.

Here's a quick tutorial on the breath. With every breath, breathing in brings in energy (O_2) and exhaling eliminates waste (CO_2). Too much energy without a good waste management system becomes an energy crisis. Holding the breath is typically a sign of the suppression of feelings. But what feelings are being suppressed? It depends on whether the breath is held on the inhalation or on the exhalation.

Anxious people often take quick short breaths, holding on the inhalation and insufficiently breathe out. They are unconsciously in a continual state of potential danger, on alert and prepared to defend themselves. Each short inhale is like a gasp or an arrested startle, alert for any sign of threat. When the breath favors short inhales, the exhalations are also withheld and too short to expel the buildup of carbon dioxide.

A panic attack can result from the buildup of carbon dioxide from insufficient release so that there is less room in the lungs for a replenishing intake of oxygen. When people can't catch their breath their anxiety increases and they enter a state that has been described as "the fear of fear."

People who are depressed typically display a habitual pattern of holding the breath on the exhalation. They are literally deflated, usually by intrusive negative thoughts and unresolved feelings of grief, remorse, guilt, or shame. For these clients, a little encouragement to take a breath can help them to become aware of the disturbing memories, images, or inner dialogues that have become habitual.

When these people are encouraged to become more present to the moment by expressing their inner thoughts and experience, the result can be an immediate shift from hopelessness into more animated feelings of anger, resentment, shame, or grief. By re-experiencing and expressing these feelings, clients have a greater possibility of resolving the issues underlying the original events and lifting their depression.

The most common impairment of the breath is in shallow or incomplete breathing. During mental activity, the breath is often barely discernible and likely only in the upper chest near the clavicle. I find it valuable to encourage clients to become aware of shallow breathing as a way of recognizing emotional triggers from the past and learning more adaptive, less reactive ways for responding to their partner. This kind of awareness has the greatest potential for partners' capacity to help each other heal from early attachment wounds and deficits.

Clients can also become more aware of themselves in the present moment just by being directed to notice how they are breathing as they react emotionally to the interactive process with their partner. When partners are facing each other and interacting during therapy, a noticeable shift in the clients' breathing patterns may not just be a reflection of what is taking place between them. It is also likely that what has been triggered is a longstanding emotional pattern that started in early childhood and has become a chronic state.

Body-to-Body Intimacy as Affect Regulation: Implicit Relational Repair

We just looked at ways that conscious breathing can increase awareness and promote a release of stress and a shift of affect. As a body-based therapist, my focus with clients in couples therapy has been to help them to become conscious of the experience of stress in the body, to recognize how they trigger and are triggered by one another, and to utilize breath awareness to ratchet down the stress so they can better hear and empathize with one another.

Gestalt therapy typically addresses a client's inability to set clear boundaries and/or conversely, a tendency to set rigid boundaries with an intimate. Relational neurobiology, on the contrary, focuses on the implicit body-to-body cues that *transcend* physical boundaries between individuals. Right brain-to-right brain signals are transmitted in nanoseconds through sensory cues in facial micro-expressions, subtle tones of voice, or small gestures. Proximity is all that is needed for an exchange to pass between individuals that can trigger each other's feelings of insecurity, shame, rejection, etc.

Much of the focus in relational neurobiology is on the implicit regulation of stress through the body-aware, intersubjectively attuned therapist who picks up subtle cues that partners themselves may not pick up on. They just know when they are feeling threatened. I've witnessed one partner get upset by something said by the other, who then replies to the upset partner, "Oh, don't be so sensitive!"

Often enough, however, the disparagement is present in the offending partner's demeanor, perhaps in a condescending smirk, a disdainful glare, an arrogant lift of the eyebrows and the "sensitive" partner gets the message. That exchange can become an opportunity to address the impact of subtle cues, and how partners' sensitivity to one another can also be a positive attribute in their capacity to bring love and fulfillment to one another.

Relational neurobiology draws attention to the unconscious repair that can take place during therapy through the nonverbal body-based interactive process itself. A therapist's expressions of empathy, concern, and compassion for each partner can have the effect of calming and soothing a dysregulating couple, thereby catalyzing a new kind of exchange between them that can de-escalate rather than escalate the disruption. Schore points out that a therapist's clinical effectiveness involves learning "a number of non-conscious functions of the therapist's right brain" that include intuition, creativity, and insight, that are communicated by the therapist to the client.

> All technique sits atop these right brain implicit skills, which deepen and expand with clinical experience: the ability to receive and express nonverbal affective communications; clinical sensitivity; use of subjectivity/intersubjectivity; empathy; and affect regulation.
> (Schore, 2012)

Marks-Tarlow (2014) also points out the importance for the intuitive therapist to pay attention to gut feelings during therapy because, "the guts have a brain of their own, being part of the enteric nervous system." The enteric nervous system extends from the mouth along the alimentary system into the stomach, small intestines, bowel and down into the rectum and is part of the autonomic nervous system along with the sympathetic and parasympathetic branches. This brain in the belly is emotionally reactive as anyone with irritable bowel syndrome (IBS) knows.

Therapist Personal Growth: The Core of Therapeutic Presence

All of the qualities of therapeutic presence reflect a developing body-based intimate connection and empathy that the therapist acquires with personal growth, professional training, and years of practice. But it is the personal growth that is most essential.

For the therapist to interact with clients in their distress, as defined earlier by Geller & Greebberg (2002) as "therapeutic presence," especially with couples, i.e., capable of being "fully in the moment on a multitude of levels, physically, emotionally, cognitively, spiritually, and relationally," and to be sensitive to the *implicit* bodily cues within herself and the *implicit* micro-expressions passing between partners—*and* not to get caught up personally in the emotions—requires a quality of presence that can only come with the therapist's personal growth.

The task of personal healing for the therapist, as much as it is for the clients he or she is treating, involves turning the lead of one's own history into gold. No matter what we have gone through in our own lives, all of it becomes fertile territory for gaining compassion, empathy, and wisdom to facilitate the growth of others. Grappling with our own emotional challenges, in our own intimate relationships and to be capable of integrating it all takes dedication and the courage to expose our vulnerabilities in trainings and peer supervision groups dedicated to personal growth.

Not having a loving mother was more of a disadvantage in my young life than I knew when I yearned for love and the elusive committed relationship I seemed incapable of achieving. But having to learn to distinguish real love from pretense and to see myself as lovable and worthy turned into an asset as a therapist. What worked for me in my own growth process gave me the tools to guide others to overcome the deficits of their past and to trust a reciprocal openness, compassion, empathy, and especially, forgiveness with a partner that enables true love and intimacy.

When a therapist's emotions are aroused by an interaction you witness or are a party to, no matter how much you may try to hide it, there is always a certain amount of "emotional leakage" that will be transmitted to another person. A nanosecond flash of anger on your face or in a gesture can trigger a client's anger or fear, even without either of you being aware that you are triggering each other's past emotional and relational history. You may also disappear for a few moments, aroused by your own unresolved emotional memories, and lose contact with your clients who are sure to feel your sudden absence. It can be very helpful to a client for a therapist to own up to what just happened.

If the therapist is feeling uneasy about something and not addressing it honestly, the client is likely to sense the disconnection, even if he doesn't know why. This is where the therapist's lifelong commitment to his or her own personal growth is essential and every session that arouses the therapist's emotions is a growth opportunity for both therapist and client.

I call this the gift of countertransference. When the therapist's own feelings are aroused, the client will sense that something has changed in the therapist. Maybe the couple is dealing with an issue that brings up some sadness in the therapist from similar unfinished business in the past. Or the therapist may feel a sudden sense of tiredness and a loss of concentration in that moment that may very well be the therapist's personal relational issue implicitly triggered by the couple's interaction.

One or both partners are likely to pick it up. They might imagine that the therapist is suddenly not as present or interested in them, or even worse, that he is disapproving of them. If in fact the therapist's own feelings have become figural for him in that moment, it's best for him to share it and own it—person-to-person, rather than hide behind the façade of clinician.

As one psychoanalyst shared in his "evolving perspective on therapist self-disclosure":

> I have gradually and cautiously liberated myself from the view that I ought to present myself as a blank screen upon which patients project their sexual and aggressive impulses and fantasies. . . . My basic stance is primarily shaped by concepts such as reciprocity, mutuality, responsiveness, symmetry, and by a concern with the intersubjective aspects of the therapeutic relationship . . . marked by authenticity, transparency, realness, and egalitarianism.
>
> (Geller, J. D., 2003)

Whatever feelings are aroused in the therapist as we witness our clients interact can be pertinent to the couple. If our experience is relevant, we can safely expect that sharing our feelings will further their progress. Learning how to communicate our inner truth, despite the fact that we may be confessing vulnerability, is the mark of an authentic human being and a truly healing presence.

3

Transformation: Restoring Evolutionary Progress

We used to think of growth as something only children did. As an adult, we might get better at our jobs or improve on certain talents, but once we were grown-ups, we were pretty much formed. People excused their bad habits by saying, "Well, you can't teach an old dog new tricks." The problem with that way of thinking starts with the observation of dog lovers that, with love, you can teach an old dog plenty.

The same is true for adult humans. We are capable of growing and evolving our entire lifespan. The myth about immutably fixed habits once had support in the now debunked theory that brain anatomy was fixed and from childhood and thereafter the only change was to decline. Since the brain couldn't change human beings couldn't change and grow either.

We now know that the brain changes its structure every day—rewires itself through thought and with every activity performed, and if certain parts of the brain are damaged other parts take over. This process is known as neuroplasticity. According to neuroscientist Norman Doidge, "The neuroplastic revolution has implications for . . . our understanding of how love, sex, grief, relationships, learning, addictions, culture, technology, and psychotherapies change our brain" (Doidge, 2007).

What we have been looking at so far is the process of growth and how psychotherapy can restart a neural, emotional, and behavioral developmental process that was interrupted in childhood through trauma or the incapacity of our primary caretakers to be sufficiently present or loving or to empathically read our needs. The early wiring of our right brains was shaped experientially through right brain-to-right brain transmissions and became the foundation for all later person-to-person interactions especially in close intimate relationships.

Now through the same kind of right brain-to-right brain transmissions, embodied relational experiences during psychotherapy and sex

53

therapy can have a powerful impact restarting a developmental growth process with regard to intimate love and gratifying sex. Since so much of who we are, and our ability to be fulfilled in life, has to do with our capacity to establish loving intimate relationships, helping our clients to repair both past and present relationships through body-to-body intimacy can reprogram their brains and transform their lives.

The Transformative Power of Pleasure

As I have consistently emphasized in all my work—in therapy, trainings, books, and articles—the capacity to experience and augment pleasure is a critical key in the process of growth and transformation. That doesn't mean to diminish the importance of confronting the pain of anxiety, grief, shame, or any of the other contracting, diminishing emotions. In facing their pain, clients need to have faith that, with the support and guidance of the therapist, they will get to the pleasures of resolution. Facing anxiety, they will find courage; facing grief they will find solace; facing shame, they will find self-forgiveness and compassion—all exhilarating, and enlivening pleasures (Resnick, 1975; 1997, 2004, 2012).

Schore (2003) points out that in the original family, the attuned caretaker who is capable of instilling in her infant the qualities of connection indicative of a secure attachment does more than just down-regulate the infant's stress and alleviate his discomfort. The most effective and loving mother also up-regulates her baby's excitement through eye-gazing and eye-averting games in face-to-face play.

> In play episodes of affect synchrony, the pair are in affective resonance . . . which creates states of positive arousal and interactive repair . . . modulates states of negative arousal . . . and are the fundamental building blocks of attachment and resilience in the face of stress.
>
> (Schore, 2003)

Elsewhere Schore states that effective therapy not only increases the regulation of negative emotions but also increases the capacity to regulate positive emotional states and to "tolerate the novelty and uncertainty that accompanies new emotional experiences such as those associated with intimacy." He suggests that a corrective emotional experience does not work only by reducing negative affect but also by increasing a client's "capacity for the positive affects that accompany intersubjective play." He states that "a psychotherapeutic growth-facilitating environment [is a potential source] for the expansion of the tolerance of positive arousal and thereby the capacity for intimacy" (Schore, 2012).

When I submitted the manuscript for my first book, *The Pleasure Zone* (1997), a cornerstone of the work was the importance of the ability to enjoy pleasure for mental and physical health and emotional well-being, yet from childhood, we often learn to resist pleasure. I adopted the notion of pleasure-resistance from my studies of Wilhelm Reich. I coined the term "low pleasure-tolerance" and I gave a multitude of examples from what I call "the eight core pleasures," the *primal pleasures* of just being, *pain relief, release and resolution*, the *elemental pleasures* of play, humor, movement and sound, the *mental pleasures* of positive thinking and a quiet mind, the *emotional pleasures* of love and liking, *the sensual pleasures* of taking delight in all the senses, the *sexual pleasures* of desire, arousal, sex play, and orgasm, and the *spiritual pleasures* of feeling a part of something good that is larger than oneself, quieting the mind and coming to terms with mortality. My publisher was very enthusiastic about the book, but she didn't like the term pleasure-tolerance and asked me to change it to something more positive. I thought about it for quite a while but ultimately, I could not come up with a term that better described the tendency that diminished the capacity for embracing life pleasures and we kept it in the book. I now stand vindicated by no less an authority than Allan Schore.

Diana Fosha in her work on transformational experience observes that pain and suffering "shrinks the sphere of life lived with zest" and that the process of transformation is rooted in an emotional experience that

> . . . can morph suffering into flourishing. . . . Positive attuned, dyadic interactions are the constituents of healthy secure attachments . . . and conducive to optimal brain growth. . . . Positive affects are the constituent phenomena of physical health, mental health, resilience and well-being.
>
> (Fosha, 2009)

Play Is the Key to the Pleasures of Love

A playful spirit and the variety of different kinds of pleasurable feelings that arise enhance learning and the possibilities for change and growth. Neuroscientist Jaak Panksepp (2009) suggests that playful activity is a key factor in the "epigenetic construction of the social brain" and shapes "the many plasticities of the brain."

Allan Schore (2012) goes further by observing that while the warm attuned mother can intuit from her baby's distress signals his or her needs at the moment and down-regulate his or her distress, it is particularly the episodes of play that generate "affect synchrony." When mother and child are in an energetic or limbic resonance there is an "amplification of vitality." These states of positive arousal can lessen the effects of negative states. Pleasurably attuned states become the building blocks of attachment and the resilience to effectively deal with stress and novelty at all stages of life.

> Schore sees play states as essentials in forging an attachment bond of mutual love. These right brain-to-right brain, growth-promoting, emotional experiences during childhood generate a relational template for the capacity to share a strong bond of mutual love as an adult. Play is also a vital factor fostering creativity by opening the right hemisphere to ambiguity, novelty, and imagination.
>
> (Eberle, 2017; An interview with Allan N. Schore. *American Journal of Play*, 9(2), 105–142)

These insights have valuable implications for working with couples on both emotional and sexual issues. As two people bring their bodies together in an extended hug, as they do in the "matching breaths exercise, their breathing rhythms and nervous systems begin to sync. Developing a greater capacity to play together does more than simply lower their stress. It can deepen their love and open up their capacity to more creatively deal with their differences. There are many ways to play together, of course. But there can be no doubt that loving sex is one of the most powerful ways that adults can play. It sure beats playing cards.

Schore consistently refers to the value of injecting opportunities for play during therapy. So does Panksepp who considers play to be "the most underutilized emotional force that could have remarkable benefits in psychotherapy." He suggests that "there is unlikely to be any stronger emotional aid than that contained in the joyous potentials of play" (Panksepp, 2009).

Neuroplasticity and Pleasure

Norman Doidge also stresses the importance of pleasure and play in changing old habits and stimulating new brain growth and new ways of doing things. Distilling the process of generating neuroplastic growth, it all boils down to three critical factors: focus, repetition, and reward— i.e, pleasure. On a conscious level, the more we *focus* attention on what we want to change, and *practice* new ways of doing it, and the more *rewarding* and pleasurable the process, the more the corresponding neural networks in the brain are altered.

When a person experiences a sense of gratification and reward for the behavior, the brain secretes neurotransmitters of dopamine and acetylcholine—two biochemical active in sexual responsiveness—which consolidate the change. The more attention, practice, and pleasure we feel with regard to the new experience the more "neural real estate" that new behavior occupies in the brain. This is the process of transformation in the brain.

Doidge (2007) emphasizes that feelings of love and sexual desire and excitement are among the most powerfully rewarding experiences:

> Love creates a generous state of mind. Because love allows us to experience as pleasurable, situations or physical features that we otherwise might not, it also allows us to unlearn negative associations, another plastic phenomenon. . . . Unlearning in love allows us to change our image of ourselves—for the better, if we have an adoring partner.
>
> (p. 116)

And when it comes to sexual pleasure, mates can help stimulate each other's brains for neuroplastic growth:

> Dopamine likes novelty . . . Fortunately, lovers can stimulate their dopamine, keeping the high alive by injecting novelty into their relationship . . . so that everything they can experience, *including each other*, excites and pleases them.
>
> (p. 116, Italics in original)

Doidge suggests taking romantic vacations or trying out new activities. For me, growth in each partner can be the most stimulating factor that two people can do for their relationship. Falling in love again with your partner as a result of positive experiences in therapy can be the greatest growth spurt of all.

Modern Roots of the Growth Model

Abraham Maslow would agree about the importance of pleasure for psychological growth and development. Maslow is credited with advancing the notion that it was time for psychologists to turn their attention to the psychology of health rather than sickness (Maslow,1962).

Maslow called this new approach "positive psychology" and made some basic assumptions: that we are all born with a biologically based inner nature that is at the least neutral or intrinsically good and if encouraged, rather than suppressed, we grow into healthy, happy, productive people. If the individual's essential inner nature is denied or suppressed in childhood, that person will suffer a kind of sickness of anxiety, depression, or despair as his or her true nature presses for actualization.

Maslow envisioned the hierarchy of needs as a pyramid in which the base of the pyramid, the widest part and the foundation for all growth, rested on the purely "physiological" needs of air, water, food, etc., and the need for basic "safety and security". From there came the psychological needs for "belonging and love" and the "esteem" needs for respect and a sense of accomplishment. The highest needs, the peak of the pyramid, he called the self-fulfillment needs of "self-actualization", which have to do with the ability to achieve one's full potential including the need for creativity.

To Maslow, individuals diagnosed as neurotic were deficient with regard to having basic needs met, especially their needs for physical and emotional safety, for respect, close loving relationships, and a sense of belonging. He observed that these empty holes could only be filled through gratifying human contact. Yet, while addressing these feelings of yearning in therapy is necessary and essential, making up for deficiencies in therapy is not enough. Human beings also have an inner drive to realize their full potential, to become what they can be, what he called "self-actualizing."

> The psychological life of the person, in many of its aspects, is lived out differently when he is deficiency-need-gratification-bent and when he is . . . growth-motivated or self-actualizing . . . Growth is, *in itself*, a rewarding and exciting process.
>
> (Maslow, 1962, Italics as in original)

Maslow's important notions of the "fully functioning person," of realizing one's human potential, and his research on self-actualizing individuals have had a significant impact on the fields of psychology and psychiatry to this day. Maslow's early writings supported the therapeutic models of, among others, the person-centered therapy of Carl Rogers and the Gestalt therapy of Fritz and Laura Perls, and contributed to the development of humanistic psychology as a distinct mode of psychotherapy.

Positive psychology has re-emerged as a distinct field in psychology with a focus on scientific research dedicated to examine what makes people and communities thrive. As the research and literature in this field has grown, it has offered interesting insights about human characteristics and communities that promote contentment, productivity, and resilience, (e.g., Csikszentmihaly, 1990; Seligman & Csikszentmihalyi, 2000; Resnick et al., 2001; Fredrickson & Losada, 2006; Resnick, 2012).

Maslow addressed the value of pleasurable experience on growth. He utilized Eric Fromm's distinction of scarcity-pleasures that involve tension-reduction from satisfying a need and abundance-pleasures that are involved in functioning at the peak of one's powers (Fromm, 1941). To Maslow, the relief that comes with satiation is "less stable, less enduring, less constant than the pleasure accompanying growth, which can go on forever."

Personal Transformation: The Integrated Self in Transformative Relationships

Gestalt therapy is founded on the recognition that in the process of early development, parts of ourselves that have been shamed and punished are disowned and pushed out of awareness. These dissociated self-parts represent unfulfilled needs, unresolved emotions, and painful memories that create inner conflict, take energy to keep suppressed, and rob us of the life force to be whole persons. According to Perls et al. (1994), these parts of the personality "have vitality and strength and many admirable qualities" and the task of psychotherapy is "to achieve full reintegration of these disintegrated parts."

There is now neurobiological evidence for the important role of integration in becoming a fully functioning individual and maximizing one's full potential. Kuhl et al. (2015) define the fully functioning individual as "characterized by a unity in thought, emotion, and action that amounts to "being someone" or having an integrated self and they highlight the important role played by positive relationships.

Rather than describe all the various regions of the brain affected by the integrated self, most importantly, the study confirms the right hemisphere of the brain that is dominant in all of these qualities. It's worth noting the seven functional characteristics of the integrated self that couples and sex therapy can emphasize to help partners to support one another's growth. I paraphrase to use less technical language. These are:

- To be connected to body-based "emotional and sensory perceptions, both negative and positive";
- To be able to sustain a "broad scope of attention," especially "to be aware when others are intruding into your personal space";
- To learn from both positive and negative experience and to have a "felt-sense of the consequences of ones actions";
- To value unconscious processing and to "make room for unconscious self-access in a quiet and relaxed atmosphere";
- To foster "self-development through integrating seemingly contradictory needs and emotions and positive and negative self-attributes into a coherent self-image";
- To develop resilience by "turning emotional vulnerability into emotional strength by down-regulating negative affect" (e.g., breathing into painful feelings to learn and grow);
- To develop the ability "to trust oneself to cope with negative feelings and to actively recruit positive feelings."

Most importantly, the authors stress that the necessary conditions for development of the integrated self comes about through intimate and affectionate relationships where individuals feel understood, accepted, and supported in their autonomy as a person. They also emphasize that the brain studies show that the integrated self is accessed through a network of several interacting brain areas primarily in the right hemisphere. That means that it is less about what is said than *how* it is said, through the nonverbal right brain-to-right brain communications of presence, empathy, and understanding that can be read in each other's facial expressions and bodily language.

All of the above self-integrative qualities can be accessed during couples therapy by developing the capacity and courage to honestly address difficult conflicts, repair unresolved emotional ruptures, and non-defensively hear and respond to each other's needs and differences.

I don't believe in compromising oneself to please the other because in compromise, neither individual is happy. But I do believe in generosity and in accommodating one another graciously or, if that's not possible, to accept each other's right to think and feel differently. Partners don't have to agree on everything—just on enough to keep the relationship loving, affectionate, and respectful.

Maslow's work on fully functioning, self-actualizing individuals continues to inspire the work of leading psychologists, neuroscientists, and authors to this day. We just looked at the notion of the integrated self in realizing greater personal fulfillment particularly through intimate relationships. Several other researchers have used Maslow's schema of self-actualization to look at whether or not committed love relationships or marriage can more directly foster individual self-actualization.

There are those who say that nowadays, couples are asking too much of marriage and already put too many expectations on their partner to be a romantic playmate, caretaker, business partner, co-parent to the children, and a great lover. Does the modern view of marriage and commitment make marriage a difficult mountain to scale?

Some say yes, modern couples expect so much from one another that they don't have the time and energy to devote to help their mate in a quest for self-actualization (Finkel et al., 2014). Others agree that couples can ask too much of one another and then harbor resentment and disappointment. Yet it is possible for a good marriage to foster qualities in each partner that can help them grow.

Aron and Aron (2014) suggest that a key attribute couples do need to cultivate is non-defensiveness. I would agree, but I would add that for many partners defensiveness is about a childhood history of shame. They trigger each other emotionally by trading blame, often in an unconscious attempt to deflect their own feelings of guilt and shame. This pattern can be identified and worked on in couples therapy, but it is typically not something that can be achieved simply by a handshake or just a promise to do better. The blame-shame pattern is particularly destructive when the couple is dealing with sexual frustration.

Relational Transformation: Body-to-Body Intimacy as Mutual Repair

In the initial couples sessions, therapists often encounter a tendency for partners to complain and punish each other subtly or overtly when they are not getting what they want. I've identified this pattern as "the punishment ethos," and it likely stems from partners' experiences of growing up in families where even loving parents punished their children by withdrawing affection or shaming them (Resnick, 1997).

Negative reactions to one another draws negative responses, but we know that it's not possible to control the emotional leakage of resentment or impatience if that is what a person is truly feeling. Painful feelings have to be identified as such for each individual, brought into the light, repaired and resolved to have a lasting impact on the couple.

Typically, that repair takes place during the couple session as one person recognizes that the automatic upwelling of resentment or shaming behavior stems from being punished or shamed by one or both parents for what was considered in the family as undesirable behavior. Sometimes I find it helpful to suggest a few individual sessions for each partner to enable a more in-depth "corrective emotional experience" to delve into the childhood history without distraction from the partner's presence.

I am continually reminding clients that you can't get positive ends through negative means. Relational transformation often depends on personal transformation. At the same time, personal transformation is vastly aided by catalyzing the couple's relationship with experiences of empathy, compassion, forgiveness, gratitude, warmth, acceptance, affection, humor, and patience. Equally important is for each partner to develop the skill to interrupt a triggered reflex to react negatively, to breathe into the painful feeling, to down-regulate anxiety and flares of anger, and eventually to develop the capacity to express one's feelings in less attacking or shaming ways and in a more conciliatory and compassionate manner.

As we address repairing painful emotional states in subsequent chapters we will focus on case examples of fostering corrective emotional experiences during couple sessions or in couples' groups. There are also times when it has proven valuable to do so in a few individual sessions rather than with the partner.

Transformative Sex: Embodied Relational Sexual Pleasure

When two people begin to "fall in love" what is "falling" is their social façade, the restraint that maintains an appropriate distance from the other, emotionally and physically. Decorum drops. The exuberance of the shared bodily experience is closely tied to each person seeing himself or herself lovingly mirrored in the other's eyes. Romantic lovers feel seen and felt, liked and adored, a playmate for laughter and adventure, someone to kiss and hold close, a partner to share sensual and sexual pleasures. Two hearts beat as one, as they say.

It's an old theory that this passionate feeling of romance lasts somewhere between three months and two and a half years. The popular notion is that if two people stay together, the heat of romance fades into a companionate love that is warm, friendly, and not sexually exciting. Psychologists Bianca Acevedo and Arthur Aron challenge this theory in their discovery that some long-term couples do manage to maintain romantic love, which they defined as having intensity, engagement, and sexual liveliness.

In their study, for all couples, whether in long-term or short-term relationships, romantic love was strongly correlated with satisfaction in the relationship. When individuals in long-term romantic marriages were compared with those in companionate marriages—warm and affectionate but not sexually engaging—those in romantic marriages were far more satisfied. The big difference between those two groups was that the romantic couples had maintained their sexual aliveness (Acevedo and Aron, 2009).

In another study, researchers tested individuals who were married ten years or longer and claimed to feel high levels of passionate love with their partners. The researchers took brain scans of these subjects while they looked at photos of their partner. The scans showed neural patterns identical to those who had just fallen in love. Once again, the deciding factor of maintaining passionate love over time appears to be cultivating a lively and fulfilling sexual connection (Acevedo et al., 2012).

Finally, in a study on optimal sex, structured interviews were conducted on 64 participants who reported having experienced "great sex" and a content analysis was run on the transcripts. Some of the key components of great sex were identified as being present, authentic, and involving deep sexual and erotic intimacy (Kleinplatz et al., 2009). The same transformative powers of pleasure and play in an emotional intimacy can be particularly transformative in erotic pleasure and play.

There can also be no doubt that many of the difficulties our clients have with their sexuality stem from the lack of education about sex they received at critical times in their sexual development that left them vulnerable to bodily shame and sexual failure during their earliest sexual encounters. When early childhood curiosity about sex is associated with parents frowning on any sign of the child's sexual interest, as an adult, unresolved family issues are likely to be transferred onto the partner and to inhibit sexual feelings. There is also the factor of the inhibition of childhood sex play that we shall see can result in a deficient capacity to engage in erotically stimulating sex play as an adult.

We fall in love with a stranger, but once two people move in together they become family. I call it "family transference" and I see it as an important element to investigate in the inhibition of erotic play and sexual feeling with one's mate. As couples explore how they have begun to treat each other as family rather than lovers, and to resolve some of the sexually inhibiting issues from the past they can begin to reclaim some of that lost playfulness with one another and their sexual spontaneity.

Therapeutic Goals: Embodied Relational Intimacy in Love and Lovemaking

Whether a couple seeks therapy to achieve a more loving interaction or a more gratifying sexual connection, the route to fulfillment depends upon developing the capacity for a more embodied relational intimacy. Irrespective of what the couples are discussing during the therapy hour, it is valuable for the empathic and attuned therapist to inject wherever possible a quality of embodied relational awareness and even playfulness into the interaction.

Here are five distinct areas of intersubjective attunement in embodied relational intimacy that can start in their day-to-day interactions and may be brought into their sensual-erotic play. These are the qualities therapists can support in couples' interactions.

Presence: Focused Attention

Presence is the ability for each partner to be focused on the other in the moment and fully engaged in whatever is happening between the two of them. When they talk to each other, they talk face-to-face, looking into each other's eyes, listening to what he or she is saying. Their faces reflect their interest and receptivity. When they begin to engage with each other with affection, they stay focused on what is happening right now between them. They hold each other and breathe together.

The opposite of presence is preoccupied and distracted. Too many couples hardly ever look into each other's eyes even when being physically intimate. Sometimes physical intimacy is mostly about cuddling while watching TV, or side-by-side, sitting up in bed checking emails on the cell phone.

Body-Based Empathy: Receiving the Other

Empathy has to do with each person feeling in their own body what the other is feeling, picking up not just from what is being said but also from experiencing it with them. When a partner can feel the other, each knows what feels good to the other because it is resonating in his or her own body, in how the other is breathing and responding to their touch. Their hands don't just touch the other but feel the partner's flesh responding to the touch.

The opposite of empathy is apathy, indifference, and detachment. What gets in the way of really seeing, hearing, or feeling the other in the moment has to do with taking the other for granted, being closed off, or feeling resentful or defensive.

Emotional Attunement—Reflecting the Other

When two people are emotionally attuned to one another, their faces subtly and unconsciously mimic one another. They become biological mirrors of one another. They look into each other's eyes and see themselves reflected back on the face of the other, whether sharing concern or enthusiasm. They feel safe and trust one another. Seeing oneself reflected back with warmth in the loving eyes of an accepting partner is a gift and a healing for those who grew up with neglect or abuse.

The opposite of emotional attunement is discordant and distant. Couples who are misattuned don't get each other. When one talks the other is preparing to refute what is being said. They avoid direct eye contact, and their faces appear tense and reflect resentment or hurt. They speak to each other in clipped tones of voice, literally from a distance, across the room. Sexually, if they do have sexual contact, they may go into their own world of fantasy and stay disconnected from one another.

Self and Interactive Affect Regulation—Down-Regulating Stress

Under stressful conditions, or sometimes during sexual contact when something isn't working, couples can learn to access qualities of embodied intimacy to work through their different needs and desires, their conflicting internal working models of sex, any insecurities and anxieties, or interference from work or family stresses. They can stroke each other lovingly and help each other to take some deep breaths to calm down.

The opposite of interactive regulation is interactive dysregulation. Couples in distress tend to agitate rather than regulate each other's stress. They provoke each other's insecurities, anxieties, and resentments. Their stress may begin at work and be brought home or arise in knee-jerk reactions to emotional triggers from their partners that set them off. Where these triggers come from and how they call forth the worst rather than the best in each partner is the deepest work of relational and sex therapy.

Self and Interactive Affect Regulation—Up-Regulating Excitement

Just getting along by working through disagreements and conflicts can be joyless and tedious and isn't enough to keep relationships thriving. Having a partner in life is also about generating vitality and romance by being playful with each other and sharing ordinary daily pleasures that keep a relationship engaged. Sharing something good about one's day and laughing about a funny encounter can be uplifting. For those who value their sexual aliveness, kissing, affectionate touching, erotic playfulness, and making love can be the most uplifting intimate engagement of all.

The opposite of loving engagement is loneliness and isolation. Many couples complain that their only recreation with one another is to sit and watch TV together or occasionally go out to dinner. They hardly ever play together actively, or look into each other's eyes with warmth and smiles.

The Right Brain Is the Right Brain for Love and Sex: Feeling the Other

Much of what we will look at as we explore these qualities of relational repair and embodied sexual intimacy is about getting out of left brain-to-left brain head trips and cultivating right brain-to-right brain body-to-body intimacy. In *The Master and His Emissary* (2009), psychiatrist, humanistic scholar, and neuroscience researcher Ian McGilchrist offers the most detailed account of the "striking differences" between the two hemispheres of the asymmetrical, lateralized lobes of the brain.

McGilchrist talks about the advantages of having two distinct views of the world when the two "cooperate." Yet the two lobes have different values and morality and often clash. He describes how our society, created by the lateralized brain, is the material manifestation of this conflicted duality. He details the implications for humanity that, when it comes to human distress and unhappiness, the values of the analytic, logic-oriented, power-driven left brain have become dominant over the embodied, intuitive right brain—the right brain that he describes as holistic, musical, poetic, the locus of the sense of self, that deals with "the entity as a whole—the *Gestalt.*"

We may admire power and intellect, but love begins in the right brain, from the time we were babies and throughout our lifespan. Love is body-to-body, heart-to-heart, playful, and full of feeling and laughter. Likewise, loving sex is also body-to-body, heart-to-heart, playful, and full of feeling and laughter.

That means sexual communication cannot speak in concepts quoting facts and figures, and delineating needs. Even worse, complaining, threatening, or shaming a partner's response as inadequate, or demanding a change only makes a partner feel bad and can cast a taint on the sexual connection for a long time. I like to say that the biggest problem in sex is making sex a problem.

Sexual language speaks softly body-to-body in right-brain dulcet tones and sweet talk, through lingering eye gazes, juicy kisses, breathing together, drawing in each other's scent (and pheromones), empathic touch, and appreciative sighs at the warmth and smoothness of skin-to-skin contact. No matter how disappointing sex can be between two people, the way to make it better is with warmth, empathy, and compassion. Kindness and caring are great motivators and can enhance the sexual connection and enrich the quality of love in the relationship as a whole.

Neurological research shows there are distinct social advantages to cultivating right brain dominant types of person-to-person interactions. To help with an understanding of the capacities cultivated with a right brain body-based intimacy, I've drawn up Table 3.1 to show the difference between what is accessed through body-based right brain engagement vs. left brain reasoned talk. The attributes delineated in this table are derived from multiple sources, especially, Schore (2012, 2014), McGilchrist (2009, 2015), and Hecht (2014).

Table 3.1 Distinguishing Left Brain vs. Right Brain Attributes

Left Brain	Right Brain
Cognitive	Somatic
Language	Imagery
Explicit	Implicit
Intellect	Intuition
Knowledge	Creativity
Slow	Fast
Closed	Open
Power	Affiliation
Judgment	Acceptance
Dominance	Vulnerability
Aggressive	Pro-Social
Anger	Forgiveness
Self-Preservation	Empathy

Part II
The Attachment-Sexuality Spectrum

4
Attachment: The Sensory Links Between Love and Libido

Since Freud, the fields of mental health and psychotherapy have long recognized the important influence of early childhood on emotional well-being. Yet there was little understanding about what made these early experiences so indelible as we enter adulthood. Now, thanks to attachment theory, brain imaging, and interdisciplinary research, there is substantial evidence to show that these early experiences become the relational templates in the brain and nervous system for self-confidence or insecurity, comfort or unease in social interactions, beliefs and expectations and especially how we love as intimate adults. All of it becomes the foundation upon which all later growth is built. This is especially true with regard to our sexuality.

As Freud wrote in 1905, though he was derided for saying so,

> In none of the accounts I have read is a chapter to be found on the erotic life of children. . . . As long ago as in the year 1896 I insisted on the significance of the years of childhood in the origin of certain important phenomena connected with sexual life.
>
> Freud (1962)

We now know that babies are indeed born sexual and that human sexual imprinting starts in infancy as it does in all mammals, especially primates.

Nothing in our development morphs into something else. The emotional events of our lives, and how they affected us in those moments, get layered over and over, up to the present moment. Like Russian Matryoshka nesting dolls—from the biggest doll on the outside that represents our adult self, all the way inward to our smallest self. It's all still in there, neural associations, emotional expectations, little traumas and big ones, and bodily cellular memory.

Affective Regulation and Dysregulation: Down-Regulating Stress, Up-Regulating Pleasure

Allan Schore identifies affect as a basic response at birth to pain or pleasure. How well the primary caretaker is capable of down-regulating the stress response by alleviating the infant's discomfort or pain becomes a key factor in the infant's sense of security and capacity to regulate his or her own discomfort or pain. An empathic and intuitive mother is more capable of addressing her infant's needs and regulates his or her stress, with a facial expression of concern or a smile of reassurance, a warm tone of voice and gentle touch. This quality of attunement between mother and infant leads to an expectation of pain relief and a more content and secure infant, child, and ultimately adult.

A preoccupied, anxious, or dysregulated parent is less empathically tuned into the infant, making her less capable of reducing the infant's distress, and thereby programming the infant for uncertainty around pain relief. Ineffectual caretaking results in an anxious, avoidant, ambivalent, or at worst a disorganized attachment style in the infant, the child, and eventually the adult. A distracted, unavailable, and neglecting parent programs the infant and child to fend for him or herself and to be less likely to be comfortable in close intimate connections.

Schore also points out that down-regulation is not the only factor in a healthy and happy baby and subsequent adult. The mother also needs to play with her baby and be able to up-regulate excitement, enjoyment, and the pleasures of delightful interaction. Playing baby games like mutual gaze, gaze avert, return gaze, or peek-a-boo is energizing to the infant and enables him or her to be in contact with the joys of life.

Attachment Styles: Internal Working Models of Love and Sex

The largely nonverbal interactions between primary caretakers and the child during early developmental stages create an inner neural and somatic template for the child's developing identity and for what to expect from others. It also programs the individual for an unconscious, automatic, and spontaneous behavioral repertoire that includes emotional reactivity to subtle sensory cues from others and reflexive defensive responses. As Schore states:

> As a result of his or her interaction with caregivers, the infant forms internal working models of attachment that are stored in right-lateralized nonverbal implicit-procedural memory. These interactive representations encode strategies of affect-regulation

and contain coping mechanisms for maintaining basic regulation and positive affect.

(Schore, 2012)

These internal working models are conscious and unconscious beliefs individuals have about themselves and others in close relationships, including their underlying emotional expectations and likely behavioral reactions to others under certain circumstances. The four most typical internal models, or attachment styles, in the individuals who present for couples and therapy are *secure, insecure anxious, insecure avoidant, and ambivalent*. A *disorganized* attachment style that is the result of severe neglect and abuse is often best treated for trauma in individual psychodynamic psychotherapy.

Here's a brief description of the kinds of attachment styles we are most likely to encounter in couples and sex therapy and the interaction between attachment style and adult sexuality.

A secure adult is one who feels worthy of love, safe and hopeful in a close loving relationship. Having close loving connections since the earliest days of neurobiological development, secure people enjoy times of closeness with the partner and also time alone, expect to work out their differences or to be able to make up after a fight, and during times of distress they often reach out to the other for love and comfort. Research shows that secure people are the most likely to enjoy sexual pleasure in the context of a loving relationship.

Insecure-anxious individuals tend to be less emotionally regulated to begin with due to deficits in their parents' ability to minister to their needs effectively. As a result, anxious people are likely to have a more reactive sympathetic nervous system and be less able to down-regulate stress. They tend to be alert for signs of rejection and may be seen by their partner as clingy and emotionally "labor-intensive," continually in need of comforting and reassurance. In a committed relationship, sex may be conflated with love and affection, and an insecure-anxious person is more likely than others to engage in sexual activity to safeguard the relationship with the partner rather than for emotional and sexual pleasure.

Insecure-avoidant attachment style is often associated with a distant, overburdened, or depressed mother. Her facial expressions may reflect detachment and lack eye contact, her voice expressionless and dull. The child may have been attended to by a father, older siblings, or nanny who themselves were not fully present. Left to play on their own, organized avoidants as opposed to disorganized may have learned to take care of themselves, to self-soothe when in pain, and to rely on their own resources at any early age. Depending on their innate resources, they may have done very well on their own and learned to prefer a lot of space in a relationship.

As adults in relationship, avoidant individuals are less comfortable with emotional closeness, and under stress often choose to be alone to self-soothe rather than seek intimate contact. Research shows that individuals with avoidant styles tend to have lower sex drives, are more likely to enjoy one-night stands and brief sexual affairs, and in a committed relationship are more likely to have sex with the partner out of a feeling of obligation rather than a desire to share sexual pleasures (Mikulincer & Shaver, 2007).

Sexual Presence Related to Attachment: Secure vs. Insecure Lovers

Hot, loving sex requires full body-mind presence from both partners who are empathically tuned into and connecting with each other. They look into and read each other's eyes and face. They are aroused by the other's eager kisses, the sounds emanating from his or her throat and deep breathing. They press into each other's body, squeezing, stroking, licking, and whispering appreciative words into each other's ears. Their arousal builds as they respond to each other's movements and the scent of the other's body. They are as tuned into themselves and to the sweaty pleasures of the moment as they are to the other's eagerness to progress into more intense body-to-body physical intimacy.

Sexually and emotionally secure lovers are comfortable with body-to-body physical intimacy and because they have a positive self-image, irrespective of their body type they have confidence in themselves as sexually desirable and worthy of the affectionate attention of their partner.

Insecure lovers typically lack confidence that they are sexually desirable or sexually competent lovers, and are more likely to be uncomfortable with their body image and body-to-body physical intimacy. As a result, they can be less capable of enjoying this quality of present-centered sensual and sexual focus. If their sexual motivation is driven more by insecurity than by desire, that will determine the cues they are alert to—any signs of approval or disapproval from the partner—rather than their shared intersubjective experience of pleasure (Davis et al., 2006).

When sex is motivated by insecurity, tense lovers may not be able to abandon the left brain self-talk to develop the right brain present-centered empathy skills to attune to the other's bodily signals. When people are in their heads talking to themselves they are distracted and not capable of playfully engaging with their partner. They are more apt to misperceive a partner's temporary slow-down to catch her breath or to change position as a rejection. If they are obsessing about whether they will get turned on, or if the man will sustain an erection, or if the woman will have an orgasm, or if this sexual encounter is working, very likely they won't and it isn't.

We've been looking at the kinds of interference that detract from being fully present in the interactive pleasures of the moment and interfere with becoming fully aroused. But sometimes the issue is not becoming aroused but rather becoming too aroused too quickly. A key feature of insecure attachment is the inability to down-regulate stress.

A man who is prone to rapid ejaculation prior to intromission or within seconds of penetration is incapable of down-regulating his excitement to a level where the pleasure can be contained and sustained long enough to spread throughout his body to become fully aroused. Women too, in a rush to climax can have premature orgasms that are more of a blip than a bang.

All of these sexual issues can be ameliorated in therapy that focuses on helping partners support greater security through loving interactions that down-regulate each other's stress rather than contribute to each other's insecurity. This is generally referred to as "earned security" when security is a product of healing adult relationships. Helping the couple to be more focused on the present, to become more empathic with each other in the moment and less reactive, and supporting each other's healing from the deficits of the past are critical features of embodied relational presence.

As the partners develop the ability to be present in the moment, to focus on the other rather than on themselves, and to breathe deeply and become more attuned to their sensual pleasures, the result doesn't just add to the likelihood of a couple's feeling greater sexual satisfaction. Being able to be more present with one's partner, to relax, get in touch with the sensory qualities of physical closeness, and share pleasure can enhance each individual's sense of self-confidence and sexual competency. Becoming more sexually secure has the reciprocal effect of contributing to feeling more emotionally secure and more secure in the relationship.

Becoming more attuned to the present through noticing the flow of sensation in the body is one of the valuable effects of meditation practice and development of mindfulness. As interpersonal neurobiologist, Dan Siegel describes it,

> Sensation is a really important bottom-up experience. It's a flow of bottom-up detail that is extremely helpful for us to be able to hold

onto the present moment, not getting lost in prior learning or worries about the future. It brings us right into the present moment and in this way is fundamental to mindfulness.

(Siegel, 2009)

Picking Up Sensory Signals: Experiential Therapy Is Sense Awareness

What does it mean to work in the present? Does it mean that past history is irrelevant? Quite the contrary. Early history is highly significant particularly in discovering how the past is present and resonating in the bodily experience of the moment.

Relational distress is a reflection of each individual's developmental history during times of stress. With the couple facing each other and looking into the other's eyes, the present-centered experiential process of sharing feelings accesses the multiple layers of their total beings going all the way back to how their young brains have been programmed from earliest interactions with mother, father, siblings, and others. Watching their faces and bodies we can begin to spot the sensory exchanges that trigger each other.

When two people start therapy, each person has an early childhood relational history that is now compounded by their current adult relational history. Working in the present means that we are looking not only at how the individuals interact moment by moment, but also how body-to-body sensory elements of their interaction may be activating past emotional triggers and knee-jerk reactions. Interactions that activate feelings of anxiety, guilt, or shame typically elicit defensive patterns that interfere with ability to resolve the issues. We are looking for how old patterns of reactivity are reflected in a couple's present interactions.

In their intersubjective interactions, both partners' pasts dovetail in their reactions to one another. Even when they act understanding of one another, past experience with understanding but controlling parents can trigger guilt feelings mixed with resentment.

One couple, dealing with the wife's lack of sexual interest in her husband, is a good case in point. He spoke to her in very soft, patient tones, his eyes wide reflecting empathy, nodding his head toward her as he spoke. They both came from loving homes. Yet as he spoke, she grew increasingly uncomfortable, looking away several times.

When she finally spoke, she said somewhat facetiously, "I appreciate that you empathize with me. But I'm feeling like the bad child who keeps screwing up and that doesn't make me feel sexy toward you."

When I asked about his measured speech, the man recognized that he had learned to speak that way growing up with a loving but demanding mother whom he would try to please by carefully explaining himself to her. He got very good at it. Unfortunately, it evoked a simmering resentment in his wife.

Or two people may have grown up feeling misunderstood and criticized, in which case they may have an interactive pattern of being critical and blaming each other, making them feel defensive and self-protective. Criticism is spoken not just with words but with dismissive body language, no matter how hard each individual may try to conceal his or her feelings. Subtle head shakes signaling no, clipped vocal tones, narrowing of the eyes, tight lips, thrusting chins. All of it can be tiny little movements and still drive up the tensions between them.

The preverbal and nonverbal foundation of this imprinting shows up in the unavoidably reactive body and subtle emotional leakage. In person-to-person interactions, there are two simultaneous conversations taking place, a left brain-to-left brain, verbal disclosure and a right brain-to-right brain, bodily disclosure. These minute emotional exchanges occur in facial micro-expressions that may last only a nanosecond—in a tone of voice that may reflect annoyance, or in a dismissive shoulder shrug that arouses anxiety.

The implicit body to-body communications that reflect the deepest emotional roots and expectations of each person's true feelings are communicated interactively and subliminally through what the eyes see, the ears hear, what is conveyed in a touch, in face-to-face close physical proximity to one another. If one person's words don't match his or her body language, the body of the other unconsciously registers the discrepancy and that can trigger an emotional reaction.

Implicit Memory

The sensory experiences of childhood are forever lodged in our emotional memory brain centers in the limbic system and the neural connections to the autonomic nervous system triggers. Early emotional reactions to sensory experiences likewise can remain in the body as visceral and muscular memories. These sense memories are typically implicit and below the threshold of conscious awareness. People can be triggered without knowing they have been triggered or recognizing the sensory element of the present encounter that is reminiscent of a past emotional event.

Sense memories from infancy and early childhood that occur prior to language are likely to remain unconsciously perceived but can still trigger feelings. They can involve picking up a microsecond of disapproval in the eyes of the other, a slight tone of annoyance in the voice or a flip gesture that may not have been noticed. But suddenly there's a heavy feeling in the chest or a sense of annoyance with the other.

Sensory Processing and Adult Attachment: Implications for Intimacy

Different attachment styles may also correlate with different styles of processing sensory stimuli. Sensory processing sensitivity has been defined as the degree to which people can detect and respond to various subtle stimuli in their environment as well as between themselves and other individuals. The original studies investigating the differences between introverts and extroverts found that individuals classified as introverts had a higher overall sensitivity to sensory stimulation and had lower thresholds to sound, pain, touch, and smell (Aron & Aron, 1997; Stelmack & Campbell, 1974).

The descriptions of introverts closely resemble individuals with avoidant attachment style, and more recent studies have found that individuals with an avoidant style do tend to be more agitated by, and to avoid, strong stimulation. They also appear to be less attentive to interpersonal cues as a coping strategy (Dunn, 2001). In contrast, anxious individuals are more attentive to interpersonal cues and tend to seek out sensory connections in relationships. In general, they are more alert to subtle sensory cues in close physical contact (Jerome & Liss, 2005).

Attentiveness to sensory stimuli is another critical factor both in intimate emotional connection and particularly in sexual connection. Avoidant individuals, perhaps because of their hypersensitivity to strong stimuli, tend to become less attuned to bodily cues and to withdraw. Anxious individuals in contrast tend to be much more attentive to body-based cues and hypersensitive to signs of rejection (Dunn, 2001).

Sense Memories: The Foundations of Emotional Programming

The senses play a key role in triggering emotional learning and processing during person-to-person interactions. The subtle emotional cues that are exchanged consciously or unconsciously between each person's body are transmitted and received through our senses.

That means there is a fundamental and intricate connection between the senses—what the body picks up—and the feelings and emotions that are triggered. And it all happens in a matter of nanoseconds. How the sense information is perceived, i.e., understood emotionally, is a reflection of each person's earliest intersubjective interactions with parents during their first years of life.

The senses are typically understood as the five ordinary senses of seeing, hearing, touch, taste and smell, and the sixth sense of intuition and gut feelings. Since there is continuing speculation on how many senses there actually are, I will take the liberty toward the end of this chapter to recognize a seventh sense and to speculate about an eighth sense.

Body-to-Body Sensing: The Link Between Love and Sex

Most therapists will seek to address the underlying and unresolved emotional issues between partners that interfere with closeness or sexual contact and how those feelings affect their ability to enjoy emotional or sexual intimacy. Here we look at something even more fundamental than emotions: the nonverbal, sensory communications that are associated relationally with triggering unresolved emotional states.

Developmentally, since sensory reception precedes differentiation of early infant affect into recognizable emotions, it makes sense to look at the role the senses play in the foundational programming of the brain, particularly the emotionally connected right limbic brain.

In Chapter 6 we take a more detailed look at the emotions. In this chapter we look at what intimates sense consciously and unconsciously from one another, how they derive personal meaning from what they sense, and how that affects them emotionally. We can see how two people bring their body-to-body relational sense memories of intimate love and sexual desire to bear on one another.

Sensory communications affect body-to-body intimacy through the five external senses of touch, seeing, hearing, taste, and smell, particularly through facial expression, tone of voice, and body language, i.e., what they read into those postures and gestures. Partners also pick up sense data from each other's body through smell and taste reception. We also have several internal senses that are conditioned to those external senses that contribute to emotional reactivity.

Body-based therapists have to be attuned to the vast assortment of sensory cues that can pass between intimates and affect their interaction. Even more importantly, it's essential for the therapist to be tuned into the variety of sensory information available to him or her as the intuitive basis for therapeutic intervention during a session. In the next chapter we will see how sense memory can affect sexual interactions and how to work with the sensory interactions to enhance body-to-body intimacy.

A Developmental History of Embodied Love: Sensory Roots

We start life in a body-to-body symbiosis with another living being. Inside her body, we can hear her heart beat and feel her movements. Outside her body we're hardwired to stay close for sustenance and soothing and to feel alarm at separation.

Schore points out that our emotional and social beginnings are closely tied into the maturation of the sensory systems. All senses begin to develop in the womb so that by the time of birth a neonate will relax to the smell of the mother, the warmth of her touch and the familiar sound of her voice. After birth, the earliest sensory exchanges between mother and infant occur through touch in body-to-body contact and stroking, eye contact and facial expressions, and in tone of voice. Smell and taste, the chemical senses, also pay key roles in this primal intimacy experience.

Around eight weeks of age, held in mother's arms, we look into her eyes and our facial muscles subtly begin to mimic her face. Nerve endings in the infant's face send impulses up to the central nervous system, shaping structures of the brain, particularly the right limbic brain and the nearby regulatory orbital prefrontal cortex, and down to the autonomic nervous system, programming sympathetic arousal or parasympathetic calming, matching the mother's emotional state.

In this duet of interactive facial exchanges between mother and infant the right hemisphere of our neonatal brain begins to download the emotions, expressions, and cellular memories of becoming a human, in this family and this culture, at this time. This right brain-to-right brain engagement is the very first body-to-body interactive exchange with another human being that begins to shape the unique individual we are to become. This embodied primal intimacy becomes the underlying foundation for all later intimacies.

Substantial research now shows that the brain is divided into right and left hemispheres and that each hemisphere is dominant for different functions. The right brain is the emotional brain, the first to develop in the womb and more directly connected to the autonomic nervous system (ANS). The left brain is dominant for language and logic and doesn't begin to develop until the child begins to understand language and to say words at around 18 to 24 months (McGilchrist, 2009; Schore, 2003).

If we look at the nature of that early imprinting we can get a layered perspective on how the nonverbal communications between intimate adults can trigger unresolved emotional pain from the past. And, on the positive side, how empathic responsiveness to an individual's painful expressions can reactivate and revitalize a developmental process in that adult.

The infant's experience-dependent right brain requires an interactive relationship with another right brain in order to mature. A key determinant of the bonding process rests on how well the mother can interactively regulate the infant's affect, i.e., stress and emotions. This initiates an imprinting process of the right limbic brain during infancy and childhood that becomes a strong determinant of an individual's sense of security or insecurity (Schore, 1994, 2003, 2012).

The limbic brain is a set of brain structures, and the most commonly known ones include the thalamus, hypothalamus, hippocampus, and amygdala, which support a variety of key functions that involve the regulation of the autonomic nervous system and emotions, perception of the emotional states of others, developing emotional memories, and the forming of social bonds. Through the psychobiological attunement between mother and infant, the mother helps regulate the infant's affect or stress, and it is through this quality of resonance in which the mother becomes a biological mirror for the infant that the infant comes to understand his or her inner experience.

This quality of "limbic resonance" has been described as a kind of harmonic interactive process of "mutual exchange and internal adaptation" whereby two individuals become attuned to each other's inner experience. This experience of looking into the eyes of the other and seeing oneself reflected back, met in kind, in an intimate emotional and physiological attunement, has been described as the essence of intimate adult loving (Lewis et al., 2000).

The Sensory Brain: From Early Development to Adult Attraction

Like Starman, we have all fallen to Earth. We drop from mother's womb to a bed or a hospital table or, as chance would have it, less hospitable environs. Rhythmically squeezed down a warm, soft, slippery narrow chute, we arrive to a world of cool air and bright light, sounds and jarring movements. Eventually, we are held against warm human flesh, rocked and cuddled gently. The sound of a human voice may be recognizable from the womb, softly intoning safety and calm. Nerve cells firing alarm become less intense and the new earthly body relaxes and sleeps. This, of course, is under the best of circumstances.

Our small healthy brains are loaded with infinite capabilities at birth: the capacity to speak any language, to remember, to reason, to fantasize pictures and stories in our mind's eye, to dream, to be creative, to love, and to be part of a social group. We know from neuroscience that we're born with more nerve cells than we will ever have again, even more than we could ever use in an entire lifetime. That's our human potential. Neurons that are activated blossom; those that remain dormant are pruned. We have inner resources that we may never tap. In fact, many of those hidden talents may be accessed only during times of stress and challenge, stimulating a new spate of brain maturation and adaptation.

What potentiates our potential is human interaction, and that interaction actually begins before birth in the womb. It starts in the nonverbal right hemisphere of the brain that is dominant at birth. Which of the brain's myriad capacities get activated and in which form depends on the experiential-relational transactions between the brain of the primary caretaker "turning on the lights" of the developing brain of the infant (Trevarthen, 1993).

Those lights get turned on through interpersonal sensory and sensual interactions between parent and infant. In fact, turning on the lights is an apt metaphor, as brain studies show, when mother and infant are in emotional synchrony, particularly at play, their brains light up in exactly the same place in the brain at exactly the same time. I think of it as nature's instant messaging.

The right brain-to-right brain social downloading process relies completely on the experiential interpersonal sensory exchanges between infant and caretaker. Through parental touch and bodily movements, parent-child eye contact and vocalizations, brain-activating signals are transmitted from the mature, sensate human brain to sensory receptors in the infant brain. Most of the studies on early attachment focus on vision, hearing, and touch as they impact the baby's body through the sense receptors of eyes, ears, and skin. As we shall see, smell and taste also are very much involved as well as other inner sense receptors.

Sense and Sense Ability: The Five Ordinary Senses

We typically think of the senses in terms of the exteroceptors, the ordinary five senses of seeing, hearing, touching, smelling, and taste that respond to external stimuli impinging on receptors in the eyes, ears, skin, nose, and mouth. In fact, there is not a great deal of agreement about how many senses there are, or even what can rightfully be called a sense. We begin here with the senses we can all agree on.

Skin and the Sense of Touch

Touch is the first sense to develop in the womb, before there are either eyes or ears, and beginning at around eight weeks gestation. During the time in utero, the walls of the uterus expand and contract, the amniotic sac pulsates, and the fetus' sense of touch is continually being stimulated. After birth, empathic touch by the primary caregiver is recognized as a critical factor for developing the capacity for affective bonding in the early maturation of the neonate brain. An early series of studies has highlighted the critical mental and physical effects of human tactile stimulation in the first two years of a baby's life.

We know that infants left in orphanages during the early 1900s in Europe and the United States and in Romania during the 1980s had high rates of mortality. Infant marasmus, literally a wasting away, was eventually traced to touch deprivation. Studies also show a connection between touch deprivation in childhood and the tendency toward greater aggression and violence in adolescents. Touch deprivation in adults can also be an important part of their emotional distress. People with high levels of skin-hunger have been found to be more lonely, depressed, and stressed and in poorer health when compared with people with moderate to low levels of skin-hunger.

There is certainly clinical evidence, that some of our clients, particularly single people, will engage in sexual activity not because they want sex but because they feel a need to be touched. In other studies, on human babies as well as with other mammals, affective touch was shown to have an analgesic effect, soothing pain.

Affectionate touch is critical for the quality of connection in an intimate relationship and there is much to recommend warm hugs and strokes between partners on a daily basis. In one study, tactile stimulation was highly correlated with overall relationship satisfaction and satisfaction with one's partner. Seven different types of non-sexual physical affection were studied including, backrubs/massages, caressing/stroking, cuddling/holding, holding hands, hugging, kissing on the face, and kissing on the lips. Resolving conflict was also found to be easier with increasing amounts of cuddling, hugging, and kissing (Gulledge et al., 2003).

Affectionate touch has an analgesic effect not just for babies but for adults as well. In a laboratory study utilizing a brief electric shock, women who held hands with their male partner during the study had lower levels of pain during the shock. Moreover, the couple's heart and respiratory rates came into sync as the woman's pain dissipated (Goldstein et al., 2017).

Other studies show that anxious individuals can be calmed by tender strokes, and depressed individuals can feel uplifted by a hug Gallace & Spence, 2010).

Hearing and Vocal Tone

The ears of the developing fetus in the womb begin to form at about nine weeks of gestation. The fetus can hear sound by 18 weeks and by the third trimester can not only make out voices, but can make out the mother's voice, responding with an increased heart rate. This suggests that the fetus becomes more alert at the sound of her voice (healthline.com). Though newborn babies can hear at birth, their immature hearing apparatus responds best to high-pitched and exaggerated vocal tones (www.webmd.com/parenting/baby/newborn-hearing).

Prosody or vocal tone is a key factor in recognition of the emotional state of the other and can have an instantaneous effect on the listener. Mothers intuit their baby's distress by the tone and intensity of the baby's cry to determine his/her needs at the moment. Is she in pain, hungry, or just tired?

Babies can also discern their mother's emotional state by the sound of her voice in combination with her facial expressions. Soft melodious tones comfort the infant and signal the mother's ease; clipped, harsh tones signal the mother's tension and will raise tension in the infant. Infants can distinguish between positive affect like laughter (rising pitch) and negative affect like crying (falling pitch) and are more likely to attend to, and show a preference for, positive affect (Beebe & Lachmann, 2002).

Adult couples are particularly sensitive to vocal tone. In a study at the University of Utah, utilizing audio-visual recordings of couples in therapy during real problem-solving interactions, they found that tone of voice was a better predictor of marital success than any other behavioral variable observed by a team of psychologists (Nasir et al., 2015).

Vision: Eye-to-Eye

In the first year of life, the visual sense plays a primary role in the forming of the attachment bond. The infant shows intense interest in the mother's face, and mother and infant are likely to spend much time in mutual gazing in a nonverbal face-to-face communication. Mother may engage her baby playfully, widening her eyes as if in surprise and smiling. Baby mirrors her smile and excitement. When the baby fusses uncomfortably mother's eyes may narrow in concern or anxiety. Her vocal tones or bodily movements accompany her facial expressions. All the while, baby's face is mirroring her face in an early form of empathy (Schore, 2003).

In this way, key structures of the experience-dependent right brain are programmed. The prefrontal cortex plays an important role in affect-regulation, and understanding and enjoying social signals and inter-action. The PFC lies on top of the limbic system, the emotional-motivational center that responds with reward and excitement to playful interactions or with aversion and inhibition to disruptions in the affective communication. The limbic system exerts major control over the ANS, triggering sympa-thetic excitement and activation or parasympathetic calming.

When mother and infant look into each other's eyes, the sympathetic nervous system is activated in each of them. When the stimulation of the gaze becomes too intense for the baby, he or she looks away, trigger-ing the parasympathetic relaxation response in both. Ideally, the mother waits until the baby re-engages and returns the gaze. This pattern of gaze, gaze avert, return gaze, and the mirroring of facial expression becomes the earliest channel for the development of empathy and understanding the emotional states of others and oneself. In this way the early develop-ing limbic system and the affective regulatory system of the prefrontal right hemisphere begin to be shaped (Schore, 2003; Tronick, 1989).

This pattern of gaze, gaze avert, return gaze, and the mirroring of facial expression remains a conduit of mutual emotional attunement in romantic attraction. In a series of independent studies on young adults in US and Canadian college pubs and singles bars, anthropologist David Givens (1983) and sex researcher Timothy Perper (1985) both found that gaze and gaze avert patterns characterized initial signs of interest between individuals that they characterized as courting signals. Each gaze lingers a little longer before looking away. When the gaze becomes more deliberate, the individuals are likely to approach one another and begin a process that with each step the likelihood of their leaving the bar together becomes inevitable.

Having an emotionally responsive facial expression is another com-forting signal in any interaction. Babies are hardwired to interact with a facially expressive mother and become distressed when the mother's face shows no sign of emotion. In a series of classic experiments, moth-ers were instructed to play naturally with their infants for two minutes after which they were to continue to face him or her but to cease any facial expression for two minutes. The results were profound. During the two-minutes of "still-face" the infants repeatedly attempted to engage the mother, at first by smiling and cooing, then becoming distressed, agitated and crying. If the mother continued to be unresponsive, the infant also became disengaged and slower to respond to her when she became responsive again (Tronick et al., 1978).

As an adult, a lack of emotional expression on the face of one's inti-mate during an encounter can automatically trigger anything from subtle uneasiness, to shame, or in some people, panic. Which of these painful emotions will be triggered depends on an individual's emotional make-up and sense of security.

Eye contact and rapid facial micro-expressions remain the most significant forms of nonverbal communication across the lifespan, particularly in physically close and emotional interactions. What's important about these emotional and memory triggers is that these implicit memories are largely unconscious right brain activation and bodily reactions that may not reach conscious, cognitive awareness.

Body Language in Movements and Gestures

A loving parent looks at his or her son or daughter with an open relaxed face and a look of affection in the eyes. The eyes linger on the face of the child, the face is soft, and there is a hint of a smile on the mouth and in the eyes. The voice is warm, deep, and gentle. The child sees him or herself mirrored in their father's and mother's face as an individual worthy of love, prized, valued, approved of, enjoyable to be with, and fun to play with. This child grows up to be an adult who takes pride in himself or herself as someone lovable and worthy and who has a lot to offer to a love mate.

Of course, parents aren't always available. Sometimes they have their own troubles, moods, bad days or evenings. They may not be as attentive as they have been, and their voice may take on a harsh tone of annoyance. Mom and Dad may have a fight and when mother picks up baby the angry expression may still be in her eyes, the set of her jaw, and in her breathing rhythm. Her rocking may be too fast and jerky, her voice more tense.

If the moods and bad days pass and the parent is back loving and attentive, the disappointment or momentary rupture in the relationship is repaired and things go back to normal, being loved and cared for. If the loving interaction continues, that child grows up to be an adult who expects good results when a relationship is stressed and is confident that two people are capable of reestablishing a loving connection after a fight or other kind of emotional withdrawal. On the other hand, if a parent's anxiety and intrusiveness or irritability and preoccupation are more the rule than the exception, these children are more likely to grow up to be an adult whose body is sensitized for signs of uneasiness or distractibility.

Smell and Taste Senses

Babies have well-developed senses of smell and taste that begin to grow in the womb and are present at birth. Both of these senses have important implications for emotional memory and sexual attraction and are directly connected to the limbic system. Smell in particular is evocative of memories of time passed, the scent of a perfume worn by your mother or a former girlfriend can immediately bring up a nostalgic memory and old feeling associated with that person.

Smell has also been associated with possibly being the "chemistry" in an initial attraction with a potential lover. Studies have shown that heterosexual women will instinctively find themselves more attracted to men whose scent is a reflection of DNA that is somewhat alike to their own but different enough to avoid in-breeding. Studies even show that a mate with desirable genes for a woman is more likely to produce better orgasms and a more satisfying sex life for both of them (Spector, 2005; www.theguardian.com/science/2005/jun/08/genetics. research).

The Sixth Sense: Interoception, Neuroception, and the Enteric Nervous System

The *interoceptors* are sense receptors that are located on every organ inside the body—including the heart, liver, lungs, blood vessels, and especially the gut—that respond to internal stimuli. These receptors respond to changes in temperature, pressure, vibration, and pain, for example, and regulate our internal environment and homeostasis. Proprioceptors are a special class of interoceptors that are located in the inner ear, limbs, and near muscles and tendons that send information to the brain about our movements and orientation in space.

What we commonly think of as the sixth sense is now increasingly understood as responding intuitively to information we have that we don't know we have through interoception. We pick up information implicitly all the time that the body reacts to emotionally, although we don't always know where that information is coming from. We just feel it, intuitively. We call it a gut feeling and it is very likely that we are accessing information subliminally, below the level of conscious awareness, and responding to body-based sense reception. More information about gut feelings is below on the enteric nervous system.

In fact, I have conjectured that while we consciously register information that comes through visible light, sound, or smell sensory spectrums, it is very likely we are still able to pick up wave lengths and stimuli that occur outside what is considered the ordinary human spectrums for reception of each of the senses. Instead of thinking of this as extrasensory perception, as though this talent is somehow magical, I suggest that this body-based sense of intuitive knowing may be more accurately described as *ultra*sensory perception (Resnick, 1997).

For example, we may be in the process of making a deal with someone and suddenly we feel our heart race or a sinking feeling in the pit of the stomach. Something just doesn't "smell right." Terms like "sniffing around for information" and "having a nose for news" are not just figures of speech. We are constantly responding to scent information without registering the source as a scent. Individuals who pay attention to their bodily signals may be rewarded with the good sense to pull back from a deal because something "smells fishy" (Resnick, 1997).

Indeed, that may be more than a metaphor. Scientists have recently discovered that olfactory and taste receptors exist on the skin and on every organ of the body—in the heart, blood vessels, liver, lungs, and kidneys—and in the reproductive system. There are even odor receptors in sperm cells that affect the movement of sperm toward the ovum. Promising research suggests that olfactory receptors in cancer tumors may respond to treatment by different combinations of herbal scents. We now know that dogs can be trained to sniff out and recognize cancer. It makes sense that olfactory and taste receptors would be valuable in regulating the internal bodily environment since smell and taste are chemoreceptors capable of responding to chemical stimuli released by internal organs (Weber et al., 2016; Altman, 2004).

Neuroception, as described by polyvagal theory developer Stephen Porges, is an inner sense related to sensory information picked up by the nervous system regarding safety and danger. Recognizing the nervous system as a sense reception network particularly identifies the role of the vagus nerve activation of the heart, lungs, and gut response under stress, and the physiological value of utilizing intentional breathing to calm stress and enhance presence. Psychologist and breath work practitioner B Grace Bullock has described how slow, deep inhales and elongated exhales activates the calming parasympathetic system, broadening the range of response to threat beyond merely escape and defense, and enhances capacity to be mindful in relationships (Porges, 2011; Bullock, *www.YogaUOnline.com*).

The Enteric Nervous System

Another important internal sense originates in the enteric nervous system, considered the second brain or the "gut brain." More specifically, this system is located in the tissue that lines the esophagus, stomach, small intestine, and colon. Many of the gastrointestinal disorders that have been linked to emotions like irritable bowel syndrome originate here. During times of stress or perceived danger sensory nerves running from the brain to the gut release hormones directly to the gut and account for the well-known experience of "feeling butterflies" in that area of the body. Signals can also originate in the gut that are transmitted to the higher brain (retrieved from www.psyking.net/id36.htm).

The Sexual Sense: The Seventh Sense of Erotoception and Sexual Pleasures

It's entirely implausible to me that sexual arousal is rarely treated as a sense in its own right but it has all the earmarks of a true sense. I think of it as the seventh sense. The genitals are not just organs of reproduction; they are sensory organs, no less than the eyes, ears, nose, mouth, skin, and gut. The clitoris, vagina, and cervix in the woman, the penis and testes of a man, and the anus in general, all contain different erotic sensory nerves. As a result, each of the different areas can produce distinct sensations when stimulated.

Female sensory nerves include the hypogastic nerves in the uterus and cervix, the pelvic nerves in the cervix and vagina, and the pudendal nerves in the clitoris. The vagus nerves have also been shown to respond to stimulation to the cervix. In men, pudendal nerves in the penis and scrotum and hypogastric nerves in the testes all respond to sensory stimulation and convey sensory signals to the brain (Komisaruk et al., 2006).

Of all the sensory organs, the clitoris holds a special position as the only organ in the human body whose sole function is for pleasure. The head of the clitoris contains over 8,000 sensory nerve endings, almost twice as many as on the head of the penis (Di Marino & Lapidi, 2014).

In fact, all of our senses can be eroticized and send sexually arousing signals directly to the pelvic region, all over the body and to the brain. Any body part that is known to be an "erogenous zone" is responding to erotoception. Aside from the obvious touching, squeezing, and oral and genital stimulation of the pelvic region, there is erotoception across a wide area of the body. Most importantly, as with every other sense, each area is positively responsive to its own distinct preferential sensory modality. When sensory signals bring pleasurable sensations to different areas of the body, we typically refer to them as sensual experiences. For example:

Starting with the top of the head and working down, there are erogenous zones in the gentle touch of the skin of the face; the breathing in of bodily aromas and the scentless inhale of pheromones; in the softness of the lips, taste and feel of an inviting mouth; in the soft whispers and warm breath in the ears; in kisses to the neck, crook of the arm and armpit; in the caresses of the breasts, chest, nipples, belly, and inner thighs;

in the squeezing and loving taps on the butt; in the licking and sucking of the fingers and toes.

Smell holds a particularly evocative place in the limbic system, and, in fact, this area of the brain was originally dubbed the rhinencephalon as it was thought of as a primitive emotional and motivational "nose-brain." But all of these different stimuli go directly to different structures in the limbic system which controls sexual experience, memory, motivation, hunger, and all the emotions from love to fear, to rage, to ecstasy.

In the same way that paying attention to the sensory potentials in any moment can enhance intuition and empathy, paying attention to the sensual potentials in the moment can enhance pleasurable feelings and a positive state of mind. Sensual experiences that are also sexually arousing are likely to inspire erotic play between partners, or for that matter, on one's own for self-pleasuring.

Sex and Transcendence: Spirituality as the Eighth Sense?

There is also the possibility that spiritual feelings may be a reflection of an eighth sense, that of enjoying a deep conviction of being a part of something good that is larger than oneself, connected to all humanity and all living things. A spiritual experience is often said to involve a sense of the eternal and reverence for a higher power, and may be associated with spiritual practices like meditating, chanting, prayer, singing hymns or ingesting certain psychotropic drugs like LSD or Ecstasy.

In a series of studies by neuroscientists, findings suggest that spiritual or religious practices may quiet regions of the parietal lobe of the brain, which are associated with having a separate sense of self (Johnstone et al., 2012). Neuroscientist Andrew Newburg ran brain scans on nuns and Buddhists who reported feelings of timelessness and self-transcendence during times of prayer and meditation. Newburg noted that the feeling of oneness often reported in spiritual experience is related to quieting the parietal lobe activity. He also found that "mystical experiences are blissful or ecstatic because they share many of the same neural pathways in the parietal and frontal lobes that are involved in sexual arousal" (Newberg, 2014).

There is a rich body of literature on sacred sex for people who report times of extraordinary lovemaking identified by the participants as transcendent experiences. These events are described as reaching realms of intense sexual pleasure that involve an exquisite loss of boundaries between two individuals, united in an orgasmic flood of feeling, soaring together into space. These moments of sexual ecstasy can become the province of those who through intense emotion can fully surrender to, and achieve a state of complete and total immersion in one another (Feuerstein, 1992).

These sexual experiences are often generated through powerful feelings of love and gratitude. As therapists, we certainly can't guarantee that our clients will achieve such a state of transcendence. Yet through repairing wounds of the past and present, and encouraging greater presence, empathy, gratitude, and forgiveness with one another, the potential for experiences of sexual ecstasy is strengthened.

Presence as Sense Awareness: Reception, Perception, Imagery, and Phenomenology

Now that we have looked at the vastness of our sensory network, we can see there is much to attend to in the present moment when we are with clients. First, there is our own sense reception in terms of what we are picking up and can become aware of from observing them. Then there are our clients' sensory experiences. We want to be able to help them become attuned to what they are getting from each other on a sensory level, how those facial or gestural cues make them feel emotionally, and what they trigger in each other as a result.

In terms of our own sense reception and especially, perception—which is the meaning we make from what we see and hear—the challenge for us is to resist the urge to figure out what's going on so we can explain it to them. If we are in our left brains and interpreting their reactions we are bringing them into their left brains. What's critical here is to get out of our heads where we may be strategizing, or interpreting. We want to lead them to make their own discoveries. It will be more meaningful for them that way.

Besides, trying to figure out what's going on takes us out of the present moment and the authentic relational interaction with our clients, which we now know is the genuine agent of healing and repair. We want to stay tuned into what we are seeing, hearing, feeling, and picking up from our inner senses.

Fritz Perls famously said, "Lose your mind and come to your senses!" Fritz studied sensory awareness with one of the leading practitioners of body awareness, Charlotte Selver. I also trained with Charlotte. Her exercises utilized very slow meditative movements that involve simple activities of noticing the breath in the body, how we "come to standing" or start to sit or move about a room. Charlotte emphasized being present and attentive to sensation. Here's a slightly edited response by Selver in answer to an interviewer about her work:

> We can help people to become more awake, and after they begin to wake up, they learn to trust their own sensations . . . They can discover they really can see, and hear, and sense, and that this alone can be a very powerful agent in one's life. People have usually learned from other people what to think. We don't have to look to other people to be told what is right. The possibility of discovering gradually that one can trust one's own reactions can be a very powerful event.
>
> (Schick, 2004)

This is particularly true for therapists. By the time, we earn our advanced degrees we have studied multiple leaders in our field, mountains of research, and numerous schools of thought. We have been supervised in our work, and we have been critiqued in our nascent attempts to be helpful to clients. We have been trained in a variety of different methods, some of which have been standardized to follow distinct steps. The approach I'm suggesting has to do with relying on your own body to pick up the salient body-to-body cues passing between partners and reaching us.

Actors often talk about how their body is their instrument. That's true for therapists as well. Our body is our instrument, and just like an actor, we can train ourselves in terms of what we see, hear, feel, and sense intuitively. In the same way, we can help our clients to recognize their programming based on what they learned for good or ill from their parents and teachers. We want to explore with them the values and judgments they may have introjected from others that may not reflect their current values or best judgments for themselves.

Much of our work can help clients to observe their own authentic sensations, how they make sense of their perception and whether their interpretations are based on an unquestioned belief system or expectations that have no basis in reality. Here's an example of a present-centered process for a couple that starts with observing their moment-to-moment sensory communication.

Present-Moment Body-to-Body Awareness: Sue and Charlie

This interaction takes place in a couples' workshop at Esalen Institute in front of 14 other couples. Sue says there are times she feels as though she just can't get through to Charlie. Charlie says he has had the exact same frustration with Sue. We are all sitting on the floor around the room on big pillows. I ask Sue and Charlie to come into the center of the room facing each other, to take a few deep breaths, hold hands, and look into each other's eyes.

I say, "Notice what you see in your partner's face and any sensations or feelings aroused in your body as you look at your partner." I immediately notice that Charlie has changed the angle of his head so that his head is now slightly thrown back, chin is pointing up, eyebrows lifted and his eyes have widened. He appears to be looking down at Sue whose head is now tilted upward to maintain eye contact.

I ask them to notice how they are feeling toward the other right now. Charlie says he feels comfortable, though he feels his heart beating more quickly, and he's looking forward to what will come next. Sue says she's feeling tense and uncomfortable, and a little anxious. She says she doesn't believe that Charlie is comfortable, that he looks defensive. Charlie looks away and gives a little snort when Sue says this; his mouth tics minutely to one side. Then his head tilts back again.

I ask Sue to describe what she sees on Charlie's face and she immediately responds, "He's looking down on me; he's judging me. I'm feeling afraid. I'm bracing myself." I can see that in her body. Her back is straight and she holds her head high, like a brave martyr or saint. Sue is thin and quite a bit smaller than Charlie who carries an air of authority on his face. He also seems braced and maybe a little inflated in his round chest.

I suggest to Sue to mirror back to Charlie how she sees him. She immediately runs to a corner of the room and stacks up two more pillows so that her head is now higher than Charlie's. She takes his hands, throws her head back, chin up, raises her eyebrows, tightens her mouth, and looks down at Charlie. She says, "I'm looking down my nose at you and I feel in charge now." Charlie laughs. He says to Sue, "Now you look like how my father looked at me. After a pause, his face darkens, "I can't believe I'm doing to you what he did to me." I now see a glimmer of sadness sweep across his face like a shadow. "I'm sorry," he whispers to Sue.

At that point, we did some process work with Charlie on his relationship with his judgmental father who was a pillar of the community as he was growing up. Then I thought it would be good to go back to the body memory he was emulating and to consciously feel it this time. He easily assumed the posture. I asked Sue to consciously feel her automatic relational response and her back goes up again, head high.

I ask Charlie to describe what he sees in Sue's face and body. He immediately says, "She's proud, strong, maybe a little superior, like she's better than me." I ask him how that makes him feel. His demeanor suddenly shifts; he drops his head now and looks squarely at Sue with a soft compassionate face. "She should be proud," he says warmly. "She's been through a lot and I love her." Sue's back relaxes, and her eyes well up in tears. She drops Charlie's hands and touches his face gently. "Thank you," she says. "I love you too."

At that point, I invite the rest of the group to join in and to give feedback to the couple in the center who were courageous, trusting, and generous in allowing us to witness their interaction. I define the only useful feedback as "how you relate personally to what you just witnessed in Sue and Charlie." Almost everyone shared feelings and memories that were triggered in them as they watched Sue and Charlie play out a body-based interaction they recognized as personally meaningful for them. Many identified with Charlie's personal work on his relationship with his father.

The kinds of sensory signals and reactivity that we see between partners either evoke a sense of trust that invites physical closeness or a sense of unease that drives a wedge between them. This is a major factor when it comes to feeling sexually attracted to and aroused with one's partner. In the next chapter, we look at how attachment style, sensory style, and early child and teenage sexuality combine to affect adult sexual interest, arousal, and the prospects for sexual pleasure in an intimate relationship.

5

Sexuality: Sexual Development, Love, and Lovemaking

Much of the research on the connection between attachment styles and adult sexuality appears to regard sexuality as beginning with puberty and teenage. Yet, there is substantial evidence that we are sexual at birth and the early cultural imprinting of sexuality and emotional associations through sensory communications starts very early and nonverbally. Freud knew this over 100 years ago, yet much of Western culture seem to still be resisting children's right to sexual discovery and any notion of "the erotic life of children."

> It is a part of popular belief about the sexual impulse that it is absent in childhood and that it first appears in the period of life known as puberty. This, though an obvious error, is a serious one in its consequences and is chiefly due to our present ignorance of the fundamental principles of the sexual life. . . . One occasionally finds in medical literature notes on the premature sexual activities of small children, about erections and masturbation and even actions resembling coitus, but these are referred to merely as exceptional . . . In the numerous writings on the development of the child the chapter on "Sexual Development" is usually passed over. Retrieved from: http://www.bartleby.com/278/2.html
>
> (Freud, 1905)

A Developmental History of Libido: Sex Before Birth

In the same way that our senses begin development in early gestation, there is substantial evidence that sexuality too begins before birth. Ultrasound examinations have shown fetuses exploring their own bodies in utero, handling their feet, head, face, genitals, and other parts of their bodies. Both male and female fetuses have been observed giving lingering attention to stimulating their genitals.

In one instance reported in the *American Journal of Obstetrics and Gynecology* (1996) a female fetus at 32 weeks gestation was observed stimulating her vulva with her fingers for close to a minute in the region of the clitoris. After a short break, the movements began again and were accompanied by leg and pelvis movements and contractions in the muscles of the trunk Giorgi and Siccardi (1996).

Male fetuses have been observed with erections in utero, stroking their penis as early as 16 weeks gestation. At birth, male newborns continue to have spontaneous erections while awake and at sleep. Female newborns' vaginas lubricate and clitorises swell within days of birth (Richardson & Schuster, 2004).

Infant and Child Sexuality

When babies begin to explore their bodies, they start to develop a body schema of their boundaries, a sense of me and not me. They suck on their fingers and toes and stroke their bellies and genitals. At first, discovering genitalia is one element in the beginning of this mental and physical body mapping, but by the second year, babies whose parents permit their explorations will intentionally rub, squeeze, stroke, and tug at their genitals while taking great delight in the activity.

As psychologist Michael Singer points out, early autoeroticism is natural in all babies and essential for healthy development.

> These early autoerotic activities are developmentally crucial for a number of reasons. They contribute to the development of intrapsychic schema of the infant's body as bounded, and hence differentiated from the external world. . . . Further, they contribute to a sense of the body-self as being a source of pleasure and potentially soothing, hence, a positive valuation and loving of one's body and self. Finally, these autoerotic activities "awaken" the person's sexuality, sensitizing him or her to sensual/erotic experience which becomes the foundation for satisfying mature sexual experience.
> (Singer, 2002)

The notion that emotionally healthy children are sexually "innocent" until puberty has been debunked, but the effects of sexual repression from our ancestors can persist in modern parents. Sexual uneasiness with regard to children has been going on a long time; in our more recent cultural history we can trace it back at least to our Victorian ancestors. This sexually repressed, and in some ways sexually obsessed, culture started around the 1840s in England and spread to America. Victorians as a rule were opposed to speaking about sex, to engaging in the "solitary vice" of masturbation, or to holding any regard for impure women who engaged in sex for any reason other than to procreate. Sexual pleasure in general was regarded as immoral and anti-religion (Foucault, 1990).

Traces of religious sexual repression have been transmitted brain-to-brain and body-to-body from adult to child for generations. Despite the good intentions of modern parents, if they are uneasy about sex because of their own family history, their nonverbal bodily cues will do the "talking" for them.

Sexually anxious parents can imprint their children to a biologically unnatural cultural or religious standard that can have lifelong implications. When family life is a sex-free zone, where sex is unseen, unspoken, and anxiety producing, the child becomes an adult who has learned to associate anxiety, shame, and secrecy with sexual feelings (Schermer-Sellers, 2017).

When parents frown, turn away, or slap the hand of an infant or child joyfully playing with his or her genitals, they transmit their discomfort directly to the child. It's an intergenerational inoculation of shame handed down from their mother and father and passed on to their son or daughter.

One client in individual therapy, Mary, described to me her state of alarm when she opened the door to her three-year-old twins' bedroom and saw one girl lying on her back legs spread while the other girl had her index finger inside the vagina of her sister and moving it in and out with auditory accompaniment, "boom, boom, boom." Both girls were giggling with delight as the mother looked at the scene in a state of shock. She felt herself tense up, told them in a clipped tone of voice to get ready for bed, and rushed out the door, slamming it by mistake.

Mary said she felt embarrassed and ashamed and hoped she hadn't ruined them for life. As we explored the complexity of her feelings, Mary recognized that she was simply reflecting her own intergenerationally transmitted experience of shame from her mother's traditional upbringing and discomfort with her sexuality. The processing work put her in touch with her genuine feelings of wanting the girls to enjoy their sexuality. She expressed the desire to get to a place where she and the girls could have an age-appropriate talk about sex and sex play where she was more empathic and positive.

Mary acknowledged that she wasn't quite there yet. Clearly, to do this for her little girls she would have to start with healing the sexually curious, playful little girl inside of herself. In the meantime, she recognized that she could take a breath and give the girls a smile if they ever again let themselves get caught being frisky.

Mary had come for therapy precisely because of her sexual distress in her marriage, and her husband was unwilling to join her in therapy. Talking about it was a great start, but there was a lot more to do to liberate her from her mother's repressive traditional values and her own feelings of sexual shame and inadequacy. That involved breathing, sensing, and re-experiencing memories that were awakened during therapy.

The fact that her husband wasn't amenable to explore his role in Mary's sexually inhibited response with him was a factor as well. That began yet another developmental track that had to do with her relationship with her husband—which presented its own complications and opportunities for growth.

Child Sex Play: Exploratory Sexual Pleasures

Juvenile sex play, a natural human developmental stage, can be observed in many other mammals from chimps to rats. In Harry Harlow's famous experiments with monkeys, female monkeys deprived of sex play as juveniles had both sexual and maternal deficiencies as adults. When male monkeys were deprived of sex play in youth, they were rendered incapable of sexual activity as adults. They were unable to read sexual signals from available females and were observed to thrust inappropriately at the female's side or face, what primatologist Harlow is said to have called, "the head-start program" (Konner, 2010; Novak & Harlow, 1975).

Babies and children are highly sensual beings. Babies are soothed by being held close to the mother's warm body and calmed by her smell. They are comforted by being rocked, talked to softly, or sung to. Most children also love physical contact; they enjoy hugging, cuddling, stroking mother's breasts, rubbing their face against a soft blanket, sticking fuzz inside their nose, or smelling a favorite toy.

Babies and young children are also sexual beings and will self-soothe and pleasure themselves by touching and holding on to their genitals. When toddlers and preschoolers grow up in a permissive home or day care center, they have been observed touching each other's genitals and spontaneously rubbing against each other with great delight. Between the ages of about three to four, children become increasingly interested in and likely to show each other their genitals, and between three and eight they can be observed "hugging, kissing, lifting each other, scuffling, sitting close to each other, and feeling jealousy when the object of their affection displays affection to someone else (Martinson, 1993).

As we have seen, playfulness with the parents during infancy and early childhood builds emotional security through the vitality and pleasure of the attachment bond and enhances the capacity for mutual love as an adult. In the same way, there can be no doubt that the societal tendency to suppress and shame child sex play has had a deleterious effect on the capacity of many adults to enjoy sexual pleasure, particularly in the context of a committed love relationship.

Children learn through play. Playing catch stimulates hand-eye coordination. Playing house is a way for preparing for assuming gender sex roles in one's own family. Psychobiologist Jaak Panksepp, who has devoted much of his research to understanding social bonds and the play mechanisms of the brain, recognizes various forms of human play.

Among these those most relevant to developing adult sexual fulfillment would likely be exploratory/sensorimotor play, relational/functional play, dramatic/symbolic play, and Panksepp's favorite, rough-and-tumble play. Although there is a great diversity to the types of playful activities, Panksepp notes that the single unifying factor for all types of play can be summarized as "fun."

A major value of play is that through play children can joyously and safely push their limits and discover their potentials. Play functions to enhance the learning of certain social (sex is social) skills, physical fitness, ability to think creatively, and problem-solving ability. Play also activates "certain types of neuronal growth that may serve to exercise and extend the range of behavioral options under the executive control of inborn emotional systems" (Panksepp, 1998).

Can there be any doubt that parents' and teachers' disapproval of children playing at being sexual can damage their sexual development and impede their ability to fully discover their erotic potentials? So, what is the alternative? My suggestion would be to show approval with smiles and encouragement while at the same time channeling the behavior so that it is done in private, away from the contaminating uneasiness of adults raised in a shame-based sex-negative culture. It's a delicate negotiation for many parents and teachers, but discovering a solution could be sexually empowering for the adults as well as the children.

Many of the individuals and couples with sexual issues can recall early experiences of "being caught" and punished for masturbating or "playing doctor" with a playmate and may still feel shame surrounding their earliest sexual encounters. In the five-day couples' retreats I co-lead with my husband, I talk about the natural stage of childhood sex play and its important role in sexual health. For the midday break, I give the assignment for each couple to sit together in a private space and to take turns candidly describing to one another their childhood exploratory experiences and how they felt about it then as a child and how they feel about it now.

The Burden of Early Stigma Can Last a Lifetime

At one Esalen couples' retreat, Sharon had a particularly profound experience sharing with her husband Owen the shame and guilt she still felt at age thirty-five about being caught playing sexually with another little girl at age seven. When the group re-convened she volunteered to share with the group her experience with the exercise. As she talked, she wept at how long she had kept this shame inside her and never confessed those feelings to Owen or anyone.

Sharon talked about how her mother had shamed her by telling the other girl's mother even though she begged her mother not to. She described how her friend's mother was alarmed and had prohibited these best friends from playing together or even talking. Sharon expressed the grief and loneliness she felt at losing her best friend with whom she shared so much more than sexual curiosity. During the exercise she began to see how the shame mingled with grief, that she experienced at age seven, had imbued sex with a tinge of disgust at herself mixed with sadness. It was a feeling she recognized that often cropped up, not only sexually, but whenever she was having "too good a time."

After telling Owen about this big secret she had carried all her life, Owen put his arms around her and said he was proud of her and grateful for her sharing this with him. She just fell into his arms and sobbed.

By taking the opportunity to share this pivotal childhood event, first with Owen and then the group, Sharon said she could feel the shame and guilt lift. She said she had been careful with her own children to not shame them but she was surprised at the pain and tears of shame that poured out of her as she was recounting the incident to her husband.

Now by pushing through her anxiety and sharing this with the group, Sharon said she was feeling a sense of pride and gratitude for the chance to unload a burden she had been carrying all her life. Several members of the group then expressed their gratitude for her courage and also revealed critical shame-induced turning points in their young lives. Some of the men and women from loving homes talked about their guilt and shame for making their parents so uneasy and distressed when they raised questions about sex or displayed any exuberance regarding sexual touching.

Failure to talk about sex with children is a failure to educate them and also a failure to protect them. When sex is secretive and seen as "naughty," children will refrain from talking to parents at all about sex, even after being abused and traumatized by a predatory adult. Several of my male and female clients who suffered unwanted sexual contact with older cousins, adults in the family, or with a teacher or religious figure said they never considered reporting it to their parents. Sex was not something talked about in the home. Some said they felt violated but were afraid they would either be blamed or not believed. One extreme example was a woman from a very traditional religious family who told me she was actually afraid her father would kill her.

Some clients who did tell a parent were told to just get over it. These people were doubly traumatized: first by the sexual assault and then by the abandonment by parents they saw as uncaring or impotent to support them.

Adolescent Sexuality

Adolescence is a stage in the child's maturation that begins with puberty and activation of the gonads, adrenals and pituitary glands secreting a host of sex and growth hormones, most notably testosterone and estrogen. Puberty can begin in some children as young as seven years old or as late as seventeen.

This is a developmental stage when the body begins a relatively rapid metamorphosis into becoming a sexual adult with more bodily hair, breasts, curves, muscles, and fully formed sex organs throbbing for attention. Adolescence is also a time of psychological and social challenges that accompany the growth spurts with changing moods and needs of the individual in the process of transition from child to adult.

The first major growth spurt of neurons and linkages to various parts of the brain occurs during the first two years of life. The second major neurobiological growth spurt occurs during adolescence. This is a transitional process that occurs over time with a proliferation of neurons, with strong connections to the amygdala, the fear and aggression center of the limbic system. At the same time, the prefrontal cortex, the memory, judgment, and planning center, is not yet fully formed, accounting somewhat for the reckless risks many of us took back then. Teenagers often make their decisions through the amygdala, the part of the brain associated with emotions, aggression, and impulsive behavior (Raising Children Network, 2017).

Adding to the neural development of the brain are the sex hormones of testosterone and estrogen, the adrenal stress hormones of cortisol and aldosterone, and growth hormones. At the same time all this is going on in the body, there is an intensifying drive for intimate sexual contact derailed by little useful information about navigating the terrain. Hence, adolescence is typically a time of moodiness, confusion, bad choices, and impulsive behavior, particularly regarding sexual activity. Add to the mix the natural shift from parents as primary attachment figures to peers as primary attachments, likewise bereft of a fully functional pre-frontal cortex and we get a perfect storm (Allen & Land, 1999).

Attachment theory views adolescence as a time of three competing behavior systems: the attachment, exploratory, and sexual systems. It's a stage in the lifespan when the adolescent naturally seeks autonomy, to be less attached to, and dependent on, parents. When peers become the primary attachment figures for their children this can be a difficult stage for parents who may feel rejected by children who actively avoid going to them for comfort or advice. That would especially be the case if the parents had little to say to their child about sex.

Teenage Sex Play: A Minefield of Challenges or a Sweet Spot of Pleasures

The teenage years are a critical developmental stage for capacity to enjoy gratifying sexual intimacy as adults. Adolescents raised by parents who were comfortable with their child's early interest in sex and talked openly about sex are more likely as teenagers to approach the prospects of sexual experience with enthusiasm. In childhood, sexual activity is impersonal, about playmates of the same age playing together and discovering each other's bodies. Teen sex play is more personal, continuous, and purposeful.

In the teenager, playfulness initiates a series of intimate activities that typically start with kissing, caressing, "making out," and enjoying the feelings of sexual arousal. The next phase progresses into "liking" someone and eventually moves into romantic feelings for someone deemed special. Though it may not last more than a season or a year, "young love" is an important phase in the developmental process leading to the adult romantic love associated with intense sexual desire.

Studies show that how teens approach their sexual awakening is strongly linked to their attachment style. Secure teens are found to enjoy sex more than their insecure peers; they are more comfortable with intimacy, more open to sexual exploration, have more sexual experiences, and are more likely to use condoms during sexual penetration. Anxious teens, as well as adults, are more likely to fall passionately in love, to become obsessed with the object of their interest, to be concerned about their sexual attractiveness, and to fear rejection. Avoidant teens fear closeness more than rejection, are less likely to date, to engage in sexual activity, and enjoy it less when they do have sex (Tracy et al., 2003).

Attachment security and insecurity play the same roles in gay and lesbian adolescents and adults as in straight adolescents and adults. Security is linked to satisfaction in same-sex relationships; anxiety is associated with passionate relationships and more break-ups; and avoidance is linked with fear of intimacy. Attachment style also affects the timing of coming out with insecure males and females coming out substantially later than secure individuals (Feeney & Noller, 2004).

Resolving Old Teenage Challenges as Adults: Sex-Esteem, Self-Esteem, and Relational Happiness

Unless tackled in therapy, difficult sexual experiences during childhood or teenage can have long-lasting effects on adult sexual and relational satisfaction throughout one's lifetime. There is also substantial evidence that unresolved early developmental sexual issues, like a pattern of sexual disappointments, can affect people's self-esteem and emotional well-being. Some of the teenage sexual risk factors that have been shown to have negative consequences on adult self-esteem include sexual naiveté and inexperience, low sex-esteem, sex abuse, and sexual shame. Low sexual esteem has been associated with lacking sexual competence in pleasuring oneself or a partner (Vasilenko et al. 2015).

On the other hand, several positive aspects of sexual development have been shown to transfer well from teenage to adult sexuality and contribute to a positive sense of self. These involve "sexual-efficacy," defined as "an individual's ability to successfully engage in and initiate a variety of sexual activities," and "sexual esteem," defined as "the tendency to view oneself as capable of relating sexually to another person and having a positive view of one's sexual self" (Rosenthal et al., 1991).

The research shows that there's an affirming ripple effect: greater sexual competency contributes to higher sexual esteem, which is linked to global self-esteem, which in turn enhances the likelihood of attracting potential romantic partners and to maintaining long-term committed romantic partnerships. Positive feelings have a way of promoting vitality and an optimistic mind-set, both of which tend to elicit positive responses from other people (Maas & Lefkowitz, 2015).

Sexual communication between parents and their adolescents, which involves transmitting "sexual values, beliefs, and expectations" and answering the teen's questions on a variety of sexual topics, is another factor that has emerged in the research as contributing to sexually healthy adults (DeLooze et. al., 2014). Talking about sex as a child and adolescent with parents enhances the ability to talk comfortably about sex as an adult with one's partner—a valuable skill to have in a romantic relationship.

Emotionally relaxed, non-judgmental, comprehensive, sex-positive conversation about a variety of sexual activities is one the major advantages of sex therapy. A sexually informed, open-minded, and articulate therapist can make up for the lack of information and sex-positive talk that many sexually troubled individuals missed out on as children.

A common question posed by new clients is "What's normal sex?" When therapists re-frame the question to be what is healthy sex, they can reassure their clients that sex is adult play and whatever two mutually consenting adults agree upon, where neither is harmed and both of them get pleasure from the experience, is healthy.

A sexually informed therapist is a sexuality educator as well as facilitator in the healing of relational distress. As such he or she welcomes all questions and can describe varieties of sexual behaviors and prescribe non-threatening sexual intimacy-affirming exercises the clients can explore in private as home play exercises. In their next session, they can talk about whether or not they actually ended up doing them. If they did, what was it like for them? Did they enjoy it? What felt good? If they didn't do it, was anything difficult or emotionally distressing? What got in their way of doing the home play?

Sexual Naiveté and Inexperience: Carrie and Ed

One young couple in their mid-twenties came for therapy because the man was having difficulty sustaining an erection during sexual activity. Ed and Carrie had been dating about a year and talking about marriage but Carrie was hesitant. Despite his protests to the contrary, she felt that Ed's lack of sexual responsiveness during sex was a sign that he wasn't physically attracted to her. Quite the contrary, he told her, he was much too attracted to her and he felt insecure about his ability to please her.

For couples with sexual issues, I typically take a sexual history with each partner not long after I have taken their family histories. When

I notice any shyness or hesitation about doing so, as I did with this couple, I offer them individual sessions for talking about prior sexual experiences. After we explore their sexual histories, I often suggest that they talk about some of their history and the feelings it raised in their next couple session.

I was delighted when after some discussion both said they would like to share their sexual history openly with their partner present. Each of them traced many of their sexual insecurities to their early teenage conflicts with their parents over sex. Neither Ed nor Carrie felt like they had ever talked frankly about sex with their parents.

The only sex discussion Ed could remember was a very unpleasant experience. He related a story about how he and a high school girlfriend were studying for an exam in his room and ended up in a hot make-out session. All of a sudden, his father gave a brief knock on the door and quickly entered the room catching them partially undressed and disheveled. The father ordered the girl to go home and she ran from the room humiliated and tearful, clutching her tee shirt to her chest. He then gave Ed an angry lecture about the dangers of teenage sex, STDs, and the risk of pregnancy as Ed sat on the tousled bed in his room while his father stood over him.

His father said Ed was being irresponsible and shameless, and if he wasn't careful, he could ruin his life. Ed had yearned for a closer connection with his somewhat formal father and the incident aroused a great deal of guilt and uneasy feelings about sex especially whenever he felt sexually aroused by a girl. Ed associated that incident with his father as the beginning of his troubles sustaining an erection during sex.

Carrie's memories about her early sexual awakening were completely separated from her relationship with her parents. She talked about how she and her parents had a good relationship during childhood, respectful but not physically affectionate, and had never talked about sex until she started to develop breasts. At that point, the parents appeared to become very anxious about her contacts with boys and how they were vehemently opposed to her having any premarital sexual contact with boys. They constantly questioned her activities when she was out with friends and kept cautioning her about postponing any sexual activity until she was married. They warned her that if she did engage in pre-marital sex she would be "used goods" and "unworthy of a good man."

For both of these young people, lacking any guidance from parents, and excoriated for sexual interest, feelings of guilt and shame were mixed up in their sexuality. They each felt sexually unworthy of the other; Ed said that he would sometimes get a flash of his father's seething face when he was attempting sexual intimacy. Flashbacks are a classic PTSD symptom of trauma and there is neurobiological evidence for these occurrences. Schore (2003) notes that an image from childhood can be indelibly imprinted in the limbic circuits as a "flashbulb memory" and stored as an implicit memory in areas of the right brain dominant for visual imagery.

Ed had even suggested to Carrie that they watch some online porn to pick up some clues about broadening their sexual skills. They did watch some sites, but neither of them was particularly aroused by what they saw. It's not unusual for young people nowadays to resort to watching porn for usable sex information to substitute for the absence of easy-going conversation with parents and their lack of sexual experience. Author Peggy Ornstein has observed in her studies with young people that with so little conversation in the home about the naturalness of sexual expression and the right to sexual pleasure, many young people today do in fact turn to the Internet and pornography for their sexual education. Ornstein laments the fact that girls are particularly deprived of information about female sexual pleasure and that too many girls see sexual pleasure as the province of males rather than females (Ornstein, 2016).

Recognizing the impossibility of stopping teens from looking at porn some educators are now attempting to educate teenagers about the misinformation in pornography. For example, in Boston classes are being offered for teenagers on "porn literacy" to counteract the expectation of aggression against women and the focus on male, not female, pleasure in what passes for hot sex in what teenagers often see online (Jones, 2018).

It's very likely that American parents' protectiveness of their daughters' "purity" is communicated nonverbally at a very early age. Studies show that while over 80% of boys masturbate between the ages of fourteen to seventeen, only about a third of girls at that age masturbate (Herbenick et al., 2010). This lack of girls' early sexual exploration of their bodily pleasures may at least partially account for the difficulty that many adult women have with regard to what has been called, "the elusive female orgasm."

The Sexual Desire Spectrum: High Libido, Low Libido, No Libido

A major concern I have with the research linking attachment and sexual behavior is the lack of control for high or low levels of libido for all sexual orientations. As a clinician who has been taking sexual histories for decades, it has become clear to me that some individuals discover genital pleasures very early on, begin to explore child sex play between the ages of three to five, and some of them, males and females alike, also report experiencing orgasms by that early age.

In the same way that babies are born with different temperaments, so too it is likely that babies are born with different levels of libido. It is generally accepted that temperament at birth isn't a life sentence if parents are educated how to effectively calm a "difficult," irritable, or reactive infant. However, parents who are stressed may be less capable of responding positively to their "fussy" infant or emotionally reactive child, and research shows that this interactive disconnect can contribute to attachment insecurity (Vaughn & Bost, 1999).

The same might be said of parents' ability to deal with a high libido infant, child, or teen. An infant or child who takes great pleasure in his or her genitals may also be found rubbing up against stuffed toys or even against a parent or grandparent's knee while sitting on their laps. How threatened and reactive parents or a relative become to the child's sexual exuberance could pair an implicit expectation of distress from a significant other with suppressing one's sexual enthusiasm as an adult.

Adults with a strong libido tend to highly value themselves as sexual beings. Testosterone (T) is the hormone associated with sexual desire in both males and females. High T males tend to be more sexually motivated, ambitious, dominant, and aggressive and to seek out positions of leadership. They are also more likely to be impulsive and easily angered, and to lack empathy, patience, and understanding.

High T females are more likely to have a strong sex drive and are generally more competitive, assertive, and socially dominant. When women with a strong libido find that they are not as sexually motivated as they used to be it bothers them. As one woman remarked to me in a first session, "I don't miss sex. What I miss is missing sex."

On the other end of the spectrum, some individuals report no sexual interest before puberty, do not remember touching themselves or masturbating as a child, and recall only a brief surge of sexual interest during young adulthood. Since most parents don't expect their infants or children to be sexual, a lack of interest in sex is not likely to raise any red flags.

Asexuality and the Right to Be Non-Sexual: Wendy and Tim

Asexuality is beginning to be viewed as a viable example of the broad range of the sexuality spectrum and human sexual variability (Bogaert, 2015).

When low libido individuals lose interest in sex, or never do build much interest, they are typically fine without sex. Here's an example:

One couple in their early thirties, Wendy and Tim, sought therapy because the wife apparently had no interest in sex. Tim said he felt completely emasculated at her total lack of interest in anything beyond an occasional kiss and a hug.

In recounting her sexual history, Wendy said she didn't feel any sexual feelings until she was about eighteen. She never masturbated or experienced orgasm, and though she remembered a few crushes as a child, and some sexual interest in boys as a teen, she felt more committed to being a good student in high school and college than to dating. She said that sex had never been a high priority for her.

Wendy felt attracted to Tim when they first met, mostly for the good man he was, and she enjoyed their initial physical contacts. But when she experienced her first ever intercourse with him, she said it felt like a "weird" thing to do. Tim said he was attracted to Wendy, loved the softness of her body, and very much wanted to please her and have her please him sexually.

Wendy's goals in therapy were to enjoy sex with Tim and to have orgasms with him. During that first session, I suggested that a good way for her to get to know her own body was to explore self-pleasuring. When she said she wouldn't even know how to go about it, we decided to discuss it in an individual session.

During that session, we talked about how she touches her body, if she enjoys putting lotion on her body or does any other type of self-massage. We did some breathing exercises that she could use first to relax, then to focus in on the sensations in her body. We talked about the possibility of her using a vibrator, which has a very high success rate for stimulating an orgasm. We also talked about the different ways she might stroke her clitoris and vagina. I asked her if she had any fantasies she could count on to arouse her, and she said she had no sexual fantasies, no favorite movie or music stars, and had never been aroused watching a movie.

That made me wonder if Wendy might be more turned on to women than to men and I asked her if she had noticed any adult crushes on her women friends or acquaintances. She said she had no sexual attraction to women and that she had some close women friends whom she cared about but would never consider being physically intimate with them. So we went back to looking at how to masturbate. I also suggested dimming the lights in the room and perhaps playing some soft music she liked, and to make sure that Tim would give her complete privacy.

When we met again in a couple's session, Wendy reported that she made two attempts at learning how to masturbate to orgasm before she gave up. "It's just so boring," she said. "I'd rather read a book." I suggested a romance novel but that didn't appeal to her either. That began a brief conversation about how Wendy and Tim could enjoy a more sensual connection even without hot sex. Then I asked them to face one another and share where they were with the other right now.

Tim told Wendy that he loved her very much and that her companionship was more important to him than sex. Wendy said she was grateful for his love and loved being with him. Tim then raised the possibility of having sexual experiences with other people, which Tim said they had talked about before starting therapy. Wendy replied that having Tim bring his sexual needs to other women would be a relief to her and she would like to consider it if they could set up some "ground rules." They both agreed to continue in couples therapy and to work on how to go about having an open relationship.

There are many possible factors that could be responsible for one or both partners' lack of interest in sex. Loss of libido may be a side effect of medication so it's always important to get a list of current medications being used by both partners.

Another major factor has to do with a continuing undercurrent of emotional pain for one or both partners, whether the emotional residue is of anxiety, resentment, or depression. These feelings may stem from the unresolved feelings of anger, shame, guilt, or grief associated with past sexual disappointments or sexual abuse. Couples therapy is a valuable resource for exploring the deeper emotional factors that can undermine the quality of mates' intimate connection, whether their pain is a result of how they may have injured one another emotionally or is a more long-standing wound from their childhoods. Usually, a pattern of emotional injury and pain in a relationship can be traced back to the original family. We explore those issues in the next section on the pain-pleasure spectrum.

Another major factor for many couples who have lost sexual interest in each other has to do with a lack of erotic skill in playfully and artfully ratcheting up excitement. Good couples sex therapy has to involve a good sex education in how to be an empathic and skillful lover and playmate. We look at how to develop these body-to-body erotic skills in the final section of this chapter.

Sexual Fluidity: Delayed Sexual Self-Discovery

When an individual indicates a long-term lack of interest in sex, rather than assume that no sex drive is the result of a low libido, it makes sense to ask whether he or she has ever been sexually attracted to a person of the same sex. There is always the possibility the individual is hooking up with the wrong gender.

One example is a couple I worked with in their late thirties where the woman apparently had no interest in sex with her husband. Even though Fran felt that Ted was a good lover and she occasionally somewhat enjoyed the experience, her mind wandered when they were making love and she had never had an orgasm with him. Like Wendy, Fran too found masturbation boring, had no mental access to sexual fantasies, and was unsuccessful at giving herself an orgasm.

Fran and Ted eventually separated, though they remained good friends. I didn't see Fran again until about a year later when she made an appointment to work individually on a new relationship. Her new lover was someone she was very much in love with, sexually turned on to, and she was having great orgasms. I was delighted to hear that and I congratulated her. The only problem for her was that this person was a woman.

What Fran wanted to work on now was to examine her feelings that it was wrong to be in a same-sex romantic relationship. Fran's negative feelings about same-sex love relationships were readily accessible. Having had earlier experience in body-based therapy with me she was quick to contact her inner voice of judgment and condemnation, her feelings of shame, her anxiety that she was defective and not normal, and a great deal of internal conflict about identifying as a lesbian. We explored her judgments about gay people that came from her upbringing, her fears about how this would affect her career, and her concerns about losing her friends whom she was afraid would feel different about her and be uncomfortable around her.

Ultimately Fran made a choice that felt right to her. She decided to come out as gay to friends and family and to give herself the right to happiness in an intimate relationship. To her surprise, her closest friends were completely accepting. Her mom, dad, and brother reluctantly accepted the news at first but rather quickly got over it and fell in love with Fran's sweetheart. An unexpected gain for her was that she made a whole new group of friends.

Staying true to oneself tends to pay dividends in terms of feeling right with the world. False friends drop out and free up the time and space for real love and friendship.

Women Are Complicated: Female Sexual Arousal and Erotic Plasticity

Women may even have difficulty recognizing when they are turned on. In a fascinating set of studies, researchers Meredith Chivers and Michael

Bailey set up a lab to test male and female arousal patterns. Their subjects were self-identified heterosexual, lesbian and gay men and women. All subjects were shown a series of video clips of a man and woman engaging in sexual activities, two women having sex, two men having sex, a man masturbating, a woman masturbating, a well-toned man walking nude on the beach, a woman doing calisthenics in the nude, and a male and female bonobo having sex. All subjects were fitted with genital devices that measured male tumescence and female blood flow and lubrication. They were also given a keypad to rate in real time how aroused they felt.

The men mostly responded in a "category specific" way. Heterosexual men responded to all the clips that had females in them, but not to the bonobos mating. Gay men responded to the clips with men, but not to the clips with women, and not to the bonobos. Their subjective ratings were consistent with their physiological reactions.

Women, on the other hand, showed a strong genital response to all the clips—including the bonobos, yet they appeared to be unaware of it. Their subjective responses were completely out of touch with their physiological responses. When straight women watched lesbian sex they reported less excitement than their vaginas showed and they reported more excitement watching a man and woman having sex than their vaginal response would indicate. They had a stronger physiological response to the woman exercising than to the man on the beach. Lesbian women showed the same inconsistencies. Though their subjective response matched their physiological response watching lesbian sex, they reported less arousal watching a man and a woman than their vaginas showed. They also didn't seem to notice that their bodies were becoming aroused watching the bonobos (Chivers & Bailey, 2005).

These data are consistent with a slew of other studies that show that female sexuality shows a greater degree of *erotic plasticity* than male sexuality. Erotic plasticity refers to "the ways in which people's sexual desires, the degree to which they feel these desires, and the ways in which they express these desires, vary depending on sociocultural factors and contextual differences." It appears that the female sex drive exhibits greater variability and flexibility in response to cultural and situational factors than the male sex drive. In contrast, male sexuality is driven more by biological factors (Vohs et al., 2004).

Then there are the studies by psychiatrist Mary Jane Sherfy who ran research projects on female sexuality utilizing physiological, anthropological, and primate studies. Sherfy found that with continuous stimulation women are not only capable of multiple orgasms but of having one orgasm after another until she and her partner drop. Her data show that for women, an orgasm can increase rather than decrease the flow of blood into the pelvic region and vagina and trigger another orgasm. Under optimal conditions some women may not feel completely satiated until they are physically exhausted (Sherfy, 1966).

All of the research indicates that perhaps it is the lack of sex-positive education for young girls, parental cautions about the value of female sexual "purity," and the shaming around body image that collectively inhibit girls from even exploring their own body to discover their vast inborn erotic potentials as women. It's never too late.

The Love-Lust Dilemma: Love for Family, Lust for Strangers

The most common sexual concern that propels couples into therapy is the loss of sexual interest in each other and the resulting insecurities and frustrations that threaten to end the relationship. In my last book (Resnick, 2012), I undertook to examine the myriad factors that could interfere with two intimates maintaining sexual desire and enthusiasm for sexual intimacies with one another.

One of the main issues is what I call the "love-lust dilemma." I see it as a dilemma because most of us want both: the reassuring and nurturing love of a life partner and the intensely pleasurable excitement of sexual discovery with a passionate lover. However, when childhood sexual interest is met with anxiety, anger, or shaming by a family member, the neural links of painful feelings associated with sex can result in the automatic inhibition of sexual feelings as two people get more "homey."

This interplay between attachment and sexuality involves the earliest programming of neural networks in the brain and the association of sexual arousal with parents' shaming facial expressions or gestures. For example, if one partner starts to act parental toward the other, whether critical or overly solicitous, the other may feel himself or herself morph into an obedient child. Definitely not a great set up for sex. As I wrote in *The Heart of Desire*:

> In our formative years, most of us learned more about stifling our sex drive than about celebrating our desires, particularly in the presence of family. The paradoxical result ... is that once a romance turns into an emotional attachment, our brains and bodies are wired to inhibit sexual excitement.
>
> (Resnick, 2012)

You might expect lustful desire to decrease between couples who have been together a long time. But I've seen couples who noticed a loss of sexual interest by one or both of them within days of simply declaring their love or once they moved in together. They report that they stopped flirting and enticing each other the way they did just weeks earlier, as though it was no longer appropriate to play at being sexy with each other.

Yet couples who do manage to keep their relationship sexually vibrant score much higher on relationship satisfaction scales than do couples who have a more companionate style relation. They also claim to still be in love with their partner, and their brain scans validate their claim. Looking at pictures of their beloved, the part of the brain associated with romance, the ventral tegmental area, which is loaded with dopaminergic neurons and is an integral part of the reward system of the brain, is particularly activated (Acevedo et al., 2012).

Sex With Someone You Love: Attachment Dynamics in Sexual Desire

We've been raised to believe that the best sex occurs when two people love each other. Unfortunately, that turns out not to be as easy as promised. What can get in the way of being fully present with one's lover, sensually and sexually, is seeing sex as a test of one's worth as a lovable, desirable man or woman. When sex is a test, calibrating one's performance becomes a distraction from the delights of one's lover and enjoying the pleasure of the connection.

There are a number of different kinds of relational dynamics that can turn hot lovers into platonic friends. For one, there is the early-imprinting factor of the home as a sex-free zone where, as children, they rarely if ever saw any sign that their parents were sexual beings. In a secure family, Mom and Dad were more likely to be viewed as partners managing a household than as lovers who like to kiss and touch each other. Yet those same children carefully watching their parents for clues as to appropriate behavior were also likely to be in touch with their own budding sexual sensations and getting the message to kill those feelings at home because "we don't do things like that here."

When children are shielded from observing physical affection between parents, and lack any parent-child conversation about sexual pleasure, even a loving home life can be the breeding ground for an opposition between love and sexual desire. Love becomes reserved for family and sexual desire becomes directed toward outsiders and strangers.

This, of course, has ramifications when two people meet, fall in love, and move in together. They fall in love with a stranger, but once they declare their love and share a home, they become family. As a result of this body-based opposition between affection and sexuality in early childhood and adolescence, the capacity to unite emotional intimacy and sexual pleasure in a committed relationship can be compromised. Their inner working models of committed intimacy tend to be non-sexual.

In the evolutionary scheme of things nature's purpose for mating behavior is not to guarantee sexual pleasure for life. It is to mix genes, make babies, and have two mates committed to being there to take care of the babies. One bird guards the nest and the eggs while the other goes out to fetch twigs and worms.

Humans have taken sexual mating to a whole new level. But when parents are continually viewed more like dedicated associates running a family, the thought of them having sex, for a child, can literally be nauseating. I've saved a cartoon where, as a teenage boy is hugging his girlfriend, she tells him she's wearing his mother's old jeans. The boy breaks away in horror and dizzily reels away, his face contorted in disgust as he says, "I think I'm gonna be sick!"

Then there is the risk factor in growing up in a less than loving and secure home, with parents who were themselves anxious and intrusive or avoidant and unavailable. The deficits of their home life, wired into their own brain and nervous system, can begin to manifest once lovers live under the same roof.

Two anxious people in a relationship are the most likely to have passionate sex for a while, but their neediness for reassurance and the volatility of the relationship may become a sexual turn-off. This is especially the case if one of them has a high libido and the other a lower libido. The one with lower libido will have more power in the relationship, a set-up for a power struggle as the more interested partner becomes the beseecher and the less interested one grants physical connection only for "good behavior."

Two avoidant people are likely to have the least sex and the least interest in reawakening a sexless relationship. They may be more concerned with the ramifications of a sexless marriage than truly missing sex. That may be tempered if one or both have a high libido. Under the circumstances, and depending on their age, how long they've been together, and a number of other factors, they may each have an occasional fling with someone else. That could occur with or without the other's implicit blessing.

One of the more challenging relational dynamics involves an insecure anxious partner with an insecure avoidant partner. What makes this a difficult relational pairing is that each of them has very different needs in response to any emotional distress, whether a simple disagreement or a serious conflict. The anxious partner needs contact and reassurance, and often sexual connection is what is most reassuring; the avoidant partner needs to be left alone, and sex is the last thing he or she wants.

There is also evidence to suggest that attachment style is related to different styles of sensory reception and processing of sensory stimulation. Some people are more sensitive to sensory input than others, have a lower threshold of activation, and a more active or passive way of responding (Aron & Aron, 1997). The evidence isn't clear as to whether they were born that way or if their sensory style is a result of attachment experiences. There is evidence of a correspondence between avoidant attachment and a likelihood of avoiding sensory stimulation. On the other hand, sensory seekers are more likely to seek relational closeness and to more actively "exert control over their circumstances, both in regard to sensory stimulation and in emotional relationships" (Jerome & Liss, 2005).

In working with couples, a factor to take into account is that one partner may be sensory seeking while the other tends to be sensory avoidant, and these differences may be a contributing factor in the discrepancy in their sexual desire. Different sensory styles may also play a part in conflicts surrounding boundary issues. In some of the sensing experiments discussed at the end of this chapter, we explore these sensory reception and response differences with couples and how we may effectively work with partners to be respectful of and to accommodate each other's sensitivities.

Sex With Someone You Love, Part Two: Feeling Responsible for Someone Else's Pleasure

Typically, having sex with someone you're just hooking up with involves no commitment. That's why it's called *casual* sex; it's relaxed, friendly, occasional, and uncommitted. By definition, it's not important. Each of you is responsible for the enjoyment you have together; you're doing it for fun and there are no consequences (one hopes). Maybe there's some element of ego stroking going on when the sex is good but you're really focused on getting excited and feeling good. Casual lovers can feel desired and desirable, and validation may be a factor, and if it doesn't feel great it doesn't feel worth it.

But for many of the couples we see, they're doing it for love, not just for enjoyment. Making love is "meaningful." That's pressure. They better do it right.

There can be all kinds of pressures to perform. They may feel that to please the partner they have to know what he or she likes, and to do it just the way he or she likes it. They also have to know what he or she doesn't like and to avoid getting carried away and doing the wrong thing at the wrong time. And they can't just lie there doing nothing because they'll never hear the end of it. That kind of inner dialogue and emotional interference can short circuit the body-to-body intimacy.

There is also the big switch that has to take place when their domestic business partner becomes the partner for sexual pleasure. When mates want to get together as lovers they have to relate to each other in a very different way. As mates they operate side-to-side as co-directors of the family firm. They are primarily present for their children and they are focused on family and household. To become lovers they need to adopt a new sensual repertoire that requires full attention and a body-to-body erotic repertoire that involves playfully invoking each other's sexiest selves. As sex therapists we have to help them learn how to transition from business partners to erotic lovers.

Body-to-Body Intimacies: Sensual Presence, Focus, and Mindful Erotic Attunement

Just as the earliest sensory interactions between parent and child are at the foundation of the bonds of love, it's the body-to-body sensory exchanges between lovers that are at the core of the sexual bond. It is in the capacity to be present to the sensual delights shared together rather than be focused on one's performance that is at the heart of a couple's prospects for sexual pleasure and fulfillment. Typically sexual activity aims for the pleasure of release and getting turned on is often a means to that end. Erotic activity is more about the pleasures of the sensual and sexual arousal. Often the more slowly and artfully arousal is achieved, the more the whole body becomes sexually awakened, the more intense and long lasting the ultimate release.

Presence is everything! Studies in sex research consistently show that present-centered attention to sensory stimuli during physical contact is the essential condition for sexual arousal (De Jong, 2009). Staying focused as lovers involves looking into each other's eyes, smelling their scent, feeling the warmth of the skin-to-skin contact, listening to the sound of their breath, whispering into each other's ear, and speaking in "right brain language" of soft vocal tones and "sweet nothings," those simple two to three word appreciations spoken in soft whispered tones.

Attention is focused on the other, and not on one's inner dialogue. If a client reports losing himself or herself in their thinking process, they can use a mindfulness procedure: to notice they were thinking and to re-direct their attention back to the partner and their senses: to look into his or her eyes, breathe in his scent, feel the warmth and smoothness of her skin, feel where their bodies are touching and how their own body is feeling.

Meditation is one of the valuable ways of developing the capacity to be present in the moment and developing mindfulness. Being mindful merely means to be able to focus on being present in the body and catching yourself when you are thinking, analyzing, and in your left brain, noting where your mind went and bringing yourself back to your body and the moment. Practicing mindful eroticism has to do with being fully present sensually and erotically with oneself and one's partner.

People who have difficulty getting aroused are more focused on what is not happening than on what is happening and the pleasurable sensations they might attend to. They are absorbed by their thoughts and often images of past failures and inner dialogues questioning their performance. Every therapy session is an opportunity for a couple to practice being face-to-face, to focus on the other, and become aware of any emotions that inhibit their presence.

They learn to take the skills of body-to-body intimacy practiced during a couple's session to their opportunities for physical intimacy at home. They can practice shuttling back and forth between dipping into the sensations of their own body and then back to appreciate the lover's face, the taste and softness of his or her lips, the warmth and smoothness of the lover's skin, and breathing in the lover's scent.

During a session, when I give a couple an experiment to focus on their partner and to notice their sensory experiences in the moment, I too am focusing on their sensory communications in the moment. What am I picking up in their eyes, in how they are breathing, in the expressions on their faces, in the stiffness or awkwardness of their bodies, in whether they are leaning toward or away from one another?

As partners work through their emotional tensions with one another and do the deeper work of repairing old emotional wounds associated with sexuality, they become more available to one another sexually. We also explore some of the ways they can become more playful with one another and see their sexual intimacy as an opportunity to play together and focus on the sensations and sensual pleasures of the moment rather than what they should be doing.

Researcher Peggy Kleinplatz and associates have been researching optimal sex over the last ten years and have found that what their subjects consistently mention as great sex has more to do with the quality of the lovers' connection than about orgasms or genital response. They talk about being fully present, immersed in the experience, deeply trusting one another, and being in sync, empathic, and genuine with one another (Kleinplatz et al., 2009).

In their latest study, the researchers put together a group of couples presenting with low desire and focused on building their skills of presence, authenticity, and trustfulness to enhance their erotic intimacy. They utilized Gestalt therapy, focusing methods, music, movement, developing conflict-resolution skills, and enhancing vulnerability.

Their methodology sounds remarkably similar to everything my husband and I do in our couples' workshops. The couples reported that re-introducing play into their sex lives was especially energizing as many of them had gotten into routines that were not inspiring them sexually. As the researchers described it:

> We did not recommend new positions, techniques, or toys. We did, however, encourage them to rediscover the delights of childhood playfulness and physicality per se.
>
> Kleinplatz et al. (2017)

Body-to-Body Intimacies: Sexual Presence and Erotic Playfulness

When two people keep making love in the same way, in the same bed, same position, and with the same results it becomes boring. I encourage couples to use the processes of sensual presence and empathic attunement in the service of sexual arousal. In some ways, erotic play takes us back to the childlike qualities of sex play that involve discovery of sexual desire and possibilities.

Children don't just touch each other when they play sexually. They make up stories and pretend. Every generation seems to discover "playing doctor." I wonder how all children all know to call sex play, "playing doctor." Could there be a "playing-doctor" region in the brain that is switched on by a gene with an early onset maturation that fades at puberty?

In any event, the best sex is focused, sensual, playful, attuned. I give my clients two caveats: (1) It does not start in a bedroom or on a bed, though it can end there. (2) It has to feel good for both lovers. Then I encourage them to get out of their heads and explore the possibilities of playful abandon. I particularly recommend candlelight, music, maybe starting by dancing with their bodies together, kissing, and just "messing around." Sexual enhancement exercises at home, particularly practicing matching breaths, support a couple's process as they work through the issues limiting their embodied relational sexual connection.

Focusing on Erotic Pleasure: Relaxed-Excitement and Slow Breathing

Many of our couples will need to change their mind-set of what they imagine erotic pleasure is supposed to look like. We can help them do that by describing a different kind of sex than they are used to. Despite the frenetic sex often depicted in the movies, the hottest sex often involves allowing the slow buildup of excitement, relaxing into their senses as their excitement builds, and being fully present to the sensuous connection with their partner.

That means that when they look at each other they focus on what they love and appreciate about what they see. They breathe slowly and deeply, drawing in the scent of the lover, they kiss and taste the lover's mouth and kisses; they feel the warmth and smoothness of the lover's body against theirs. If they speak, they speak softly and lovingly, in brief words and tones of appreciation. As they move together and touch each other they listen for the sounds of their lover's breath and soft hums of pleasure that trigger each other's arousal even more.

In this way they are practicing being tuned into each other so they can feel what the other is feeling empathically. They can do that by also being attuned to the beating of their own heart, the warmth of their belly breathing openly and relaxed, letting the warmth and the breath spread into the pelvic floor and into their genitals—present to the lover's body and to their own.

This isn't the only way to make love, but it's a good start. When they can do this, they can also branch out and become more playful and exploratory.

The Ripple Effect: Self-Esteem and Gratitude

The ability for partners in a relationship to enjoy physical pleasure with one another generates an undercurrent of good feelings that contributes to satisfaction in a relationship. Studies show that when both partners in a relationship feel sexually fulfilled, they are more likely to feel overall satisfaction with the relationship in general (Sprecher & Cate, 2004).

One study showed that having sex with a partner on one day positively affected the quality of the couple's interactions the following day and their ratings of their overall relational satisfaction. The effect was particularly strong for anxious individuals and suggested that having sex can temporarily alleviate an anxious person's insecurities. One notable gender difference appeared showing that for anxious men just having sex the day before raised their positive appraisals of the relationship, while for women it was the *quality* of the sex that determined their appraisals of the relationship (Birnbaum et al., 2006). Every woman will be able to relate to that.

There is a deep connection between relational satisfaction and sexual fulfillment. Part of that is what the late, distinguished professor Mildred Hope Witkin (1993) identified as the ripple effect in successful sex therapy. Just like it is for teenagers, when partners' sexual distress is relieved, it enhances their self-esteem and they feel better about their relationship.

When a woman who has never had an orgasm learns to let go to the point where she can experience climax, she has achieved an important accomplishment, not only for herself but for her partner as well. The same is true for a man who has overcome his difficulty sustaining an erection and is now able to focus on his partner and be present, enhancing their body-to-body intimacy. Likewise, for partners lacking sexual experience, learning how to sexually please one another brings shared relational contentment, increasing adult self-esteem just as sexual success for a teenager also enhances self-esteem.

Empirical studies have also made the connection between sexual well-being and subjective well-being. In one study, "a positive evaluation of one's sex life is closely associated with an overall feeling of happiness." In another study researchers concluded that, "at any adult age, sexuality indeed can be considered an important element of well-being" (Laumann et al., 1994; Hooghe, 2012).

Fulfilling sexual intimacy in a relationship fosters each person's feelings of gratitude as his or her partner develops the empathy to kiss as each likes to be kissed, to touch as each likes to be touched, and to value each other as erotic playmates.

In the next chapter we go into the more complex repair work to heal ruptures in the couple's relationship and the unresolved wounds of early childhood at the foundation of the partners' relational challenges.

Part III
The Pain-Pleasure Spectrum

6

Pain: Emotional Healing
Awakens Pleasure

Emotions are therapists' stock in trade. Helping our clients come to terms with their feelings, release stuck emotional expression, and direct the energy release toward healing, health, and happiness is the path to lasting results in therapy.

Emotions Are Painful or Pleasurable

On the most basic level of personal experience, emotions are either painful or pleasurable sensations in the body. Emotions can feel good, like love and enthusiasm, or feel bad, like fear and shame. In general, painful "bad" feelings contract the muscles and viscera, preparing us to fight or run away, or to harden and close off the body in a protective sheath of muscular armor (Reich, 1961, 1980).

Pleasurable good feelings are non-defensive and expansive. We feel energized yet relaxed, open to the possibilities for emotional and physical nourishment through exploration, adventure, and play. Loving intimate relationships are life's greatest joys. The ability to feel loved and loving toward one another, to trust each other's support, to thoroughly enjoy each other's company, to repair misattunements and injuries in a way that strengthens and deepens the relationship, and to share intimate, arousing, fulfilling sexual pleasure are the blessings offered by effective embodied relational sex therapy.

In couples therapy, we look for the opportunities to examine the painful emotions that partners trigger in one another that limit their intimate pleasures. To do so, we need to identify each individual's underlying vulnerabilities and propensities to react to their intimate in the way that they do. We want to help them to recognize how they learned to react that way, and to resolve underlying painful emotions that persist from their past that get in the way of interacting with pleasurable emotions of love, empathy, and enthusiasm for each other's company.

Affect, Emotions, and Feelings: Implicit and Explicit Sensory Triggers

In fact, we can distinguish between three qualities that are normally lumped together when we talk about emotions: *affect*, a biological arousal to stress; *emotions*, which have either a positive or negative valence; and *feelings*, which are sensations in various parts of the body. Affect rouses the body, while emotions and feelings activate the body and impel movement away from pain and toward pleasure. Affect and emotions are givens; when you're stressed you're stressed, and when you're sad you're sad. Feelings are more complicated.

All aspects of emotion are aroused by the senses: the five exteroceptors of seeing, hearing, touching, tasting, and smelling; the multiple kinds of interoceptors on every organ of the body including neuroception, proprioception, and erotoception; and the special realm of inner feelings that come from the heart and the gut—what I think of as our "truth detectors."

Damasio (1994) distinguishes between primary and secondary emotions. Primary emotions correspond to Schore's notion of "primary affect". Again, this is the notion that certain states of activation are wired at birth to respond to inner or outer stimuli in a "preorganized" way. For a baby, hunger would be the trigger for crying. For an adult, a growling sound, or being approached by an intimidating stranger, is detected in the limbic system, in the amygdala, triggering a bodily state we identify as fear, and a reflexive reaction like moving away.

Secondary emotions are acquired through lived experience and are associated with memories, mental imagery, and thoughts. Emotions can be biologically triggered by real situational dangers or rewards as well as by imagined ones. These conditioned emotions, based on past experience, trigger the autonomic nervous system, which releases hormones and neurotransmitters into the blood stream, like adrenalin leading to a rapid heartbeat, a tightening of the gut, and flight-fight-freeze or pleasurably exciting reactions. These visceral responses also activate the muscles of the face and skeletal system, which manifest in emotionally salient facial expressions and body postures.

The third part of the emotional process involves feelings. Only after the emotion is triggered will the activation become consciously perceived as positive or negative feelings. If a sensory trigger is obvious, like a partner's tight mouth and pinched brow, it may bring to mind an explicit memory of a parent's disapproving look. But it doesn't have to be an explicitly recalled memory. You don't have to know that the expression on your partner's face is unconsciously triggering in you an old association and a feeling of shame. But you can feel that something just happened and it makes you feel bad.

Making the Implicit Explicit: Exploring Mental Imagery and Emotions in Personal Work

When an emotion is triggered, changes in bodily states may briefly be accompanied by mental images from past events flashing in the mind's eye like Schore's description of a flashbulb memory. While interacting with another person, we are not necessarily aware of the mental imagery that mediates between a sense memory and becoming emotionally activated.

In body-based therapy, we can foster the conditions to track the connection between the sensory trigger and the emotional body state. We saw a good example of this in Chapter 4 with Sue and Charlie. When they sat opposite each other at the couple's workshop, Sue felt that Charlie was looking down on her and she responded with fear, bracing herself for criticism. When she mimicked Charlie's body language, he immediately recognized that he was embodying his critical father. Charlie became saddened that he had taken on his father's persona; he recognized he was doing to Sue what his father had done to him. That became an opportunity for Charlie to do personal work on his relationship with his father.

I asked Sue to move back to give him some personal space and I asked Charlie to close his eyes, take some deep breaths, and check in with his body. He said he was feeling sad that he had become like his father. He felt a lump in his throat, a heavy feeling on his chest, and his gut was tight. I asked if he could get an image of his father in his mind's eye, as his father looked to him as a boy. He said he could see him. I asked, "How old would you have been then?" "About eight," he replied. "Be that eight-year old, Charlie. Feel yourself as him," I instructed.

I asked what memory was coming back to him. "I've been suspended from school for getting into a fight with another kid and I'm telling him I was just defending myself. He doesn't believe me and when I protest he gets furious with me for talking back to him." "What do you do then," I ask. "Nothing," he says. "It's no use, if I keep talking he might take a swat at me. I can't risk it." "Has he ever taken a swat at you?" I ask. Charlie just nods his head, and I can see he's just too choked up to talk.

"What's happening now?" I ask. "I feel like a coward. I feel ashamed of myself."

I can tell that Charlie is holding a lot of feeling inside himself. He's hanging his head, his shoulders are hunched over and he's leaning on his arms braced on his lap; he's barely breathing. This is hard on Sue and I can see her getting ready to reach out to comfort him; I stop her with a silent shake of my head. Charlie needs his space to feel what he's feeling and to deal with it with resources he has now that he didn't have then.

I say, "You're no coward, Charlie. You have every right to feel sad and afraid. He's a bully. Let him know who you are." Charlie covers his face with both hands and his tears begin to flow. Sue is quietly weeping now too in her own space, a great example of intersubjective communication of emotion and empathy. We get them both some tissues.

After a few minutes, Charlie straightens his back, eyes closed, but we know he's seeing his father. He says, "I admired you; I wanted to grow up and be like you. But you *were* a bully and I knew it. You drank too much on weekends and you made me and Mom feel like we weren't good enough for you. But she was better than you. And I tried so hard to please you and nothing I ever did was good enough for you. I'm a good kid and you don't see me. I'm ashamed of you and that's the truth. I love you and I'm ashamed of you and I feel sorry for you."

After a few moments, Charlie opens his eyes and nods his head yes like he's discovering a truth he had always known deep inside. He looks around and spots Sue, and she moves over to him and they hug. Charlie takes a deep breath and lets himself be comforted by Sue. That's when we got back to their work together, his expression of gratitude and love for Sue and finally, the appreciations for sharing from the rest of the group.

Emotions Are Motivational: Pressure Builds to Restore Equilibrium

This piece of work is a good example of what we mean by resolving unresolved feelings. When emotions are activated, we are triggered to act in a specific way to resolve the sensed need or danger, and to restore homeostasis and well-being. If we don't act on the impetus, the activation remains in the system, held in check by the musculature of that particular emotional state.

The word emotion is derived from the Latin *emovere* to move out and from the French word *émouvoir*, meaning to stir up, to excite. Emotion is energy in motion. The body is activated away from pain, toward the possibility of resolving the threat or discomfort, and restoring equilibrium.

Both good and bad feelings generate motoric impulses, pressing for discharge. Essentially, the body is saying, "Do something!" The movements associated with high arousal fear are flight, to run away; to fight and try to destroy it; or to freeze and play dead, which is nature's way of conserving energy.

Emotional Resolution: Vocal and Physical Release

In the same way that our feelings energize the body and are reflexively expressed in physical action, there is also a buildup of internal energy that needs to be discharged in vocal expression and physical movement. Much of the attachment research on emotional vocalization emphasizes the parent's vocal tones and the effect on the child in response to a parent's voice signaling empathy, impatience, or annoyance.

The focus of Wilhelm Reich's work that inspired body-based somatic therapies like Gestalt and Bioenergetics was not on the parent's vocal expression, but rather on how parents may block their children's vocal expression of emotions. Punishing children for feeling angry or expressing anger at being treated unfairly or for showing fear and acting "cowardly" prevents the child from developing the ability to resolve feelings effectively in a satisfying self-affirming manner, and releasing them from the body.

Reich emphasized the need for the individual as an adult to uncover these blocked emotions in therapy and to safely express the suppressed feelings in emotionally salient bodily movements and vocalizations as expressive sounds or in truthful and courageous, words.

Unresolved Emotions: Chronic Emotional States Become Traits

Just on a physical level, the natural emotional response cycle starts with an exteroceptive sensory stimulation or an interoceptive sensation that releases various neurotransmitters that trigger the body to react and resolve the activation.

Movements associated with discomfort or pain, to protect or defend oneself, may be in response to a physiological need or to a psychological activation to a perceived personal attack. As Reich showed, when the emotion is blocked because expression is forbidden or dangerous, the impetus to act is blocked by an instinctive holding of the breath and a tensing of the muscles to resist movement. The emotional impetus is arrested, and the emotion remains unresolved (Reich, 1980).

Movements associated with pleasure are to head toward whatever is experienced as inviting. When parents punish their children for being too exuberant, too curious and exploratory, telling them to sit still and stop fidgeting, those messages can set them up for a lifetime of feeling like they are too much and need to diminish themselves to hold themselves in check to be acceptable. Holding themselves "in," they hold themselves back from pleasure.

Pleasure is invigorating and energizing, and inspires attraction to novel experiences. Securely attached children feel safe to venture out. They have their parents as a secure base to start out from and as a safe haven to return to when they feel threatened. That enables secure children to be more adventuresome, and they are more likely to explore their environment and be creative.

But even securely attached children will be blocked from certain pleasures when they are about to do something dangerous, like put a finger in a lit candle. Unfortunately, for some parents, sexual pleasure represents a dangerous exploration. When a child starts to play with his genitals, a slap on the hand sends a powerful message that certain pleasures are off limits. Over the months and years, nonverbal messages of disapproval send powerful inhibitory signals to budding young bodies.

People who learn from childhood to hold themselves back from expressing their true feelings end up with a backlog of feelings in the body held in check by shallow breathing and chronic muscular tensions. Eventually, chronically withheld emotion becomes trait-like, or characterological, etched into a person's facial expressions, body posture, and inhibited movement patterns.

With loving parental guidance during childhood, triggered emotions can be effectively channeled to release tension and become a positive learning experience. Without learning to channel painful expression in productive ways, over the years, one inhibited expression leads to another. Unless the forbidden emotion is effectively released, the individual takes on the appearance of a sad or angry person, someone who elicits a feeling of sympathy from others or sets off an alarm that he is quick to take offense and to keep away.

There is also evidence that blocked emotion can lead to stress-related illness. Emotional stress can be a risk factor for high blood pressure, migraines, bronchial asthma, heart disease, gastrointestinal problems, and chronic pain, and can interfere with healing a variety of illnesses like diabetes and cancer.

Blocked Emotions in the Body: Physical and Sexual Manifestations

The body-based couples therapist notices the clients' body and facial expressions to intuit what may be at the core of some of the issues the two people are encountering with one another. Here are some examples that signal possible chronic emotional blockages that can be observed in a person's face, posture, and movements. It's important to recognize that possible effects on sexuality are complex, highly individualistic for different men and women, and sometimes contrary to what you might expect.

Anger is associated with feeling hurt and victimized and an impulse to attack or defend oneself. Chronic unresolved anger can be seen in a combative posture and a quickness to flare up or to take offense. The eyes are narrowed, the lip and jaw are tight, the upper back and the chest can be puffed out in a display of dominance. While a habitually angry person can generate fear and a lack of sexual desire in his or her partner, the emotion has also been linked to an increase of sexual desire and aggressive lustful sex in some angry men and women (e.g., Iannuzzo et al., 2014).

Fear is an impulse to run or hide. When suppressed, the body takes on a submissive look; the head bows, the chest hollows, and the shoulders roll forward, like a turtle pulling his head into his shell; eyes may look up from the lowered head or sideways rather than make direct eye contact. Depending on the individual's level of libido, fear can result in a dampening of desire with one's partner or the emotion can have a heightening effect on sexual arousal for individuals who relish being a sexual submissive.

Despair or unresolved grief is all about suppressing tears and not fully mourning for what was lost. The person just looks sad, the mouth is turned down, the head hangs, and there's no energy. When grief is not fully mourned it turns into depression and is associated with immobility and hopelessness. In general, depression reduces sexual interest or motivation.

Guilt is self-punishment either for doing the wrong thing or not doing the right thing. When feelings of guilt have been aroused at the recognition that one has injured someone, whether intentional or unintentional, it has a positive value and activates a need to make amends toward the injured party. As a chronic state, however, guilt is very destructive as the emotion is essentially anger turned inward and involves living with an inner accusatory voice of constant self-criticism. A chronically guilty person can be highly critical of others as well. While it may seem odd, guilt as well as shame can be eroticized and linked to sexual desire.

Chronic Shame: Programmed for Failure

Like guilt, shame activates an inner voice of self-judgment and self-punishment, but not just about what one has done wrong but how one is defective. Unlike guilt, which has a possible resolution if one were to make amends, with shame, there is nothing the person feels he or she can do to be good enough. As in guilt, people with chronic shame may have difficulty making eye contact, the head sinks into their rounded shoulders, and the body appears limp. However, some people have learned to adopt a compensatory stance with a puffed out chest, holding themselves stiffly erect, head held high in a look of pseudo pride, though they can be deflated like a popped balloon with an exposing or diminishing comment from another.

Personality and attachment theorists and clinicians place special emphasis on the central role played by chronic shame in traumatized and insecure clients (e.g., DeYoung, 2015). Recognizing and helping repair and resolve shame dynamics between partners are especially critical tasks for couples and sex therapists.

To Schore (2012), therapists have been overly focused on clients' hyperaroused sympathetic-dominant states of anxiety-fear and aggression-rage while ignoring the key role played by the hypo-aroused parasympathetic-dominant state of clients in states of shame, particularly in social and interpersonal relationships. Chronic states of shame can be recognized in clients who present in therapy with a sense of helplessness and despair about their situation and a tendency to withdraw and "attempt to avoid attention and become unseen." These people typically give up too quickly rather than rally their resources to go after the change they crave.

Looking again at Sue and Charlie, Charlie had been in individual therapy and had been able to conquer his low expectations of himself and tendencies to withdraw socially, which he recognized as connected to his relationship with his father. But it was in the couple's group that he was able to see the remnants of his shame patterns in how he was treating his wife.

When he started out confronting his father in the group, he withered at first, but then with the support of the group, Sue, and myself, he was able to summon up his courage and his energy. He said he felt like a coward for not having stood up to his father. With Sue, he had been acting out the judgmental bully, a compensatory means of feeling more noble than this noble woman who had her own unfinished business from childhood. At the end of his work, he no longer saw his father as powerful but as limited and he felt his own strength connected to his feelings of compassion and admiration for his wife.

Studies consistently show that anxiously attached adults are more prone to shame and guilt than either secure or avoidant adults. When they are shamed or criticized, anxious individuals may become dys-regulated and fervently defensive, which can trigger them into painful bouts of self-hate and despair. Avoidant individuals sensitive to shame are more likely to emotionally cut the other off, sealing off their hearts and shunning any direct contact with him or her—avoiding eye-contact, speaking, touching, or acknowledging the other in any way (Lopez et al., 1997).

Sexual Shame: Unique Role in Sexual Arousal

While it might seem that the powerlessness and worthlessness that go along with the feelings of shame would undermine sexual arousal, there is evidence that just the opposite occurs for some people. Over the years, I have encountered couples where one person wanted to spice up their sexual encounters with playing out what might be described as shame-based erotic scenarios.

One woman who was having difficulty getting turned on to her husband said that she would love it if would spank her while they were flirting and coming on to each other. He refused, saying that he had been an abused child and wouldn't consider abusing her in the service of their sexual pleasure. She was clear, however, that she would consider playful spanking as play and not at all abusive. I agreed that if it was something she had requested, slapping her butt with no desire to hurt her but to pleasure her couldn't rightfully be considered abuse. I also observed that gentle slapping on the buttocks could release tension and assist in letting go to sexual arousal. That made sense to him and made her very happy— and their sex life improved markedly.

Utilizing handcuffs or blindfolds and other paraphernalia and sex toys can also spice up sex play for some couples. Another possible alternative that can become acceptable for some couples involves the occasional use of shame-invoking fantasy. On the other hand, I have also encountered couples where one person's desire to experiment with bondage and submission or cross-dressing while making love did not meet with the partner's approval and it was nipped in the bud.

Sex researcher Jack Morin has cast some light on the connection between shame and eroticism. Morin (1995) compiled stories of peak erotic experiences from a diverse group of responders and found an aspect of eroticism that appeared frequently in responders' stories. He called it the "naughtiness factor" and described it as an excitement that comes with violating taboos. He suggested that when early sexual prohibitions are accompanied by punishment or shaming, breaking the rules may be experienced as self-assertion and contribute to self-esteem.

Another possible factor linking shame and sexual excitement is classical conditioning. When sexual arousal is accompanied by being caught and shamed for masturbation or engaging in any kind of forbidden sex play, shame and humiliation may become neurobiologically linked with intense sexual arousal.

One young man came for therapy because he was distraught over his sexual fantasies. He came from a very religious family and his masturbation fantasies ever since he could remember involved his being beaten up by women. He was afraid that his fantasies boded badly for finding a woman to love that he could be turned on to. We were able to trace his earliest experiences of sexual excitement at being taunted by his two older sisters for being "a dirty little boy." Turned out he did meet a woman to love and contrary to his fears she was sweet and loving and still he was turned on to her.

Among sexually compulsive individuals, and the mostly males who engage in various paraphilias like foot fetishes, exhibitionism, voyeurism, and cross-dressing, the experience of shame is a key factor in driving up the erotic intensity of the experience. For that reason, many of these people do not seek treatment unless they are caught in illegal activities like pedophilia, peeping toms, or exposing themselves in public places.

However, it is also possible for some men and women to enjoy acting out fantasy scenes that involve humiliation without it being a detriment to themselves or to others. Mutually consenting adults who enjoy kinky sex that may involve BDSM, contained whipping, or scenes with one person being submissive to a dominant typically involve "safe words" that stop the proceedings when one person is no longer enjoying the game.

In general, the sex therapy community agrees that to honor sexual diversity is to recognize that whatever two (or more) mutually consenting adults agree to that doesn't cause harm to anyone and brings pleasure to all is healthy. That acceptance includes "vanilla sex," which is normative sex that involves either opposite-sex or same-sex couples expressing their affection for one another through sex play. When couples don't agree about the kind of sex that turns them on, that becomes a relational negotiation. Accommodating one another's sexual preferences by touching in the way one likes to be touched or trying new ways of playing at sex can be a way of expressing love as long as there is no emotional coercion of a reluctant partner.

Sexual Harassment at the Workplace: The Toxic Mix of Erotic Shame and Power

In his powerful book, *The Function of the Orgasm*, Reich made some poignant observations when he directed his attention to his male patients' fantasies when they masturbated. He found that "not in a single patient was the act of masturbation accompanied by the phantasy of experiencing pleasure in the normal sex act." I presume that meant sexual intercourse. Instead, he found the penis "was a means of proving potency" and the fantasies of his patients consisted of proving oneself as a man, picturing a rape, or "being beaten, bound, tortured, or eating feces" (Reich, 1961).

I have no doubt that some of what we have witnessed in the recent landslide of sexual misconduct charges against powerful men involves this very factor of erotic shame. Too often we hear that sexual harassment has nothing to do with sex; that it's all about power. On the contrary, I see sexual harassment as very much about sex— for the perpetrator—and its potency comes from being mixed with guilt and shame.

All the stories of sexual harassment involve some aspect of paraphilia: exhibitionism, where the man exposes himself to the woman or masturbates in front of her; dominance, in forcing a woman to sexually submit; and humiliation of the person who is likely to be experiencing fear or shame during the episode. Men in lesser positions have also been harassed, groped by more senior men looking for sexual favors. These can be intensely arousing experiences for the sexual predator who typically enjoys high status as a leader in his field and the shame or fear depicted by the victim only intensifies the perpetrator's arousal.

Without effective therapy for post-traumatic stress, this kind of incident can wound a victim for life. However, I am a firm believer in post-traumatic growth. Confronting the inner wound with the therapist's warm acceptance, support, empathy, compassion, patience, and encouragement inspires the client's courage to go into the pain on a body-based physiological level through breathing into the wound of shame. To feel it in its many layers—the suppressed or dissociated fear, disgust, rage, shame, guilt, and submission—is to eject it from one's body and to feel clean again.

And always, the courage to move into and through that tunnel, to face the witch's brew of painful emotions with courage ignited by the breath is to stand up to the defiler. To be full-throated with the words, bodily movements, unwavering determination, and skill to defend oneself is to taste freedom. At that point, the task in therapy is to keep facing the demons, and by doing so, build the skill level-by-level to protect one's personal space and sexual boundaries.

There is a silver lining to exposing this occupational, multicultural, tacitly accepted sexual assault, thanks to all the courageous women and men, newly empowered by their numbers, who have come forward. The national dialogue on sexual predation has been cathartic and has spread globally. Bringing it into the light has had an invigorating effect on opening up the cultural conversation on sex, and has advanced society's sexual awareness.

By encouraging the people who have fallen victim to sexual abuse to speak out, shame can turn to pride. This openness about sex may empower others to assert their sexual rights and sovereignty over their own body in their own families. Most of the people who have spoken out come from the ranks of successful women and men in the arts, business, technology, and government, but ordinary individuals are also being harassed in their own homes or on the job.

In particular, I have worked with women clients in traditional relationships who in the course of their work reveal an unconsciously held belief that having sex without pleasure is their responsibility to a husband who works hard to support their family. Perhaps a more open dialogue about sex in the news or on social media will inspire the women who don't go to therapy to learn how to talk more openly, though delicately, at home about their sexual feelings or to seek therapy. Hopefully, these public revelations will awaken parents to the necessity for raising sex-positive respectful boys and girls who, through more open conversations about sex at home, are better equipped as men and women to safely set sexual boundaries.

Corrective Emotional Experience: Re-Creating the Past in the Present

The most transformative work in therapy occurs when chronic emotions are identified as such, and the client is guided back to the original painful event or series of events to re-experience and to emotionally resolve the imprinted emotion in a way that achieves closure and inspires growth.

Gestalt therapy was founded on re-doing the past in the present and has developed the quintessential body-based experiential method for facilitating this work. The essence of Gestalt practice is founded on turning pain into pleasure or, as I like to say, turning lead into gold. The originators of Gestalt therapy during the early 1940s were clearly familiar with the concepts of corrective emotional experience and built it into the present-centered experiential process work that became Gestalt therapy.

Alexander and French (1946) were the first to suggest that contrary to Freud's formula for catharsis as the key to working through trauma, something more was needed—and that something more was a "corrective emotional experience." They defined the essential factor as re-exposing the client to the original traumatic experience, and with the support of the therapist, for the client to re-experience the traumatic event with a new, more positive, result.

There are several types of corrective emotional experiences. One occurs between the therapist and the client in individual therapy. In showing the client the authentic compassion and empathy he or she did not receive in childhood, the therapist encourages the client to explore withheld painful feelings about being punished, shamed, or violated by a parent or significant person in the client's young life (Hartman & Zimberoff, 2004).

Another kind of corrective experience can occur in couples therapy between partners, when the therapist models a quality of empathy that guides the partners to re-connect with love and empathy for each other as the most effective means for resolving their disappointments with one another.

In my experience, the most powerful corrective experiences occur when the individual client recognizes the connection between a present emotional blockage and a past event. Through the use of imagery and breath awareness, the client can re-experience the prototypical, emotionally inhibiting, life-shaping childhood trauma. What makes this "corrective" and not just cathartic is to re-do the experience and to express the emotions originally suppressed in *a self-affirming way*.

Hartman and Zimberoff refer to this type of work as age-regression through hypnosis. I find that utilizing deep, intentional breathing and focusing on the original imagery from childhood has the same effect, with the added advantage that the individual does not have to attribute his or her success to any non-ordinary state of consciousness other than deep relaxation—which after all is what hypnosis is all about.

In this kind of experiential, present-centered, body-based corrective emotional experience, we go back into the person's childhood, which is still there in memory, simply layered over like the Russian nesting dolls. The therapeutic objective is to create a safe environment for the client to re-experience the early developmental disruption and to repair it in a manner that feels good and validates their individuality, autonomy, and worthiness. The healing process can generate the kind of personal agency that can restore healthy developmental growth.

In the work with Charlie, we went back to his original experience with his father and instead of cowering in shame, with my urging and support Charlie stood up to him. In doing so, he experienced a new sense of power and agency and a release of the shame that made him compulsively attempt to re-assert himself by shaming Sue. This is a classic situation for male clients with overbearing fathers who end up in therapy with a variety of emotional and sexual difficulties.

Corrective Couple Experiences: Gestalt Processing Face-to-Face and Side-by-Side

What we are looking at here involves individual growth as much as relational growth. Sometimes in a couple's session a painful childhood event comes up for one partner. I tell clients that couples therapy is a good place to work on it since the painful event in the partner's past is typically relevant to what the couple is working on. Some want to do the work in an individual session, in order to reserve the couple's sessions for their interaction. Most opt to be present for each other's deeper work.

Here's an example of a male couple in a six-year relationship where they each opted to be present for each other's deeper work.

Resolving Old Wounds as a Team: Cory and Dave

Cory was an attractive man with an expressive dancer's body who at age thirty-five was ten years younger than his husband Dave. Dave's body seemed stiff and contained in comparison and it was he who had insisted they come for therapy. Dave said that he was fed up with Cory's flirtatious behavior with other men in his presence. Dave was clearly in pain, his voice was gravely and he sighed often. He complained that it was disrespectful for Cory to come on to their friends and that it didn't seem possible to have friends at their house or to go out to parties without Cory coming on to someone.

Cory flared, saying he was insulted and he denied that he was flirtatious. "I'm just being friendly and having fun," he insisted, "and I can't take your suspiciousness and jealousy. I love you so much," he said leaning forward his voice softer, "and I want to be with you forever but I can't take your drama." Dave's face got even sadder and he seemed deflated.

When I asked them how this conflict had affected their sex life, Dave replied dryly, "What sex? There is no sex." Cory protested, "I can't have sex with you anymore. I know that's a part of what makes you jealous when you see me being friendly with our friends. But I'm just too annoyed with you. I get tense when you touch me," he told Dave. "Your jealousy is a turn-off."

In the next two sessions we looked at the differences in their backgrounds and how each was bringing old wounds into their relationship. Cory was an only child and by age six, knew he was different from other boys he played with; his parents knew it too. He liked to play dress up and dance around the house, waving scarfs and making up dance steps. His mother found him amusing, but his father was less enthusiastic. Cory said he tried to get his father to like him, but nothing he did worked so he began to do the opposite, to see how far he could provoke him. When he started to study dance at age twelve his father almost completely avoided being with him.

Dave had his own wounds from childhood. He was a shy child with a little sister who was three years younger and a "born charmer." Even though he felt loved by both parents, it was clear to him that he didn't light up his parents the way his sister did. She was more of the performer in their household and he was the intellectual, the one who studied and got good grades.

Dave's school accomplishments made his parents happy and proud of him but they still didn't seem to be that interested. Dave kept to himself, read a lot, played video games, and excelled at school. He said he liked his little sister because she was hard not to like but he also resented her. Dave came out as gay at age seventeen, which shocked his parents, but his younger sister said she knew it all along.

Dave described a dinner party at the home of another gay couple and a few of their friends. It was clear to him that Cory really hit it off with a new man neither of them had known before. Cory said he wasn't turned on to the guy sexually, but they shared some big laughs together and really connected on a political level. He knew Dave was watching them from the corner of his eye and was getting uncomfortable. When I asked if Cory made any attempt to include Dave, he replied that it would have been uncomfortable and he was enjoying himself too much.

Dave said he sat there at the party watching Cory and the other fellow and he got "more and more pissed." He finally got up and told Cory to get a ride home and he left by himself. When Cory got home they had a big fight.

Does it matter which came first, Dave's jealousy or Cory's coldness toward him and warmth toward other men in his presence? And what was really going on with Cory? It seemed to me that his behavior toward Dave, knowing his insecurities, looked punishing. I asked Cory about that straight out and he owned up to being resentful and maybe wanting to get even. Dave said he was beginning to think this relationship was hopeless.

I assured Cory and Dave that having wounds to work on together was the great value of being in an intimate relationship. I like to tell clients that no one can escape from childhood without some wounds because we're all vulnerable and that some element of pain seems to be nature's way of inspiring growth. I talk about how we're born with more neurons than we could possibly use and that it is with challenge that we access our potential and make use of resources we otherwise wouldn't know we have.

Besides, without issues to work on that enable each person to grow through their intimacy, a relationship could easily stagnate. Intimate love relationships are our adult opportunity to repair wounds of the past that keep us stuck in old emotional patterns. After hearing this couple share with each other what they most love and appreciate about the other, in their first session, I could honestly see that they shared a deep love.

I told them that the issues that brought them to therapy could be "the shit that makes their garden grow." This was their chance to work as a team to grow the relationship into a more loving and sexually fulfilling, lifelong bond. They liked that. I gave them "matching breaths" to do at home that were focused on non-sexual extended hugs and breathing together, and suggested that, when they talked to each other, they make sure they do so face-to-face, looking into each other's eyes.

In the next sessions, we looked at their different attachment styles, how Cory had entertained his mother and relished attention, and how Dave tended to be more of a loner and not as attentive to Cory when they were at home together. In some ways, Cory treated Dave like he treated his father, provoking him as a way of getting his attention.

Dave's patterns clearly grew out of the lack of attention he himself got at home and the jealousy he began to acknowledge that he felt at his sister being the center of interest in his family. Dave never allowed himself to feel jealous of his sister but here he was with Cory, who thrived on connection and loved an audience, just like his sister.

It was time that Dave allowed himself to recognize that he envied Cory's social ease just as he had envied his sister. It was time that Cory owned that he was treating Dave like his father and that his "family transference" was interfering with his feeling sexual desire for him.

Healing Through Body-to-Body Intimacy: Embodying Empathy, Repair, Resolution, and Physical Affection/Sexual Pleasure

The work in each session always begins with a catch-up: any insights or feelings from the previous session, how home play exercises went, and anything they may want to focus on in the present session. Then we go to work. I ask that they close their eyes, take some deep breaths, scan their bodies from the inside for feelings of tension or emotion, turn and face each other and share where they are with one another.

Working with Dave and Cory was a delight because they loved each other deeply and were both eager to grow their relationship. The more they recognized how the patterns they evolved intersubjectively as a couple reflected a composite of each of their early relational patterns, the more they each took responsibility for their contribution to their emotional conflict together.

My therapeutic goals in embodied relational couples therapy all revolve around one overriding objective: to work through the couple's impasse via enhancing their body-to-body intimacy. The four-fold path of empathy, repair, resolution, and physical affection is not sequential but simultaneous and in no particular order. Yet each step along the way furthers the facility by which any next step is taken.

One session may focus on repair of a present conflict and how their early history is impacting their feelings and behaviors. We may go back to the suppressed or dissociated emotion that has been triggered in one or both and see how a relational injury triggers old emotional wounds. We can use the opportunity to focus on one of them to express the suppressed feelings from the family history without directing it at the partner. Then we can go back to the partner to reinforce the connection between the current event and the past to reaffirm how, with *empathy* and support, each partner is an integral part of the other's growth. Feelings of relief and a surge of pleasurable excitement come with feelings of personal affirmation, of a partner's acceptance and *resolution*. Finally, we explore how intimates can turn their loving empathy, feeling seen and accepted, into body-to-body *affection* and sensual and *sexual pleasure*.

Let's see how this work progressed with Dave and Cory.

Repair and Resolution

Given our cultural history with same-sex love and sexuality, many gay men and lesbians have experienced some degree of parental or family rejection and shaming. Both Cory and Dave recounted early memories of feeling unaccepted by their family, though Cory was culturally more gender nonconforming in his physical mannerisms and clothing choices.

Cory was a sensitive child and tended to cling to his mother while he felt little connection with his father. He felt rejected by his father and he suppressed the rage he felt toward him. But he did learn how to stir his father's emotions, albeit negatively, by taunting him with his behavior, playing dress up in dance costumes, and doing ballet pirouettes and jetés around the house.

Dave was more independent and said he guessed he was gay at puberty when he realized that he only fantasized about boys when he masturbated. He suspected that his parents secretly knew that he was gay and that's why they were less interested in him than his sister. He told himself that he didn't need them to accept him and he felt that excelling at school and later in business was the best route for him to achieve personal recognition. He dated in his early twenties but was largely uninterested in the men he went out with until he met Cory. Cory excited him and he loved and admired his freedom of expression and physical attractiveness.

During a session, when we would reach an emotional impasse we would look for how the current emotional trigger reminded one or the other of a past familial event. We might at that point or later during the session go back to the spontaneous memory evoked by the current interaction. Through deep breaths and inner focus on the visual imagery—what Damasio calls "movies of the mind"— we might look for what is left over from the past to re-do in a self-affirming way.

The beauty of doing this work in each other's presence is how much empathy for one another this kind of work generates. They identified with each other's pain and felt compassion for their shared sense of being different from other people. When Cory worked he typically felt free to rage and sob. Dave was uncharacteristically tender toward him in those moments.

Dave was more restrained when he worked on past slights he felt with his parents although he did allow himself to dialogue with his sister and to tell her that he envied her and felt competitive with her. When he stepped into her being metaphorically, he represented her as loving toward him and shared that as a child she had admired him too and that she still did. His eyes did get moist during the work and Cory too welled up with compassion. I too was very touched by Dave's uncharacteristic openness and vulnerability.

Empathy and Affection

As Cory and Dave delved into their backgrounds they clearly grew emotionally closer. They were doing the home-play experiments more regularly, holding each other for extended hugs, breathing together, and being more affectionate with each other at home. Cory knew that he desired physical closeness more than Dave did and felt that Dave was being generous with him and he was grateful. Dave laughed when Cory shared that and he protested that he was also enjoying the hugs though he didn't need them quite as often as Cory did.

They still hadn't invited any friends to their home nor had they resumed their sexual connection since they started therapy. Dave had not brought up the issue of sex for a while and then, one day at the beginning of a session, Cory started with a declaration: "Let's talk about sex." He looked very animated, a little anxious perhaps, while Dave, ever cool, just said "Okay." I perked up and said, "Great, turn and face each other."

Cory started with,

> My sweetheart, I owe you an admission and an apology. I did want to make you jealous. I felt like you didn't appreciate me and that if you saw how other men responded to me you would want me more. I know I caused you pain and I'm so, so, sorry.

He reached out and touched Dave on the knee. Dave was sitting sideways on the couch facing Cory and barely moved but smiled a brief smile and put his hand over Cory's.

Cory and I were focused on Dave who sat very still and said nothing for a few very long minutes when Dave suddenly shifted uncomfortably and we could see his face was flushed and he was fighting back tears. He coughed a bit and looked down and I whispered to him softly, "Breathe." He had been holding his breath and when he allowed the air to gush in, his body jerked and a few tears began to roll down his face. He cleared his throat, and the sound that came out was husky and deep. It almost looked like he didn't know how to cry.

This time instead of saying anything, I just leaned toward Dave and exhaled deeply a few times. When he turned to look at me I looked him in the eyes and gave him a big smile. He laughed and mimicked my exhale and then broke down and let himself cry softly for just a few moments. Then he threw his arms around Cory and held him tight. I felt honored to be present to this moment and sat by quietly.

Cory had expressed deep remorse for causing Dave pain. There was no doubt that Cory's remorse was deeply felt and from his heart. His emotion, coming not from shame but from love, was eliciting an equally deep, felt-sense of forgiveness. This was indeed a genuine expression of body-to-body loving empathy coming from both of them. Nothing more needed to be said. They stood up, each man hugged me, and they left my office holding hands.

The next time I saw them was two weeks later and they came into the office looking relaxed with a kind of healthy glow. They told me that they had taken some time off for a romantic holiday at a lovely hotel on the beach and fell in love all over again. They were just starting to get physical again and the experience of lovemaking was different than it had ever been before with anyone. They could feel the arousal all over their bodies and it was very sensual and sexy.

It was clear to me that Cory was sexually more comfortable and experienced and he was thrilled to be Dave's sexual guru. In the past, Dave was the one who knew more about fine dining or art and the theater. But now it was Cory's turn to be the more knowledgeable one and he just warmed to the task, letting Dave know that he felt like they were starting a new relationship.

Cory and Dave make appointments now and then when some issue comes up that they want to look into more deeply and want my input. I'm always delighted to see them. Each time I see them I can tell their bond is solid and they have evolved a relationship that works for them both.

Resolving Painful Emotions Releases Pleasurable Emotions

The beauty of corrective emotional experiences lies in how working through the unresolved pain is always a pleasure. When clients face the fears they avoided in childhood and re-do the traumatic event with a new personally assertive ending they experience the exhilaration of their courage and resolution. When they feel their anger and confront the neglectful or abusive parent of their childhood, they can let go of the poison of chronic resentment and ultimately may come to forgive and feel compassion for the inadequate mother or father. When they stand up to the shaming parent or teacher, they gain a sense of pride. The outcome of resolving a chronic painful emotion is always a pleasure.

More Complicated Work: Repair After an Affair

The work I have described so far has not looked at the most serious relational ruptures of all, those with unrelenting physical and emotional abuse, chronic addiction, or a pattern of secretive affairs that can involve lying and financial loss. This work often involves more complex lifestyle issues and is beyond the scope and focus of this book.

However, corrective emotional experiences can be utilized with individuals who were suddenly left or betrayed by a spouse who decided he or she no longer wanted to remain in the relationship. The work often starts with expressing their rage toward the former spouse, then their grief, and sometimes their shame. At some point, they may be able to recognize their own willingness to stay and suffer in a relationship that wasn't working. When they are able to let that relationship go and even feel compassion for the betraying or abandoning partner, the emotion is always one of relief, a renewed sense of personal agency, and hope for a better future.

I also see couples where one person has been discovered in an affair and the straying partner expresses remorse. The expression of remorse is key to allowing the partners to do the hard work of repairing the relationship.

My experience working with couples after an affair has been very powerful, particularly when there is an acknowledgement of guilt, expressions of grief, and the partner who feels betrayed is also willing to acknowledge ways in which he or she contributed to the estrangement between them. The process can take a long time, sometimes two or three years, because of the likelihood of PTSD flashbacks on the part of the one who feels betrayed and feelings of reactivated guilt and shame on the part of the betrayer. The couples who have stayed with it have prospered by staying together with greater love, typically better sex with each other, and tremendous appreciation for what they went through together.

In the next chapter, we take a broader view of the wide assortment of pleasures that can enrich our daily lives. These pleasures include sensory awareness, sensual and sexual delights, the pleasures of health and emotional well-being, playfulness, creativity, feeling good feelings and thinking good thoughts, and having the courage to imagine the best future rather than to prepare for the worst. We can see how pleasurable activities and positive emotions inspire physical and emotional health and are the keys to personal and relational transformation.

7

Pleasure: The Transformative Power of Body-to-Body Intimacy

Western civilization tends to have mixed feelings about pleasure. After all, we have a puritanical history going back to a time when exuberance was looked upon with disgust, children were to be restrained from being too spirited, and contraptions were invented to keep boys from masturbating under the covers in bed at night. Girls were deemed sexually pure and good women were assumed to be lacking in sexual desire (Miller, 1983; Foucault, 1990; Groneman, 2001).

We may have come a long way from those days, but the suspiciousness about feeling too good has been handed down from one generation to the next and we are still in the process of weeding out its destructive roots. As Oxford pain researchers Siri Leknes and Irene Tracey (2008) have pointed out:

> The Calvinistic focus on moderation, or even abstinence, of pleasure has deep roots in Western culture and is powerfully connected with shame. Whereas excessive reliance on shame and stoicism might cause unnecessary suffering, extreme pleasure-seeking and pain avoidance (hedonism) can have undesirable consequences such as drug addiction and obesity. However, the inability to take pleasure in everyday rewards is also a form of suffering.

In *The Pleasure Zone*, I wrote about how being shamed for demonstrating exuberance and excitement during childhood could result in low-pleasure tolerance—an inability to allow oneself the ordinary pleasures of daily life that foster physical health, healing of illness, and emotional well-being. Working toward a corrective emotional experience with empathic relational support is one of the most effective approaches for uncovering early shame programming and reclaiming the everyday contentment of loving relationships (Resnick, 1997). Here's a great example of the pleasures that become available when working through early shame programming associated with feelings of pleasure.

Reclaiming Pleasure Can Transform a Life

A while ago, a man in his early fifties contacted me with an unusual sex problem for a man. He told me that he had no difficulty having sex with his wife, nor did he have any trouble sustaining an erection for the duration of their contact or controlling his ejaculation. He added that he is pleased that his wife is enthusiastic about their lovemaking and that she almost always enjoys powerful orgasms. The problem he has suffered most of his adult life, he told me, is that he derives no pleasure from orgasm.

When I suggested that he come in with his wife for couples therapy, Chet told me that he wasn't ready to work with her on this issue, that it was an embarrassment, and that he didn't want to trouble her. He asked if I would be willing to start just with him and I said I would.

In our first session, Chet's face was devoid of expression as he described his feelings during sex. He said he enjoys the connection with his wife Gloria but at a certain point, the pleasant sensation stops and the ejaculation occurs quickly after that. When I asked about how that compares with the sensation he feels during masturbation he said it was similar in that he gets some pleasure from the arousal but that at a certain point the sensation stops and he ejaculates. Again he told me that it was embarrassing. When I asked what was embarrassing, he replied, "that my body doesn't work." When we talked about how he felt about the rest of his life, his work and relationships with his wife and grown son, he said that his relationship with his wife was good but that he wished he were closer with his only child.

As to his profession as an engineer, he despaired that he didn't progress further in his work and he said that he thought it was because "he never went all in." He said that throughout his life he felt like he never went all in. When I asked what he meant by that, he replied that he felt like he held himself back because of his fear of failure, and that if he didn't try too hard he couldn't fail. When I asked about his relationship with his son, there too he felt like "he didn't give it his all." He explained that he wasn't at ease with his son because his son had problems and he was uncomfortable with his son's intensity; he acknowledged that he tended to be preoccupied judging himself when they were together.

Those phrases "not going all in" or "not giving his all" I heard as shame, and likely metaphors for holding himself back in sex and not just in his family, and work. He often mentioned stopping himself out of embarrassment, a clear indicator of chronic shame (de Young, 2015). We looked at how he might not be going all in or giving his all sexually as well, that he might not be fully present with his wife or even fully focused when he masturbated. I noted that as good as his relationship was with his wife, there too he hadn't given her his all because he hadn't shared with her his sexual frustrations even though it troubled him. He acknowledged he was troubled but said he didn't want her to be troubled too. Yet not sharing more deeply with her might at least partly be affecting his sexuality.

Chet suffered from a good deal of shame around feelings of pleasure. He frequently talked about being embarrassed and not giving something his all, or going all in, fearing the possible intensity of the experience. He noted that he was not being fully present at anything. He lived his life at the midpoint, never experiencing the exhilaration of going all in and giving everything he had for the thrill of it, irrespective of the approval of others. The breath work helped him feel his feelings more and being more present not just during sex but also in his relationships with his wife and son.

Chet was a textbook case of a shame-based man living a hypo-aroused, parasympathetically biased lifestyle that kept him from realizing his potential with his family and in his work. But it was the absence of sexual pleasure and full release through orgasm that brought him to therapy. Sexual arousal depends on both sympathetic arousal as well as parasympathetic relaxation—what I call "the pleasure of relaxed-excitement." Chet's avoidance of risk or challenge kept him under-stimulated.

When we looked into the childhood experiences that led Chet to live an under-stimulated life, the work transformed his entire life. He described his mother as non-demonstrative and his parents as showing little affection for him or for one another. Then he zeroed in on one particular experience that for him was the moment that changed him from a fun-loving enthusiastic boy to a cautious, shameful, self-demeaning child. He felt that one incident was the terrible moment when his life changed.

Chet was around age twelve when came home from school one day feeling wonderful about how well he had done in class, gaining praise from a teacher and a pat on the back from a buddy. He ran in to tell his folks sitting at the kitchen table, exclaiming, "I feel great!" His father shot up from the table furious, repeatedly poked his index finger into Chet's chest and shouted, "In this house, we don't talk like that."

Another event took place soon after that when he was walking to school with a close friend who started giving him grief about getting straight A's. Once again he got the message not to stand out. At that point he said he never gave his all in school again and though he did well, he never again "went all in."

As he was relating the story, Chet stopped for a moment saying that even then he felt all choked up. From that time on he felt he shouldn't be too big for his britches. "But what can you do," he said, more like a statement than a question. "You can't change the past." "Oh yes you can," I said. "Let's re-do it." I explained to Chet that the significant moment of his shutting down was not something he could have done differently when he was twelve. His father was too threatening and his mother didn't and couldn't support him. But that moment was still in there and with the resources he has today and with my support he could find that exuberant Chet again and reclaim him. He said he would try.

I asked Chet to take a few deep breaths, to imagine himself as that boy again, and to put himself back in that moment with his father. As Chet started to breathe deeply I could see him getting tense. "What's happening?" I asked. He said he was feeling sick to his stomach and he felt fear. He was embarrassed that it had taken him so long to deal with this and he blamed himself. I told him I understood how difficult this was and that I admired his courage and his willingness now to go back into the pain.

The next breath was a deep sigh and he sat there silently with his eyes closed and I could tell he was back there in that moment re-experiencing it. Finally, he said, "I don't know what to say." So I fed him a line; I suggested, "I have a right to be excited, I have a right to feel great." He stammered, "I have a right to feel great." A spontaneous rush of air filled his lungs. He exhaled in a semi-laugh, repeated the lines and went on from there. "I have a right to feel great. I have a right to excitement. I have a right to joy. I wish you and Mom could be happier. I wish you could have lived happier lives. I love you."

That session was only the beginning. He had experienced deep feelings, and he was impressed with the experience of full deep spontaneous breaths. But in the next session he talked about feeling uncertain, like he was losing control, feeling sad, and also like he was increasingly in touch with how often he felt fear or anxiety. The experience of going back into the past had opened up a developmental process that had been interrupted just as he was entering puberty. We did more experimenting with feeling his fear in his body, how he naturally became tense all over, especially in his chest and belly, and how to breathe into his fear and feel his excitement.

We covered a lot of territory in the next three months of sessions working on being more open with his wife and his son and taking more risks at work. We also talked about his becoming aware of how he might be holding his breath during sex. I reminded him continually about breathing more deeply and focusing on his wife rather than on himself when they were making love.

In the last session, he came in saying, "I'm actually doing better." When I responded that he sounded surprised, he said, "I *am* surprised." He talked about how the earlier work "talking back to his father" was so unfamiliar to him that it opened his eyes. Not talking back was how he responded to a lot of situations, and he saw that life could be a dialogue instead of like something that just happens to him. He said he now lets himself feel his fear instead of hiding from it and when he does he finds that the fear drops away.

Finally, Chet was pleased that the buildup to orgasm was stronger and the sensation of orgasm was more intense. He related his greater sexual enjoyment to becoming more adept at recognizing when he felt afraid and instead of seeing his fear as something that was wrong with him, he saw it more as a challenge. The only problem would be to not breathe into it and take it on. He summed up his experience so far in therapy and what he learned the most was "being able to hold on to pleasure—to hang out in it rather than being afraid of it."

Chet did all this transformative work in individual therapy. I've suggested to him that he consider taking the next step of coming into couples therapy with his wife and to continue his exploration with her. I also think it would be valuable for him to come in for a few sessions with his son. Whether or not he does any more work in therapy, I feel gratified by the enormous progress he has made. Spurred on initially by a sexual issue, this man's entire life has been transformed.

Pleasure Is More Than the Absence of Pain: Expansion, Exploration, and Forward Movement

On the simplest level, the difference between painful and pleasurable experiences and emotions is the difference between contraction and expansion. When a child is loved and honored for whomever he or she truly is, the empathy, compassion, support, and encouragement feed the child's metabolic energy and inspire the child's capacity to channel that energy productively.

The secure child can venture out to explore the world because she feels safe and has been given tools to indulge her curiosity and to investigate new realms of experience. When the child feels threatened, the parent is there as a safe haven to return to for comfort and protection.

Not only does a parent's affection and encouragement support exploration but a loving, empathic, and encouraging parent also provides a positive behavioral model that builds that individual's adult repertoire of supportive skills toward his or her own mate and children.

Although some researchers argue that, unlike pain, which triggers an autonomic reaction to run in fear or attack in anger, positive emotions engender no such action tendencies (Fredrickson & Branigan, 2005). I respectfully disagree. When something feels good, it provides energy. A child who sees something that she likes she feels herself drawn to it; she knows exactly which way to move—forward! Pleasurable experience moves us toward the person, place, thing, or experience that led to reward.

Pleasurable feelings are motivating and typically very specific, directing a beeline toward the rewarding stimulus. Feelings of love, gratitude, and enthusiasm upon encountering a friend or lover spontaneously move us energetically toward the person to embrace him or her. Excitement, appreciation, and curiosity are expansive sensations. Experiencing pleasure is a state of arousal telling us that whatever it is that we are doing to keep doing it.

Pleasure provides direction to the movement much better than pain.

Painful sensation generates a physiological impulse to contract. Not only do the muscles of the body contract; when people experience pain, their world contracts. Pain is a signal that something is wrong and a sign to avoid anything associated with that feeling. Pain doesn't necessarily inform direction. It just signals us to go anywhere but here.

Yet despite the fact that the autonomic nervous system has been triggered, movement in response to painful feeling is often inhibited. We don't often run when we are afraid, particularly when the fear is generated by our own fearful imagination. We may also freeze in fear. Most of us resist throwing a punch at people, no matter how angry we may get at them.

That's precisely why unexpressed pain can cause illness—instead of expressing the toxic energy and finding closure, it's held in the body. Emotional pain is physically painful; physical pain typically evokes fear and anxiety, possibly grief, and sometimes shame.

Where the emotional pain is felt in the body is significant. Emotions like shame, guilt, fear, grief, and resentment can cause tension and pain in what I think of as the emotional center of the body: in the head and face, throat, the chest and heart, belly and gut, in the diaphragm and small and large intestines. Despite the fact that we can feel emotion all over the body, in the hands as they automatically tense into fists when we get angry or in the legs when we feel like kicking someone in the shins. But much of our information about feelings can be most easily accessed by focusing in to the area between the top of the head and the pelvic region. Whether the origin of the pain is an emotional or a physical one, the assault is on the individual's well-being,

Chronic emotional pain takes its toll on the body's ability to repair injuries or return to homeostasis, producing the conditions for psychosomatic illness and lowering a person's resistance to disease. When the locus of the contraction is in the chest, the stress causes wear and tear on the heart. If the locus of the contraction and stress hormones is in the gut, irritable bowel syndrome may result.

Pleasurable feelings have consistently been shown to enhance resistance to disease. Positive emotions speed recovery from the visceral effects of negative emotions and are shown to optimize physical health and emotional well-being (Ornstein & Sobel, 1989).

A Plethora of Pleasures: Sensory, Emotional, Sexual, and Spiritual

All pleasures are motivating, and we have vast inner resources for nurturing healthy pleasures. Many pleasures, like eating, drinking, sleeping, moving, loving, and making love satisfy basic needs and restore homeostatic balance, though we continually refine our tastes and pleasures as we get older. With primary needs met, social motivations and creative inspirations take over. What all pleasures have in common are the subjective feelings of liking, wanting more, and gravitating toward what beckons.

Pleasures that nurture the body and generate positive emotions, loving relationships, and spiritual connection have been shown to be at the foundation of the lives lived by happy people. In the past, therapists were prone to specifically focus on resolving pain, and assumed that once the problem was identified and resolved, pleasure and well-being would naturally follow. We now know better. Resolving the pain in therapy and terminating therapy there is going halfway up the mountain—that's the literal definition of mediocrity.

Exploring and resolving pain is necessary but not sufficient. That's true for any type of therapy and especially for couples and sex therapy. Recognizing early childhood programming and adult tendencies to resist pleasure and practicing a wide spectrum of delights is the other half of the healing journey. Pleasurable exploration and reclaiming playfulness are essentials for therapy to be truly transformative.

Hedonic and Eudaemonic Pleasures: The Connections Between Sensory Pleasure and Emotional Well-Being

Positive psychologists have attributed human happiness and well-being to two kinds of pleasures that appear to be distinct from one another: hedonic pleasures and eudaemonic well-being. Hedonic pleasures have been largely associated with positive emotions and sensory pleasures while eudaemonic pleasures are associated primarily with living a meaningful and engaging life. Eudaemonia is the subjective well-being that comes with experiencing one's life as valuable, meaningful, and engaging (Berridge & Kringelbach, 2011).

Hedonic pleasures should not be conflated with hedonism. Hedonism is typically understood as a lifestyle where emotional entanglements are to be avoided and the main focus of life is to accumulate pleasures. The pursuit of sensory pleasures to the exclusion of anything else is compulsivity. As pleasure theorist and founder of Bioenergetics Alexander Lowen pointed out in a lecture half a century ago, "If a good steak can excite our palates, two good steaks can give us indigestion."

Too much food, drink, sex, and material wealth with none of the richness, expansiveness, and growth that comes from confronting challenge and learning from the sometimes painful complications of human connection is developmentally limiting. But as the research shows, there is certainly value in appreciating sensory and emotional pleasures in combination with the more enduring eudaimonic pleasures of leading a life that is experienced as having value to oneself and to others.

That was what I was getting at when I was promoting *The Pleasure Zone* one afternoon on television on *The O'Reilly Factor*. Responding to Bill O'Reilly's questions, I was explaining how pleasurable experience is a key to physical health and emotional well-being and yet many of us have learned to hold ourselves back from feeling as good as we can. I talked about the value of letting go of pleasure-resistance and embracing playfulness and the emotional, sensual, sexual, and spiritual pleasures that support health and happiness. O'Reilly looked at me in mock horror and exclaimed, "But Dr. Resnick, what you are espousing is hedonism!" I laughed at his challenge. "Yes," I shot back, "but it's an 'enlightened hedonism.'"

The Neuroscience of Pleasure and Well-Being

While hedonic pleasures and eudaemonic meaningfulness appear to be very different, empirical studies on well-being show that individuals who score high on one scale also tend to score high on the other. That is, happy people tend to feel more pleasure in life, while those more likely to value emotional and sensory pleasures are also apt to think of themselves as happy.

Since hedonic and eudaemonic pleasures tend to "co-occur in the same happy people," neurobiologists were able to find "hedonic hotspots" in subcortical structures in the reward circuit of the brain that were most active during pleasurable experience. These areas are the *nucleus accumbens*, which is activated by dopamine and associated with reward and sexual desire and by serotonin that is associated with elevated mood, memory, and sexual desire; the *ventral pallidum*, which is also associated with reward, bonding, and incentive motivation; and the *brainstem*, which plays an important role in connecting the sensory systems to the cortex, and regulating heart and respiratory function, consciousness, and sleep (Berridge & Kringleback, 2011).

The researchers also found that the network of hedonic hotspots forms an integrated circuit so that the more hotspots that are activated the greater the subjective experience of pleasure. Recruiting greater sources of pleasure makes the experience "nicer than usual." Under those circumstances, "neurochemical activation of hedonic hotspots creates a brain wellspring for intense pleasure . . . generating high hedonic peaks of sensory pleasure" (Peciña et al., 2006).

Well-being itself is viewed as an ongoing state of "hedonic resilience," where pleasures are frequent and sustained, and not necessarily tied to any one source. In other words, the capacity to take delight in all the senses adds to the feeling of happiness.

Perhaps it involves taking the time to witness a lovely sunset, reflect over a painting, or enjoy a mate's smile; to listen to music, get a massage, smell the roses, eat slowly and relish one's food, enjoy one's creativity, write a poem, play a game just for the fun of it, laugh heartily, meditate and experience a quiet mind, think good thoughts, feel grateful, enjoy the company of friends, sing in a choir, dance, feel a part of the community and preserve a sense of a spiritual connection to something good that is larger than oneself.

In the same way, taking the time to make love and to allow the excitement to build erotically also takes focusing in on the full contingent of senses: looking into your lover's eyes, listening to his or her breaths and whispers, feeling the warmth and smoothness of his or her skin, smelling the scent of sexual arousal, tasting your kisses and drinking in every delicious sensuous moment of your body-to-body sexual intimacy.

Physical affection needs to be a part of daily life and not just relegated to the times when couples begin to make love. When I see couples for the first time whose presenting complaint is that they don't have sex, my first question is "do you kiss?" The answer most often is "no." That's where the work starts—not with helping them regain the desire to make love but to regain the desire to kiss.

Studies show that more frequent expressions of physical affection in couples like hugging, kissing, and holding hands contribute to romantic feelings and greater relationship satisfaction (Gulledge et al., 2003). When couples work through their personal and interpersonal pain together and are more attuned empathically, their body-to-body intimacy and gratitude supports and is supported by physical affection—hugging, kissing, and erotic playfulness.

Positive Emotions Broaden Experience and Growth

Despite my differences with some assertions, I find the work of positive psychologists Barbara Fredrickson and colleagues on the "broaden-and-build theory" to be significant. A substantial body of their research demonstrates that positive emotions are highly adaptive. Good feelings have been shown to broaden the scope of attention and enhance cognitive and behavioral repertoires (Fredrickson & Branigan, 2005). From a Darwinian perspective, positive emotions are recognized as evolutionarily adaptive for our ancestors in building social relationships, family connections, and child caring (Berridge & Kringelbach, 2011).

Pleasurable Experiences and Emotions Contribute to Personal Evolution

Pleasurable experiences don't just contribute to the evolution of the species. By enhancing a person's capacity to build loving relationships and to relish the simple joys of daily life, shared relational pleasures also contribute to the personal evolution of each individual. Enhanced by the capacity to focus on a loved one, to be empathically present in an emotional exchange as well as in a sexual encounter builds strong bonds.

Pleasure has been associated with greater creativity, a preference for a wider variety of experience, a greater flexibility of response, and the "ability to integrate diverse material" (Isen et al., 1987). Neurobiologically, pleasurable emotions have been linked to "increases in brain dopamine levels, particularly in the prefrontal cortex (PFC) and in the anterior cingulate," an area of the brain that connects the prefrontal cortex and the emotional limbic system. Since a specific function of the PFC is "the active maintenance of patterns of activity that represent goals and the means to achieve them" (Miller & Cohen, 2001), pleasurable emotions would appear to have the effect of neurobiologically supporting the ability to realize our aspirations. That certainly includes relational aspirations.

The research corroborates my observation that pleasure is expansive and pain is contracting. The "broaden-and-build" theorists note that negative emotions narrow individuals' thought and action repertoires while with positive emotions they "pursue a wider range of thoughts and actions than is typical." When people are feeling good, they are more likely to be playful, to explore their environs, to relish and to integrate their experience.

All these studies show that positive emotions, from high activation amusement to low activation contentment, contribute to people's capacity to be more attentive, perceptive, creative, playful, sociable, and more likely to have positive thoughts and to achieve their goals (Fredrickson & Losada, 2006).

A Body-Based Awareness of Positive Emotions

So far we've been looking at positive emotions as cognitive and neurological events, but all emotions are felt in the body. We recognize that painful emotions like fear, anger, and shame are contracting and pleasurable emotions are expansive, but there is more to somatically experiencing our body-based feelings.

In some ways it may be easier to recognize our painful feelings than to recognize our pleasurable feelings. When we take a few deep breaths to awaken bodily awareness and focus in on sensations in the face, torso, belly, and pelvis, we can pick out areas of tension. When we are afraid we can feel the tension in our chest and belly, a rapid heartbeat, maybe sweaty hands.

Love is experienced as warmth. We describe an empathically attuned individual as showing warmth, and watching an act of kindness is often expressed as "heartwarming." There are plenty of synonyms for "emotional warmth" including, love, empathy, affection, generosity, sensitivity, kindness, and closeness. Yet, most of the people I've encountered in therapy don't have as well developed a vocabulary for pleasurable feelings as they do for painful feelings.

It can be helpful to ask clients how they know they are feeling good by asking them where they feel good in the body. If they don't know, we may be able to help them find it. We can ask if it has to do with energy, like having a bubbly excited feeling all over or specifically in the chest. Or they may just feel at peace and content. They may notice an urge to touch or embrace their partner, or to smile or laugh. They may also be enjoying a general overall feeling of well-being and happiness.

Expressing Good Feelings

Aside from shame, which can be hard for people to acknowledge, most clients have no problem identifying painful emotions. They may say that they are feeling anxious, angry, frustrated, disappointed, devastated, or depressed. When people feel good, however, many don't seem to have a vocabulary for describing the feeling. They may simply say, "Good."

I notice the same lack of detail with couples at the beginning of a session, when they agree that things have been going well. I always have to ask them, "What's good?" At that point, they may offer a description of a positive outcome of an event in terms of how they avoided a fight or had a nice lovemaking experience.

Of course, I'm always pleased to hear about their positive interactions. But I also want to know how that makes them feel emotionally toward one another as a result of these positive experiences. I want them to know that positive feelings are as significant to identify and to build on as painful feelings are to distinguish and work through. One of the ways we can utilize good feelings to help broaden and build an intimate relationship in couples work is to help them broaden and build their ability to identify their good feelings.

Verbalizing positive feelings in couples therapy involves expressing appreciation and articulating what they are grateful for in each other. The better they express positive emotions, the more aware they can become of the nuances of their good feelings and how expressing their good feelings toward one another, in itself, is rewarding and reinforcing.

Therapists can especially help clients connect with their capacity to feel empathy. We can tell them that all emotions are catching. We use the term "emotional contagion" to describe how one partner's annoyed tone of voice or angry yelling injects the other with the same negative feeling and that's how the negativity escalates. I think of it as spreading an emotional infection.

Empathy is a kind of positive contagion. Looking into the eyes of the other with love, sensing their pain, and being open to their vulnerability imparts compassion for one another. Learning to be compassionate toward a partner can help in becoming more self-compassionate and forgiving toward oneself and one's own imperfections.

The therapy session is as much about building a positive and pleasurable emotional repertoire and the capacity to mutually soothe and regulate each other's distress as it is about resolving conflicts and negotiating differences. For some clients, witnessing and experiencing the therapist's support and empathy models emotional skills they can learn, that they may never have witnessed in their original family growing up. The more they look at each other and acknowledge the positive feelings they have for each other—for an act of kindness or instances of growth—the more those positive interactions will increase.

If a couple starts a session by saying that things are good, I will ask them to face each other and to share what's good. As always, one person speaks at a time without interruption so they can grow their listening skills. That's when their vocabulary of positives expands. They can share appreciations, notice each other's signs of growth, acknowledge each other's kindness, honesty, generosity, patience, tender gestures, and times of sensitive, playful, and enjoyable lovemaking. Their smiles and body language in those moments of grateful sharing reinforce their expanded intimate repertoires.

I like to end each session—even the difficult ones—with sharing appreciations for anything that the other expressed or explored during that session. I may have to encourage them with something like: "Go on, find something nice to say—but you have to mean it!" Not uncommonly, a partner expresses an appreciation that surprises and delights the other. At other times, the only thing one can find to say to the other is "I appreciate that you're here." When I ask, "And how does that make you feel?" he or she may say something like, "hopeful." That's ending on a positive note.

Romantic Love Can Last a Lifetime: Enhancing Health and Well-Being

Originally, the theory was that romantic love may bring two people together but eventually the romance fades and what keeps them together is companionate love. We now know that dwindling romance in long-term relationships is not necessarily inevitable. Research over the last few years has shown that some couples are able to retain romantic feelings and those who do tend to be happier and more satisfied with each other than couples in companionate relationships.

In a 2009 study, psychologists Bianca Acevedo and Arthur Aron used brain scans to study a group of individuals in long-term relationships who scored high on romantic love on a questionnaire assessing relational satisfaction. They compared their brain scans and responses on the questionnaire to those of individuals who scored lower on the scale but were still moderately satisfied in a friendship-style relationship. They had both groups undergo brain scans while looking at photos of their partners and found that individuals in long-term romantic relationships showed the same brain responses associated with romantic love as people in short-term romantic relationships, but they had none of the obsessive characteristics of the new romances. Those in companionate relationships did not show a comparable brain scan looking at their partner's photo.

Essentially the results of the study show that it is possible to maintain long-term highly fulfilling passionate love relationships. Even more significantly, the key to doing so involves maintaining sexual liveliness in the relationship.

Some corollary effects are also worth noting. People in long-term romantic relationships tended to be more content with themselves. They scored higher on self-esteem and overall happiness and were in better physical health than those in warm, friendly long-term relationships that lacked sexual engagement. Also noteworthy was the finding that enjoying long-term sexually engaging relationships enabled individuals with insecure attachment styles to become secure.

To understand what might enable a long-term partner's love to foster security in someone who began the relationship insecure, we can refer to the early relations between parent and infant/child and the positive relational qualities of that intersubjective interaction that contribute to a child's security. These qualities entail body-to-body closeness (holding and comforting the baby), empathy, providing a secure base (encouraging exploration and personal development), and when the child is threatened or hurt being a safe haven to return to for comforting. A long-term loving relationship that is emotionally, physically, and sexually intimate provides all those qualities of skin-on-skin contact, warmth, empathy, and a safe haven that effects a rewiring of the neuroplastic brain and nervous system.

These data are an affirmation of what I have come to believe: with genuine love, it's never too late to have a happy childhood.

Other studies provide further evidence for the salubrious effects of romantic adult relationships and marital happiness. There's evidence that brains show "interpersonal synchronization," and become better attuned on a cooperative task than do friends or two strangers (Pan et al., 2017). Heart rate and breathing also synchronize, and when one person is subjected to a painful stimulus under experimental conditions, an intimate partner's touch has an analgesic effect, and the greater the partner's empathy, the better the pain was diminished (Goldstein et al., 2017).

Given all the research that now shows the emotional, physical, and quality of life benefits of enjoying a more affectionate and sexually lively relationship, therapists can set their sights higher in terms of what we can aim for in couples and sex therapy. As Acevedo and Aron (2009) write:

> The possibility of long-term romantic love sets a standard that couples (and marital therapists) can strive for that is higher than seems to have been considered realistic. . . . [A] shocking recognition that a long-term marriage does not necessarily kill the romance in one's relationship may give some couples the inspiration they need, even if challenging, to make changes that will enhance their relationship quality (and thus general well-being).
>
> (p. 64)

Clearly, the key factor to enhance romance and reap the benefits requires a more concerted effort for couples therapists to include sexual aliveness and pleasurable connection in the repair and enhancement of partner's body-to-body loving interactions.

Erotic Pleasures: Moving Beyond the Sexual Routine

I often hear couples talk about who initiates sex, and just the thought of one person "initiating sex" while the other has to accept or decline sounds boring to me and I imagine sets a tone for a stilted kind of lovemaking. When I ask a couple what that means, I hear a rather narrow set of likely approaches made by the higher libido partner toward the less sexually invested partner. They range from one extreme of a verbal invitation of "Hey, wanna have sex?" to another extreme in a sudden, unexpected display of physical attention by one partner moving in on the intimate space of the other in a way that can feel violating.

It makes no sense for a couple who abstain from pleasurable physical contact Monday through Saturday, to expect to be aroused on Sunday mornings by a routine offering of the same predictably limited results. Even pancakes every Sunday morning for years would likely grow tiresome unless the syrup and toppings were varied.

So what's the alternative to weeklong celibacy punctuated by a *de rigueur* weekend romp? I think of it as a menu of possibilities for keeping a warm glow going. Basically, it involves a daily body-to-body presence: a lingering kiss or two in the morning before departing, a sustained hug and a kiss upon returning, an appreciative kiss, smile, squeeze, a few words of appreciation every so often, eye contact while chatting, dimming the lights and playing some soft music and slow dancing cheek to cheek is always nice and cuddling in bed before drifting off can enhance the quality of the night's sleep.

Naturally, there will be times the couple has a disagreement or one or both are just not into it, but they can still aim to be present in the body. Eye contact helps. Smiles help. Warm touches are especially good. A sympathetic ear when one of them is down is always appreciated. Laughing, dancing, playing together, and respecting each other's differences all contribute to relational happiness.

Pleasurable Wanting: Tension-Reduction Sex vs. Ecstatic Sex

Clearly, there are many different kinds of pleasure and ways of understanding pleasure. One interesting notion is Erich Fromm's distinction between scarcity pleasures and abundance pleasures. Fromm noted that pleasures derived from satisfying a state of need are different from those enjoyed coming from a state of abundance. Pleasure derived from satisfying a hunger he identified as *relief* while the pleasures associated with appetite he recognized as *joy*.

Fromm made a similar distinction with regard to sex. He suggested that Freud's concept of sex was equivalent to hunger, an urge generated by a physiological tension and satisfaction brought relief. But the kind of sexual desire and pleasure that corresponds to appetite is the enjoyment that comes from a sense of abundance and freedom and is an expression of sensual and emotional capability (Fromm, 1941).

I have made a similar kind of distinction between tension-reduction sex and ecstatic sex.

Tension-reduction sex is where having an orgasm is an important way to relieve not just sexual need, but more often than not, generalized stress accumulated during a tense day. For some people, tension-reduction sex is a way to get a good night's sleep without taking a sleeping pill. Ecstatic sex is more like a death-rebirth-into-a-higher-plane experience than a one-bright-moment-then-total-wipeout kind of thing. . . . In ecstatic sex, pleasure is not just the release of pressure but also something powerfully expansive—physiologically, emotionally, and spiritually (Resnick, 1997).

The buildup of tensions can be physical from not taking energetic breaks during the day; or emotional, induced by frustration, resentment, anxiety, and self-doubt; or it can be sexual when masturbation or partnered sex is not an option. For the insecure partner, having sex may be used for emotional reassurance of desirability of a partner's love. Then tension-reduction may be more of an emotional relief than a sexual release. A consistent pattern of using sex for something other than mutual pleasure and loving connection can grow very stale. When a couple's sexual pattern is usually in bed at night before going to sleep, I call it "the last weary act of a long weary day" (Resnick, 2012).

There is no doubt that some sexual experiences can be so loving and emotionally beautiful that both lovers feel transported, like they are soaring in space together to another plane of existence. We've already noted that that there are some sexual circuits in the brain that are also activated during times of spiritual ecstasy. This kind of experience may occur when lovers have been reunited after some time apart or when a deep sense of gratitude or other kinds of profound feelings have been triggered.

Sex doesn't have to be ecstatic to be better than tension-reduction sex. I encourage couples to keep a "starter" growing and to recognize that their arousal will grow with a few hugs and kisses each day as a daily kind of nourishment. As the research shows, couples that kiss, hug, and hold hands on a daily basis have greater satisfaction in their relationship. They are certainly more likely to be sensually attuned to one another when they are physically close in a pleasurable way, even if it's only for 30 seconds at a time. Those seconds can add up to a more extended affectionate or sexual encounter.

In fact, not all tension is negative. In Maslow's descriptions of self-actualizing people he noticed that many of them were able to postpone gratification by learning to savor the state of need. He called it "pleasurable wanting." Lovers who take their time making love, allowing their excitement to build, then back off and relish the arousal before starting up their erotic play again find that their arousal will build and the more intense the arousal, the more intense the physical and sexual release and joyful connection (Maslow, 1962).

Mindful Eroticism: Attending to Erotic Pleasures

Broadening the spectrum of erotic pleasures between partners begins with body-to-body presence and a focus on the sensual awakening and energetic stirrings of their own bodies. When partners engage sexually in slow, focused sensual connection, breathing deeply, looking into each other's eyes in full body-to-body presence and playful attunement sexual energy can charge the whole body with intensely pleasurable desire. I think of it as "mindful eroticism."

As somatic psychotherapist Marie Thouin-Savard describes it:

> As with most healing modalities involving a strong relational and even spiritual component, somatic sexology practices blur the lines habitually drawn between therapy, education, and spiritual

practice by addressing eroticism as a holistic phenomenon, instead of a purely physiological and cognitive-behavioral one. Also, the experiential and often multifaceted nature of those methods (blending emotional, physical, and spiritual dimensions into erotically focused practices) challenges the binary between sexual function and dysfunction, which is foundational to the field of sexology... Often, participants and clients seek out experiential methods not only to "fix" their sexual problems, but to explore their erotic potentials.

(Thouin-Savard, in press)

Focus is everything when it comes to being attuned to the pleasure potentials of the moment. In one study, for example, individuals whose attention was focused on the sensory experience of eating chocolate reported more pleasure than individuals engaged in a distraction task while eating the chocolate (LeBel & Dube, 2001). These results certainly have important implications for people who have difficulty controlling their weight due to a habit of mindless eating. The same can be said for people involved in the beginning intimacies of kissing and caressing their partner while engaging in distracting mental dialogues with themselves or fantasizing a porn movie in their heads rather than playfully engaging with their partner.

The Venn Couple: The Transformative Power of Love, Pleasure, and Balancing Autonomy and Interdependence

No doubt you're familiar with the Venn diagram depicting two identical overlapping circles that provides a visual depiction delineating the area of overlap between two spheres in the center and their area of difference as everything outside the overlap. For a couple, the area of overlap would represent the common territory of shared interests, activities, responsibilities, mutual friends, and time spent together.

The areas in each circle that do not overlap would represent their lives independent of one another. That might include involvement in different professions, jobs, distinct daily responsibilities, hobbies, personal friends, and time spent apart.

Confluent, Divergent, and Balanced Relationships

The area where their lives intersect could be relatively large so there is not a lot of room outside the overlap to have much time alone or to explore personal interests, friends, or family on one's own.

Or the area of overlap could be relatively small so that it looks like these two people have little in common or don't share much of a life together. They may have a family and a home together but otherwise they may have different jobs, different friends, few common interests, and are apt to take vacations separately.

When the circles overlap almost completely we might describe those relationships as *confluent* or enmeshed. There are a number of risks for those relationships. One big risk is monotony due to the lack of outside stimulation they can bring to share with one another. Another is the possibility that one of them is highly controlling and demanding and the other partner is conflict-aversive and just defers to keep the peace. There is also the possibility that both of them are suppressing parts of themselves in order to keep the peace because their original families were enmeshed and that's their working model of relationship. Those relationships tend to be non-sexual as they are like old shoes with one another and likely fearful of independence.

When the circles barely overlap, it indicates that those two people lead separate lives, appear to have very little in common, and the relationship might be considered *divergent*, which is a strong indicator that the relationship is in jeopardy of ending.

The happiest couples are those who are fairly well *balanced* between sharing a fulfilling intimate life while still retaining their independence to pursue their own personal interests. When partners can support a balance of autonomy and interdependence those are likely to be the happiest relationships and most likely to retain romantic and sexual interest in one another.

Irrespective of whether a couple presents with emotional difficulties or sexual difficulties effective couples and sex therapy has to address a radical imbalance between autonomy and interdependence. That means addressing the imbalance is part of the problem and has to be part of the solution.

Achieving Mutual Fulfillment: Supporting a Self-Actualizing Process

A loving relationship is a work in progress in the same way that each individual is also a work in progress on a path of growth, whether through therapy or just through getting older and wiser. Growth takes time, and there can be setbacks along the way.

Maslow points out that most of the self-actualized individuals he has studied are older, as age and experience do have their rewards for growth-motivated individuals. Difficult circumstances, whether health, financial, environmental, or political turbulence, can also create challenges for growth. The ability to fulfill one's dreams or at least to continue to enjoy the process of learning and growing is what it takes for us all.

Helping couples to enjoy their sexuality is an important step for two people to actualize their potential for happiness and pleasure together. Sexuality combines mind, body, and spirit. And when two people together can throw off the shackles of whatever keeps them from the fullness of pleasure their bodies can bring, they have truly "mutated up" together.

Clearly, for therapists to facilitate this quality of growth in others, we have to go through the process ourselves since our right brain-to-right brain communication with our clients is our most profound influence in therapy.

> Psychotherapy is as specific as any attachment ... a therapy's results are particular to *that* relationship. A patient doesn't become generically healthier, he becomes more like the therapist. . . . That makes selecting one's therapist a life decision with (in mild terms) extensive repercussions. An uncomfortably large number of therapies yield neutral results. . . . But if therapy *works*, it transforms a patient's limbic brain and his emotional landscape forever.
>
> (Lewis et al., 2000)

So far we've looked at some of the key areas to explore in integrating couples and sex therapy. We have focused on helping each person to explore parts of themselves they may have dissociated and disowned to support them to become a more integrated and whole person so that their couple relationship can be more loving and fulfilling for each of them. We have seen how partners can be more present with one another, experience how their intersubjective relational process is a part of each individual's emotional and sexual growth, and how each individual's growth can grow the relationship.

We have seen how therapies that focus primarily on ameliorating pain are leaving out the most transformative part of the growth process—how to expand capacity to celebrate the joys of life. To interactively expand their relationship together in a way that serves each of them mentally, emotionally, sexually, and spiritually requires that they share more times of peace and contentment together while building on their capacity to share expansive levels of enthusiasm and pleasure.

In the final chapter, we will put it all together in a systematic approach I call Embodied Relational Sex Therapy™ (ERST).

Part IV
The Cognitive-Somatic-Experiential-Behavioral Spectrum

8

Embodied Relational Sex Therapy™: A Neurobiological-Gestalt Integration of Couples and Sex Therapy

Traditionally, psychotherapeutic approaches have been viewed in either/ or terms: cognitive-behavioral therapies or somatic-experiential therapies. What I have described in this book is a more inclusive approach. In the same way that we recognize that it isn't whether nature or nurture underlies mental distress or whether light travels either as a particle or a wave. In each case it is both. And when it comes to cognitive-behavioral or somatic-experiential, it can also be both.

Whether through individual, couples, group, or sex therapy, the best way to facilitate growth in our clients is to use a full spectrum of the resources we have within our rich field of psychological theory, research, and insightful discourse. The richness of our resources also includes our personal human resources of authenticity, warmth, intuition, creativity, humor, and playfulness. As therapists and educators our professional development is very closely tied to our personal development.

From a Cognitive Description to a Somatic Focus to an Experiential Process to a Behavioral Practice

When couples come for therapy, they want to talk about what's bothering them. Often they will say that a big part of their distress with their partner is a lack of communication. They don't feel heard or understood by their partner. They may not recognize yet that there is another more subtle, body-based communication that is taking place between them that also affects their distress. Very likely, they also don't feel seen, heard, or felt. That's a lack of positive body-to-body communication.

Cognitive understanding about what works and doesn't work is critical for helping clients fulfill their desires. Good sex therapy has to include a sexual re-education because most of our clients' original education about sex as children was negative and shaming.

And we are certainly aiming for behavioral change. That's what our clients are looking for, and they want to see results. Cognitive and behavioral change is a necessary aspect of therapy. But by itself, it is not sufficient. The question is: what's the best way to get from a cognitive re-framing of the issues to lasting behavioral change?

While a left brain, cognitive-behavioral approach may be helpful when the goal is to target voluntary motor control, current neurobiological research consistently supports a right brain somatic-experiential approach for the deeper work of getting to the unconscious realm of healing emotional wounds resulting from early parent-child relational deficits.

Inconsistent empathy during childhood or ineffectual down-regulating of a child's stress or pain and lack of playful up-regulating interactive joy and pleasure leaves its mark on the structure of the right brain prefrontal cortex, the development of the emotion-processing limbic system, and how the autonomic nervous system is wired. As Allan Schore has written, "It is now clear that psychotherapeutic changes in conscious cognitions alone, without changes in emotion processing are limited" (Schore, 2012).

With warmth, empathy, genuine love, and support from parents in childhood, an individual grows up confident and secure. With parents who themselves are insecure, tense, anxious, angry, or depressed and unable to give their child the love and support to discover their true selves, individuals grow up with unresolved pain and a brain and nervous system that is over-reactive and poorly integrated. There are all kinds of trauma to the developing brain and nervous system: "big T" Trauma and "little t" trauma, from serious abuse to inconsistency and neglect. Some things just can't be changed simply by talking—even with an empathic therapist.

My focus in therapy with couples is to help them develop their ability to be authentic, empathic, and playful both emotionally and sexually, with one another. In that way they will be better able to feel and express their love with each other and develop dormant qualities within themselves.

- To be authentic, each individual has to be capable of knowing what he or she truly feels.
- To be empathic, each needs to be fully present and open to the other.
- To be playful, they need to drop their defenses and risk abandon, trusting that the other will not turn on them and become hurtful.

Starting Left Brain With Right Brain Undertones

As I see it, the most effective couples therapy to accomplish these goals starts left brain, moves right brain to make some body-based discoveries, and at some point goes left to articulate and understand what just happened. We start cognitive with couples talking about what they want to achieve in therapy. The therapist provides new information related to the issues and reframes the problem as an opportunity to repair from emotional deficits or injuries from the past and to grow. Then we shift right to a focus on somatic awareness and on the tensions, sensations, and emotions that each individual can detect within his or her body.

From there we can begin to experientially process present-moment intersubjectively co-created interactions utilizing breath, sensory awareness, and emotional experience. When partners trigger each other we can identify and help trace those feelings back to their origin in childhood and then guide them to safely release the blocked emotions to repair a childhood wound and achieve closure. From there we can return to the cognitive and connect the dots to the current body-to-body emotional and sexual communications between partners. Moving forward, we can play and explore the pleasures of practicing new life-affirming behaviors.

In other words, we move between the cognitive and the somatic—from the new way of looking at the issues, then into a focus on authentic bodily experience and experientially processing whatever comes up emotionally, then back to a cognitive understanding and what just happened, then back to the body and more experiential processing. We can end with trying out a new potentially pleasurable behavior and having clients take it home and "play with it." In that way, the deeper work of somatic-experiential processing mediates between cognitive understanding and lasting behavioral change.

Though I do a great deal of couples work in groups, the process I'm outlining here focuses on long-term weekly or bimonthly sessions. Group work is more condensed, but in some ways can be even more powerful as couples witness each other's work. They learn from each other and the courage each individual displays in revealing their innermost vulnerabilities. They discover that in the safe atmosphere of the couples group, exposing their shame brings praise, support, and admiration, and that in turn brings a sense of relief and pride in themselves. Many of the couples I work with in a group recognize that their work is only beginning and they continue to work with me on an ongoing basis.

What follows in this closing chapter is the step-by-step process from the first session, progressing deeper and deeper into a couple's individual and relational challenges, open to the surprises, setbacks, repairs, rebounds and, when they stay with it, arriving at a place where their love is reaffirmed and stronger than before. They are more affectionate and making love creatively in a way that works for them both.

The First Session: The Experiential Intake

I recommend starting a written record for each couple during the first session by taking notes on the salient words and phrases each person says to the other and in response to our questions. The intake follows this format:

The Presenting Problem

As indicated in Chapter 1, every first session starts with a couple saying what they are looking for in therapy and with the therapist asking questions. The questions we need to ask involve getting each person to give his or her point of view on how they view the problem, what they have tried so far, what if anything has helped, and their goals for therapy. In the course of the conversation we are all getting to know each other.

From there we have a set format for proceeding with an experiential process-oriented intake. However we may express it at the moment, we want them to know that every problem is an opportunity to grow, that growth involves both their individual growth and how their ways of interacting with each other will grow. We want them to know that we are not just focusing on problems but also building on their strengths as a couple.

Sharing Loves and Appreciations

In order to be clear what those strengths are we ask them to turn and face each other and to share with one another what they most love and appreciate about one another. We ask them to do it this way: first one person speaks and completes without any interruption from the other, and then the other speaks and completes without any interruption. To emphasize that they are to talk to each other and not to the therapist, we can tell them that we will be eavesdropping but it is more important they talk to each other and not to us.

When they are both finished we can ask them, "How are you each feeling right now?" Usually, after this dialogue they both feel good because they have been appreciated and we want them to notice and articulate their good feelings. We may also want to comment on some of the nice things they have said to each other and ask if there were any surprises. There usually are. Not uncommonly, partners do not verbalize appreciation for the "little things" they do for one another or for the qualities they observe in the other that they like but fail to acknowledge, even to themselves.

Identifying the Changes You Want

At this point partners have achieved a certain level of good feelings toward one another that lays the groundwork for the next task. We can ask them to share with one another, "How would you like the relationship to change and more specifically, how would you like the other to change?" We might add, "What would you like more of, and what would you like less of?" Here we can see if they want the same things and we can watch how they say what they want. We remind them to do it in the same way: first one person speaks and completes without any interruption, and then the other speaks and completes without any interruption.

Any Requests?

This is each person's opportunity to be direct with the partner and to specifically ask for what they want. We can see if they know how to make a request or if they end up complaining and only talk about what they don't want. Do they ask nicely? Are they shaming and judgmental? What do they seem to avoid asking for? We can also ask if they notice any feelings come up in this exchange and where they notice the feelings in their body. Sometimes people don't know how to make a request and instead will make a demand or a threat, wiping out whatever good will they may have accrued through the process.

Recognizing Your Contribution to the Problem

Finally, we might ask, "How do you see yourself contributing to the issues between you?" This last question shows whether both partners take responsibility for how they may be contributing to the distress between them, i.e., their intersubjective participation in the problem. When partners are compassionate and forthcoming, you may hear them say things like: "I know I can be critical at times." "I see how hurt you get when I turn away when you want to kiss." "I yell when I'm stressed and that makes you crazy." "I sometimes use sex to punish you." I always positively acknowledge partners when they own up to their part in the problem.

Goals for Therapy

Finally, we can ask each of them to specify their ultimate goals for therapy. This tells us whether they are both on the same page in terms of their motivations. During the course of therapy, knowing what they say they want also allows us to refer to those goals when they have made progress and then backslide into relational patterns that derail them. We can let them know, "If this is your goal, you can't get there from here. Rather than play out those old relational patterns, what feelings are coming up for you that you need to address and express?"

During this entire process, which is primarily based in language communications, somatically attuned therapists are also watching the partners' face-to-face and body-to-body communications. We are also alert to our own interoceptive cues and intuitive alerts. We might notice a lack of eye contact at times, particularly during the requests for changes, facial grimaces, shifts in body postures, or emotional signs like flushing or fighting back tears. We can make note of these and ask about it when they complete the exercise.

The Cognitive-to-Somatic Transition: Tuning into the BodyConscious Breathing

At some point in the session we are ready to shift from the cognitive to the somatic part of the intake. I want them to know that whether we are aiming for emotional, behavioral, and/or sexual change, we need to get into the underlying emotional tensions and feelings that may be at the root of their difficulties. To make new discoveries instead of repetitively going back and forth over old ground, we need to access those feelings directly in the body.

From there we take a few deep sighs in and out of the mouth and I then ask them to focus in on their inner felt-sense awareness for any tension or tightness in their "emotional center," the area between the top of the head, face and jaw, throat, upper chest, diaphragm, belly, and pelvic region and to make a mental note of where they hold tension. I tell them that where they hold tension in is significant. I ask them to turn and face their partner, and to notice any shift in their feelings.

Sharing Feelings

I ask them to share how they are feeling toward the other right now and if anything came up during this process that was surprising. If they are in touch with feelings, I ask where in their body they are feeling those feelings and to point to it. Typically, people who have not done any body-based therapy will display tense torsos though they may not necessarily be in touch with the tension or even think of it as significant. Some couples are immediately ready to share feelings and I will simply watch how they interact and make observations about their body-based cues and ask them questions about present-centered bodily reactions and emotions.

At any point during the session, I will share my observations about how they are communicating emotionally both on a verbal and on a nonverbal level and ask if any of the patterns I'm noticing reflect familiar patterns from their own original families.

If this is a double session and there is still time I take a family history from each of them to identify relational patterns they may be triggering in one another. If not, I will be sure to do that in the next session. I make a point of ending the first session with the matching breaths exercise to practice at home.

Matching Breaths: Holding and Breathing in Sync

If we haven't done any breathing together yet, I start by demonstrating the deep sighing breath—breathing in deeply through the mouth into the throat and letting it go through the mouth in a full throated un-vocalized "hah."

At the office: I start this exercise by having a couple either standing or sitting, wrap their arms around each other and put their right cheek-to-right cheek together so that their mouths are just below each other's ear. At home they can also do this lying down.

I ask one partner to be the leader and to take slow deep sighs, in and out through the mouth and for the second partner to synchronize his or her inhales and exhales to the first partner.

After four or five breaths I ask the second partner to now be the leader and for the first to match his or her breaths to the new leader.

After four or five breaths, I then say now neither of you leads and both of you follow. Synchronize your breaths by slowly breathing in together and out together.

At the end of the exercise, I suggest they look into each other's eyes, say thank you and give each other a little kiss.

At home: They are instructed to go straight into synchronizing their breaths without taking turns leading.

In the beginning of the next session, I will ask the couple if anything stood out for them in the last session, if there were any highlights, and if they did the home-play exercise. If they did it, I will ask how it was. If they didn't, I will ask what got in their way and if that issue typically gets in the way of their closeness. That reflection can be the jumping off point for the rest of that session.

The Somatic-to-Experiential Transition: Tracking Ongoing Experience

Here's an account of one couple's transition from the first session to subsequent sessions and how matching breaths at home was evocative of a relational interaction that led to a valuable session at the office and to a deeper and more erotic body-to-body intimacy.

Jayne and Matt are a couple in their mid-thirties, married for nine years with two daughters aged five and two. Their presenting problem is that Jayne has lost all interest in sex and that Matt has a high libido. He wants to give Jayne the space she needs but it has been hard on him. He knows he's been impatient with Jayne and he wants her to desire him again.

Jayne replies that it's hard for her to be in her body these days, that she feels anxious a lot, and that sex is confusing to her now. When I ask Jayne to say more about her feelings she talks about the responsibilities of raising two children and fixing meals, and that she misses going to her job at the ad agency and working with colleagues.

When I ask how they are both feeling right now, Jayne says she's tense and can feel it in her throat, chest, and shoulders. Matt says he has some tension in his neck but otherwise he's okay. At that point, I suggest that we look at the strengths of their relationship and I ask them to turn and face each other and share their "loves and appreciations." They have many loving things to say to each other and I can see Jayne noticeably relax during their exchange. When we get to the changes they would like to see, they primarily refer to housekeeping issues, about hanging up clothing, and cleaning up after themselves. When I ask if there is anything else they want from the other Matt volunteers that he has a tendency to avoid confrontation and he would prefer less conflict.

Their family diagrams revealed very different family constellations. Matt came from a large family of two boys and two younger sisters with all of them, including the father, equally constellating around a large circle labeled Mom. Matt was close to his mother who demanded obedience. He said he saw a lot of affection between his parents but they also quarreled a lot. Matt didn't remember having sexual feelings or masturbating until puberty. When he was thirteen his mother opened a book about sex and showed him diagrams depicting genitals and explained intercourse.

Jayne's parents divorced when she was six and her younger sister was four. They lived with their depressed mother who was occasionally affectionate. Both little girls tried very hard to please the mother though it wasn't easy. The girls visited with the father every three to six months. Jayne respected him but she was also afraid of him. Neither parent talked to Jayne about sex, but she remembered playing doctor and other sex-like games with a girlfriend from about age six. She learned more about sex from her girlfriend at age eleven. We talked about some of the differences and similarities in their childhood experiences and I gave Jayne and Matt the matching breaths exercise to do at home.

In the next session, both Jayne and Matt said that they found the first session to be illuminating and commented on the reality of their very different backgrounds, which until then they had not recognized as having much relevance. They both said they felt relieved and reassured by looking at their strengths. Jayne especially said that she felt safe and found the session validating. They did the breathing exercise at home a few times and found it relaxing. Yet they had some stresses during the week relating to their older girl's school and the two-year-old being difficult and in the session they wanted to talk about the situation, which we did.

We used the opportunity to look at how they tended to ratchet up each other's anxiety during the session by challenging each other. We referred to the childhood experiences with their mothers and fathers and did some breathing exercises together. They noted that taking some deep breaths by themselves and then holding and breathing together made them more relaxed and better able to focus in the moment. We talked about how they could help regulate each other's stress. They said they felt a lot better and were pleased they were able to tackle some home issues during the session.

The third session was particularly illuminating. They came in both saying that they were doing a lot better. They had done some breathing together and Matt remarked that he enjoyed the connectivity of it and experienced it as an intimate time together. Jayne noted that she found it very calming though she felt that Matt had another agenda. That upset Matt and he came back at Jayne saying that she is always monitoring the situation to keep it cerebral rather than letting it become more emotional or physical.

Jayne protested that this was not cerebral—it was real for her. I was fascinated how what started out so positive so quickly turned into hurt feelings.

Jayne complained that Matt was leading the breathing and that he wasn't following her and that she felt duped and taken advantage of. Matt said he got lost in the experience. Jayne said she felt abandoned, that it was horrible for her to try to lead and then to feel like Matt was not with her.

At that point Jayne fell silent and sat back looking forlorn, like nothing was ever going to work for her; her head hung, her eyes were closed, her face looked sad, and her shoulders slumped. Matt just watched her. Neither said anything.

Meanwhile I recognized this pattern as what was limiting Jayne's interest in Matt sexually. I took the opportunity to make the link between matching breaths and sexual connection. I interrupted their silence by saying, "You know, really good sex is like matching breaths. Two bodies come into sync together and follow each other's rhythms so that they are both leading and following. When one person does all the leading and the other does all the following, the follower is going to get bored."

Jayne's head and shoulders popped up. She sat straight up and a definitive "Yes" shot out of her mouth in a half shout-half whisper. "Yes," she said again more vocalized with a look of surprise on her face. "Yes," she said to Matt now more forcefully, angrily.

> You are always in control. You reason with me like a child. You're the one that's cerebral. That certainly doesn't turn me on. If you're going to be in control, then sweep me off my feet. I have to read romance novels to get turned on to have sex with you. You complain that I don't like foreplay. I don't like being "done to" your way while I have to take it and fake it.

Matt just stared blankly at Jayne like he was in shock.

We talked more about sex and what each wanted more of and less of with each other. I also wondered if this experience of who is in control during lovemaking or in other areas of their life together might relate to each of their relationships with their mother, since it was the mother at the center in each of their young lives. Jayne said that this issue with Matt was also a constant pattern for her with her mother. She continually felt drawn in by the mother and when she went she felt abandoned. She felt drawn in to Matt and totally relaxed into the breathing but when he wasn't following her she felt like a chump and became livid.

Matt said he had the complete opposite experience as a child. He felt his mother was always tuned into him, that she always knew what he was experiencing and he always felt protected by her. Matt's mother may have been too good at reading his energy because he said she also would "blackmail" him. When she wasn't pleased with him she would shame him so he felt she was really in control. That could be what made it so difficult for him to relinquish control.

The other thing that stood out for me was in their sexual history. Jayne was in touch with her sexuality from age six and that meant she could get into sex play and that's what turned her on. She got plenty of sex play in reading romance novels and that was her substitute for arousing "foreplay." Matt was the dutiful child and his mother was almost like a mind reader with him and she would shame him when she didn't like something. He also was raised in a religious family where there was no mention of sex all through his childhood. Very likely, if he had any sexual feelings he was apt to suppress them, since his mother "always knew what he was experiencing."

At the end of the session, Matt turned to Jayne with a soft look of compassion in his eyes, took her hand in both of his and said, "I got it." Jayne stiffened at first but softened as she studied Matt's face. Then she took a deep breath and very softly said, "Thank you." Matt smiled and shook his head.

That session became a pivotal one for continuing the work on aligning Jayne and Matt's sexual attunement. We focused on having Jayne be the one to approach Matt for physical connection and holding, and for her to lead the breathing and have Matt follow her. With his early experience, he was the one who always set the pace. With Jayne, it was always her mother and she had to adjust to her mother's rhythms. Now it was Matt's turn to learn to follow as well as lead and it was Jayne opportunity to lead as well as follow. Using matching breaths as a model, Matt learned to follow and that became an empowering experience for Jayne. With some of the touching and erotic experiences they came to explore together, Matt was able to enjoy a more erotic sexual experience than the pattern he was "hooked on" earlier and Jayne was able to reconnect with a spirit of sexual playfulness and the authentic pleasures of body-to-body sexual intimacy.

The Experiential to Behavioral Transition: Replacing Mindless Habits With Mindful Presence

Offering the couple body-to-body interactive exercises to play with, both during the session and at home, enhances their ability to be conscious of their inner experience from one moment to the next. Tracking inner experience may start with a bodily feeling of tension in the emotional center, say the throat or chest, proceed to a building of emotion, then to a memory and the urge to express feelings.

Present-moment mindfulness gives an individual an experience of his or her authentic self and their right to feel what they are feeling. A present focus in therapy helps partners develop skills of self-knowing by tracking their ongoing experience, taking the time to reflect on their mixed feelings and inner truths, and making conscious choices.

These skills are particularly valuable when it comes to achieving the often-stated goals of greater emotional closeness, intimate sharing, and sexual fulfillment. Practicing a moment-by-moment inner felt-sense of empathic and erotic attunement with one's partner involves moving slowly at least at first to savor the multiple sensual pleasures of true connection with one's partner.

Besides practicing matching breaths, here are two other exercises I give my clients at the office and suggest that they practice at home.

Home-Play: Body-to-Body Intimate Pleasures

Nonverbal Sensing: Silent Communion and Interoceptive Awareness

At the office: Here's an example of a basic set of sensory processes I may give a couple for facilitating a playful sensual interaction:

- Take a deep inhale, feel your belly fill, your rib cage widen and your chest lift, and blow out through slightly puckered lips all the way down to the last bit of breath, using your abs at the bottom of the exhale to push out more air. Then do it two more times.
- Notice if there is any tension or tightness anywhere in your body and take a few deep sighing breaths, breathing in and out through the mouth to relax.
- Turn and face your partner and take hands. Notice if you feel anything different now in your body as you look into your partner's eyes.
- Now notice if there is any part of their face that particularly pleases you, and see if you can find where in your body you are feeling pleased. Allow yourself to close your eyes and check in with yourself anytime you feel like and come back to looking at your partner's face whenever you're ready. I usually give them three to four minutes to do this part of the exercise.
- Now one person leans in toward the other, put your lips to his or her ear, and softly whisper something sweet. Then the other partner does the same.
- Share with one another what that was like for you and any discoveries you've made.
- Thank each other for playing with you.

At home: I suggest they sit opposite each other, take a few deep sighs, notice if there is any tension in the body, and then just take hands and look into each other's eyes for a few minutes. Allow yourself to close your eyes and check in with yourself anytime you feel like and come back to looking at your partner's face whenever you're ready. If your partner has his or her eyes closed, keep looking as long as you feel like. When you both have your eyes open, one of you whispers something sweet into the other's ear and the other partner does the same. When you are both ready to stop, thank each other for playing with you.

Exploring Playful and Mindful Eroticism: Creating the Erotic Bubble

One of the erotic appeals of an affair is often that it is secretive. Lovers meet at a hotel specifically for pleasure and playful sex and since they are typically not a part of each other's domestic life, they are in an erotic bubble together that is protected from the mundane chores and responsibilities of everyday life. Life partners can create for themselves the same kind of erotic bubble that can amplify their eroticism with one another.

At the office: When they are ready to move beyond their sexual routine and explore their erotic potentials together at home, I suggest that they start by making a date to meet for sex, even though the meeting will be at home. We can talk together about some of the elements they might create together for their tryst. If finances permit, some couples with children may opt to hire a baby-sitter and schedule a date at a hotel to safeguard against intrusions and feel freer to be focused on each other.

At home: On the day of their planned tryst, it's best if they can refrain from any talk about domestic problems or responsibilities before meeting. If they are apart they might talk briefly on the phone and share anticipations and playful flirting.

They may want to start with a snack or light dinner or a drink if alcohol is not a problem. The goal of the tryst is only for pleasure and play. It's not even to have orgasms, though that may happen.

These are the elements I encourage them to explore:

- Dress for the date in a way that makes you feel sexy.
- Create a sexy mood through dim lights or candlelight.
- Choose music for a slow sensual dance and movement.
- Expand your erotic repertoire. Some of the sensual activities and sex play you can engage in before any genital activity are holding, matching breaths, kissing, stroking, caressing, squeezing, flirting, talking sexy, and just having fun together however you do that.

Pleasure Therapy: The Healing Powers of Playfulness

Therapy provides partners with a relatively safe place to bring up their frustrations, resentments, and unfulfilled desires. But that can't be all that takes place during the therapy session. The research lends support for injecting opportunities during the session for clients to explore more positive interactions that have a greater likelihood of eliciting positive emotions. Those can be in the form of the therapist offering a behavioral option to play out and experience how a more positive or conciliatory approach is likely to elicit a more amenable response.

Many of our clients have a limited repertoire for positive interactions because they rarely witnessed positive interactions between their parents, particularly when the parents had disagreements or conflict. Mom and Dad may have been more likely to attack each other or to punish each other by avoiding contact than to work things out. They may rarely have seen parents display affection toward one another. Under those circumstances, clients may lack models for empathy, compassion, or thoughtful accommodation rather than resentful compromise. Their default mode of response will be what they witnessed their parents do.

Even when clients attempt to avoid repeating their parents' bad habits, their emotional programming and repertoire in an intimate relationship can be very limited. The therapist, then, becomes a model for empathy, compassion, negotiation, interacting from a place of tenderness rather than toughness, and being playful.

The same can be said about sex. Sexual activity is typically done in private so people don't have the same opportunity to broaden their sexual repertoires by watching skilled lovers in the flesh make love. Nowadays most young people—boys as well as girls—get their information about sex from R-rated movies and online pornography. Of course, what they are seeing is an act, a fictionalized depiction of sex for the benefit of voyeurs not for the enjoyment of the partners. They may be good actors, but they are doing it for the money not for pleasure.

When therapy stresses bodily awareness in the moment and offers couples playful interactive experiments that include a focus on the different areas of the body—their face, chest, gut, belly, and pelvic regions, noticing tension and practicing methods of breathing deeply and letting go—they are developing valuable skills to bring home. Present-moment mindfulness transfers to their home life, not just for difficult emotional discussions but also for pleasurable affection and sexual explorations.

The same is true for psychotherapists. To do our best work, we too have to continually be in the process of growth or we grow stale. With continued personal and professional growth we can maintain the excitement, confidence, persistence, creativity, playfulness, and gratification that comes with experience at our craft over the years. Our clients grow through a combination of our efforts and theirs. We learn from them. They teach us what works and what doesn't work, and when we acknowledge them when we have been amiss and learn from them, we all grow. With authenticity, the bond between therapist and client grows stronger and the therapeutic alliance becomes more resilient. What a blessing it is when our work is a nurturing process of discovery for us as well as for our clients.

Afterword

There are familial, social, and cultural implications of this work for raising and educating healthy humans as well as for the training and educating of therapists, teachers, and all health professionals. I would be remiss if I didn't underscore what this body of research tells us about how to nurture infants, children, and adolescents to become healthy and happy adults capable of creating healthy, happy, and loving relationships.

Mothers who take the time to hold their infants in arms and cuddle with their children, who look into their eyes with loving smiles, comfort them when they cry, and play and laugh with them, lay the foundation for their daughters and sons to be secure. In this way, children access their native ability to grow strong and be resilient in the face of change. Males who are the primary caretakers and nurture infants can also be good mothers.

Parents who outsource the care of infants and children to nannies and daycare centers for a greater percentage of time than they are with them set up the neural foundation of their children to become more like their caretakers than like them.

Human sexuality is multifaceted, present at birth, and is an integral part of human development. Just as learning to speak a language, read a book, and ride a bicycle have critical periods when development is easiest through playful activity, so too does sexuality have critical periods when children discover the natural pleasures of the body through playful activity. Parents and caretakers can channel this activity to be safe and socially adaptive in the same way that learning to read a book and ride a bike can be safe and adaptive. Shaming, punishing, and denying children's sexual desire and natural inclinations to explore sexual knowledge can program them for a lifetime of unfulfilling intimate relationships.

Social and religious policies that prescribe adolescent celibacy set up pre-teens and teenagers to feel shame and inadequacy during a critical period of sexual learning when they might be learning to safely enjoy experimentation and develop a sense of sexual efficacy and esteem. Developing sexual skills can prepare adults for loving and erotic pleasures with a mate they love and can commit to. Without that period of experimentation in adolescence adults often feel they missed out and can hunger for that experimentation as an adult when doing so can jeopardize their committed relationship.

Lesbian, gay, bisexual, and transgender people are normal, not defective, and are a natural part of the biodiverse spectrum of human sexuality. If allowed to be who they are, they typically discover their sexuality in their earliest childhood by the age of four or five. LGBT people occur in every culture on earth, including native peoples around the globe where, except for Western civilization and religious communities, they are often honored as having special human abilities. If we examine our artistic communities we are likely to find a predominance of gender nonconforming individuals who add immeasurable richness to the cultural life of our society.

As a result of what we now know about the interplay between attachment history and sexual development, sexual health, healing, and education must be an integral part of the training of all psychologists, psychiatrists, social workers, counselors, educators, teachers, and health professionals of all kinds who come in contact with children and patients. In that way, professionals in a position of helping others can be sexually healthy themselves and respectful of the sexual diversity of the people they serve.

Now this book is complete. May you be happy, be playful, breathe deeply, love fully, and inspire others to do the same.

Appendix: Family Closeness Profile (FCP)

O = Female
Δ = Male

Name_____

DOB_____

Town, State_____

Today's Date_____

Creating a Family Closeness Diagram

1. Draw a diagram below of your family as you were growing up *until the age of 12*. Do it this way: If every female is a circle and every male is a triangle, assign a symbol to every member of your immediate family. Your mother and any sisters would be circles; your father and any brothers would be triangles; you are (a circle or triangle).

2. Show the emotional closeness or distance between every member of the family by how close or distant you felt to them and how you sensed they were with one another. I am interested in *how it felt to you then*, when you were growing up, not how you see it now. Transgenders may use the symbol corresponding to identity.

3. Start with placing your mother's circle and your father's triangle to the degree you same them as emotionally close or distant. If you were closer to one parent than to the other, put your symbol next to that parent. Place any brothers or sisters in that matrix as to how you saw it then. Label each symbol by name. Draw only one matrix for the entire family.

4. If there was any change or traumatic event that changed your family life, draw two diagrams—one before the childhood-changing event, and one after.

5. When you are finished, hand me your diagram. Thank you.

Creating a Family Legend

1. **Mother's name and current Age =**
2. **Father's name and current Age =**
3. **Name and current age of siblings from oldest to youngest, including client, placed in order of birth. If there are two diagrams, before and after, create a legend for each. Include anyone now deceased with age and year of death.**

Biographical Details

1. **Three adjectives:** Give me three adjectives, that is, three descriptive words that express what it was like for you growing up in this family. Again, I am interested in how it *felt for you then*, and not how you understand it now.

   1 a. How was it (first word)?

   1 b. How was it (second word)?

   1 c. How was it (third word)?

2. **Describe the relationship as you saw it then between your mother and your father.** Were they ever affectionate in front of you? Did they ever fight in front of you?

3. **Describe your relationship with your mother.** Was she affectionate with you?

4. **Describe your relationship with your father.** Was he affectionate with you?

5. **Describe your relationships with your siblings.**

6. **Describe any traumas, illnesses, or accidents growing up.**

7. **Were you raised in any religion?**

Family Sexual Attitudes

1. **Many people become aware of sexual feelings at an early age and can remember stimulating themselves or playing doctor with playmates.** How old were you when you began having sexual feelings? Do you remember early childhood sex play with a friend? If so, how did you feel about it then? How do you feel about it now?

2. **As a child or teenager, were you ever surprised by either parent while masturbating or engaging in sexual activity with a friend?** If so, how did your parent react? How did you feel about it then? How do you feel about it now?

3. **As a child or teenager, did you ever experience unwanted touch or sexual assault by any member of your extended family, or at any time by anyone?** If so, how old were you and did you tell anybody? How did you feel about it then? How do you feel about it now?

4. **Is there anything I haven't asked you about your childhood or teenage years that I should know about? Thank you.**

*****

References

Acevedo, B. P., & Aron, A. (2009). Does a long-term relationship kill romantic love? *Review of General Psychology, 13*(1), 59–65.

Acevedo, B. P., Aron, A., Fisher, H. E., & Brown, L. L. (2012). Neural correlates of long-term intense romantic love. *Social Cognitive and Affective Neuroscience, 7*(2), 145–159. doi:10.1093/scan/nsq092

Alexander, F., & French, T. M. (1946). *Psychoanalytic therapy: Principles and application.* New York, NY: Ronald Press.

Allen, J. P., & Land, D. (1999). Attachment in adolescence. In J. Cassidy & P. R. Shaver (Eds.), *Handbook of attachment: Theory, research and clinical applications* (pp. 319–335). New York, NY: Guilford Press.

Altman, A. K. (2004). Retrieved from www.nytimes.com/2014/10/14/science/smell-turns-up-in-unexpected-places.html

Aron, E. N., & Aron, A. (1997). Sensory-processing sensitivity and its relation to introversion and emotionality. *Journal of Personality and Social Psychology, 73*(2), 345–368.

Aron, E. N., & Aron, A. (2014). Climbing diotoma's mountain: Marriage and achieving our highest goals. *Psychological Inquiry, 25*(1), 47–52. doi:10.1080/1047840X.2014.878521

Beebe, B., & Lachmann, F. M. (2002). *Infant research and adult treatment: Co-constructing interactions.* Hillsdale, NJ: The Analytic Press.

Berridge, K. C., & Kringelbach, M. L. (2011). Building a neuroscience of pleasure and well-being. *Psychology of Well-Being: Theory, Research and Practice, 1*(3), 1–26. doi:10.1186/2211-1522-1-3

Birnbaum, G. E., Reis, H. T., Mikulincer, M., Gillath, O., & Orpaz, A. (2006). When sex is more than just sex: Attachment orientations, sexual experience, and relationship quality. *Journal of Personality and Social Psychology, 91*(5), 929–943. Retrieved from http://dx.doi.org/10.1037/0022-3514.91.5.929

Bogaert, A. F. (2015). Asexuality: What it is and why it matters. *Journal of Sex Research, 52*(4), 362–379. doi:10.1080/00224499.2015.1015713

Boston Change Process Study Group. (2010). Forms of relational meaning: Issues in the relations between the implicit and reflective-verbal domains. *The International Journal of Relational Perspectives, 18*(2), 125–148. Retrieved from https://doi.org/10.1080/10481880801909351

Bridges, M. R. (2006). Activating the corrective emotional experience. *Journal of Clinical Psychology: In Session, 62*(5), 551–568.

Britton, P., & Dunlap, R. (2017). *Designing and leading a successful SAR: A guide for sex therapists, sexuality educators, and sexologists.* New York, NY: Routledge.

Buber, M. (1958). *I and Thou.* New York, NY: Charles Scribner's Sons.

Bullock, B. G. Poly-vagal theory: The way it works . . . Retrieved from www.yogauonline.com/yoga-for-stress-relief/tapping-power-vagus-nerve-how-your-breath-can-change-your-relationships

Burke, T. J., & Young, V. J. (2011). Sexual transformations and intimate behaviors in romantic relationships. *Journal of Sex Research, 49*(5), 454–463. doi:10.1080/00224499.2011.569977

Chivers, M. L., & Bailey, J. M. (2005). A sex difference in features that elicit genital response. *Biological Psychology, 70*(2), 115–120. Retrieved from https://doi.org/10.1016/j.biopsycho.2004.12.002

Ciocca, G., Limoncin, E., Di Tommaso, S., Mollaioli, D., Gravina, G. L., Marcozzi, A., . . . Jannini, E. A. (2015). Attachment styles and sexual dysfunctions: A case-control study. *International Journal of Impotence Research, 27*, 81–85. doi:10.1038/ijir.2014.33

Csikszentmihalyi, M. (1982). If we are so rich, why aren't we happy? *American Psychologist, 54*(10), 821–827.

Damasio, A. R. (1994). *Descartes' error: Emotion, reason, and the human brain.* New York, NY: G. P. Putnam's Sons.

Davis, D., Shaver, P. R., Widaman, K., Vernon, M. L., Follette, W. C., & Beitz, K. (2006). "I can't get no satisfaction": Insecure attachment, inhibited sexual communication, and sexual dissatisfaction. *Personal Relationships, 13*(4), 465–483. doi:10.1111/j.1475-6811.2006.00130.x

De Jong, D. C. (2009). The role of attention in sexual arousal: Implications for treatment of sexual dysfunction. *Journal of Sex Therapy, 46*(2–3), 237–248. doi:10.1080/00224490902747230.

De Looze, M., Constantine, N. A., Jerman, P. Vermeulen-Smit, E. & Ter Bogt, T. (2014). Parent–adolescent sexual communication and its association with adolescent sexual behaviors: a nationally representative analysis in the Netherlands. *The Journal of Sex Research, 52*(3), 257–268. https://doi.org/10.1080/00224499.2013.858307

DeYoung, P. (2015). *Understanding and treating chronic shame.* New York, NY: Routledge.

Di Marino, V., & Lapidi, H. (2014). *Anatomic study of the clitoris and the bulbo-clitoral organ.* Heidelberg, Dordrecht: Springer.

Doidge, N. (2007). *The brain that changes itself.* New York, NY: Penguin Books.

Dunn, W. (2001). The sensations of everyday life: Empirical, theoretical, and pragmatic considerations. *The Journal of Occupational Therapy, 55*(6), 608–620. doi:10.5014/ajot.55.6.608

Eberle, S. (2017). Playing on the right side of the brain: An interview with Allan N. Schore. *American Journal of Play, 9*(2), 105–142.

Ellison, C. R. (2012). Sexual choreography: "Am I enjoying this right now?" not "How am I doing?" In P. Kleinplatz (Ed.), *New directions in sex therapy* (2nd ed., pp. 141–160). New York, NY: Routledge.

The Enteric Nervous System. (n.d.). Retrieved from www.psyking.net/id36.htm

Feeney, J. A., & Noller, P. (2004). Attachment and sexuality in close relationships. In J. H. Harvey, A. Wenzel, & S. Sprecher (Eds.), *The handbook of sexuality in close relationships.* Mahwah, NJ: Lawrence Erlbaum Associates.

Feuerstein, G. (1992). *Sacred sexuality: The erotic spirit in the world's great religions.* New York, NY: Jeremy P. Tarcher.

Finkel, E. J., Hui, C. M., Carswell, K. L., & Larson, G. M. (2014). The suffocation of marriage: Climbing mount Maslow without enough oxygen. *Psychological Inquiry, 25,* 1–41. Retrieved from https://doi.org/10.1080/1047840X.2014.863723

Fosha, D. (2009). Emotion and recognition at work: Energy, vitality, truth, desire & the emergent phenomenology of transformational experience. In D. Fosha, D. J. Siegel, & M. Solomon (Eds.), *The healing power of emotion* (pp. 172–203). New York, NY: W. W. Norton.

Foucault, M. (1990). *The use of pleasure: The history of sexuality, Vol.2.* (R. Hurley, Trans.). NY: Vintage Books. (Original work published 1983).

Fredrickson, B. L., & Branigan, C. (2005). Positive emotions broaden the scope of attention and thought-action repertoires. *Cognition and Emotion, 19*(3), 313–332. doi:10.1080/02699930441000238

Freud, S. (1962). *Three essays on the theory of sexuality.* New York, NY: Basic Books. (Original work published in 1905.)

Fromm, E. (1941). *Man for himself: An inquiry into the psychology of ethics.* New York, NY: Holt, Rinehart & Winston.

Gallace, A., & Spence, C. (2010). The science of interpersonal touch: An overview. *Neuroscience & Biobehavioral Reviews, 34*(2), 246–259. doi:10.1016/j.neubiorev.2008.10.004

Geller, J. D. (2003). Self-disclosure in psychoanalytic-existential therapy. *Journal of Clinical Psychology, 59,* 541–554. doi:10.1002/jclp.10158

Geller, S. M. (2013). Therapeutic presence: An essential way of being. In M. Cooper, P. F. Schimd, M. O'hara, & A. C. Bohart (Eds.), *The handbook of person-centered psychotherapy and counselling* (2nd ed., pp. 209–222). Basingstoke, UK: Palgrave Macmillan.

Geller, S. M., & Greenberg, L. S. (2002). Therapeutic presence: Therapists' experience of presence in the psychotherapy encounter. *Person-Centered and Experiential Psychotherapies, 1*(1–2), 71–86. Retrieved from http://dx.doi.org/10.1080/14779757.2002.9688279

Giorgi, G., & Siccardi, M. (1996). Ultrasonographic observation of a female fetus' sexual behavior in utero. *American Journal of Obstetrics and Gynecology, 175*(3–1), 753.

Givens, D. B. (1983). *Love signals: How to attract a mate.* New York, NY: Crown.

Goldstein, P., Weissman-Fogel, I., & Shamay-Tsoory, S. G. (2017). The role of touch in regulating inter-partner physiological coupling during empathy for pain. *Scientific Reports, 7*(3252), 1–12.

Groneman, C. (2001). *Nymphomania: A history.* New York, NY: Norton Paperback.

Gulledge, A. K., Gulledge, M. H., & Stahmannn, R. F. (2003). Romantic physical affection types and relationship satisfaction. *American Journal of Family Therapy, 31*(4), 233–242. Retrieved from https://doi.org/10.1080/01926180390201936

Hartman, D., & Zimberoff, M. A. (2004). Corrective emotional experience in the therapeutic process. *Journal of Heart-Centered Therapies, 7*(2), 3–84.

Hecht, D. (2014). Cerebral lateralization of pro-and anti-social tendencies. *Experimental Neurobiology*, 23(1), 1–27. doi:10.5607/en.2014.23.1.1

Herbenick, D., Reece, M., Schick, V., Sanders, S. A., Dodge, B., & Fortenberry, J. D. (2010). Sexual behavior in the United States: Results from a national probability sample of men and women ages 14–94. *Journal of Sex Medicine, 7*, 255–265.

Hill, D. (2015). *Affect regulation theory: A clinical model*. New York, NY: W. W. Norton.

Hooghe, M. (2012). Is sexual well-being part of subjective well-being?: An empirical analysis of Belgian (Flemish) Survey data using an extended well-being scale. *Journal of Sex Research, 49*(2–3), 264–273.

Iannuzzo, G., Pandolfo, G., Bonadonna, A., Lorusso, S., Crucitti, M., Lanza, G., ... Bruno, A. (2014). The relationship between anger and sexual behavior: A review of theories and research. *Mediterranean Journal of Clinical Psychology, 2*(1).

Isen, A. M., Daubman, K. A., & Nowicki, G. P. (1987). Positive affect facilitates creative problem solving. *Journal of Personality and Social Psychology, 52*(6), 1122–1131. Retrieved from http://dx.doi.org/10.1037/0022-3514.52.6.1122

Jerome, E. M., & Liss, M. (2005). Relationships between sensory processing style, adult attachment, and coping. *Personality and Individual Differences, 38*(6), 1341–1352. doi:10.1016/j.paid.2004.08.016

Joannides, P. (2009). *Guide to getting it on* (6th ed.). Waldport, OR: Goofy Foot Press.

Johnson, S., & Zuccarini, D. (2010). Integrating sex and attachment in emotionally focused couple therapy. *Journal of Marital and Family Therapy, 36*(4), 431–445. doi:10.111 1/j.1752–0606.2009.00155

Johnstone, B., Bodling, A., Cohen, D., Christ, S. E., & Wegrzyn, A. (2012). Right parietal lobe-related "selflessness" as the neuropsychological basis of spiritual transcendence. *International Journal for the Psychology of Religion, 22*(4), 267–284. Retrieved from http://dx.doi.org/10.1080/10508619.2012.657524

Jones, M. (2018). What teenagers are learning from online porn. *New York Times Magazine*. Retrieved from www.nytimes.com/2018/02/07/magazine/teenagers-learning-online-porn-literacy-sex-education.html

Kleinplatz, P. J. (2012). Is that all there is? A new critique of the goals of sex therapy. In P. Kleinplatz (Ed.), *New directions in sex therapy* (2nd ed., pp. 101–118). New York, NY: Routledge.

Kleinplatz, P. J., Menard, A. D., Paquet, M. P., Paradis, N., Campbell, M., Zuccarino, D., & Mehak, L. (2009). The components of optimal sexuality: A portrait of great sex. *Canadian Journal of Human Sexuality, 18*(1–2), 1–13.

Kleinplatz, P. J., Paradis, N., Charest, M., Lawless, S., Neufeld, M., Neufeld, R., ... Rosen, L. (2017). From sexual desire discrepancies to desirable sex: Creating the optimal connection, *Journal of Sex and Marital Therapy*, 1–12. doi:10.1080/0092623x.2017.1405309

Komisaruk, B. R., Beyer-Flores, C., & Whipple, B. (2006). *The science of orgasm*. Baltimore, MD: John Hopkins University Press.

Konner, M. (2010). *The evolution of childhood: Relationships, emotion, mind*. Cambridge, MA: Harvard University Press.

Kuhl, J., Quinn, M., & Koole, S. L. (2015). Being Someone: The integrated self as a neuropsychological system. *Social and Personality Psychology Compass, 9*(3), 115–132.

Latner, J. (1973). *The Gestalt therapy book*. New York, NY: Julian Press.

Laumann, E. O., Gagnon, J. H., Michael, R. T., & Michaels, S. (1994). *The social organization of sexuality: Sexual practices in the United States*. Chicago, IL: University of Chicago.

LeBel, J. L., & Dube, L. (2001, June). *The impact of sensory knowledge and attentional focus on pleasure and on behavioral responses to hedonic stimuli*. Paper presented at the 13th annual American Psychological Society Convention, Toronto, Ontario, Canada.

Leknes, S., & Tracey, I. (2008). A common neurobiology for pain and pleasure. *Nature Reviews Neuroscience, 9*(4), 314–320. doi:10.1038/nrn2333

Lewis, T., Amini, F., & Lannon, R. (2000). *A general theory of love*. New York, NY: Random House.

Lopez, F. G., Gover, M. R., Leskela, J., Sauer, E. M., Schirmer, L., & Wyssmann, J. (1997). Attachment styles, shame, guilt, and collaborative problem-solving orientations. *Personal Relationships, 4*(2), 187–199. doi:10.1111/j.1475-6811.1997.tb00138.x

Maas, M. K., & Lefkowitz, E. S. (2015). Sexual esteem in emerging adulthood: Associations with sexual behavior, contraceptive use, and romantic relationships. *Journal of Sex Research, 52*(7), 795–806. doi:10.1080/00224499.2014.945112

Marks-Tarlow, T. (2014). The interpersonal neurobiology of clinical intuition. *Smith College Studies in Social Work, 84*(2–3), 219–236. Retrieved from https://doi.org/10.1080/00377317.2014.9 23712

Martinson, F. M. (1993). Childhood sexuality. In B. Wolman & J. Money (Eds.), *Handbook of human sexuality*. Northvale, NJ: Jason Aronson Inc.

Maslow, A. H. (1962). *Toward a psychology of being*. Princeton, NJ: Van Nostrand.

McCarthy, B., & McCarthy, E. (2003). *Rekindling desire: A step by step program to help low-sex and no-sex marriages*. New York, NY: Brunner-Routledge.

McGilchrist, I. (2009). *The master and his emissary: The divided brain and the making of the western world*. New Haven, CT: Yale University Press.

McGilchrist, I. (2015). Divine understanding and the divided brain. In J. Clausen & N. Levy (Eds.), *Handbook of neuroethics*. New York, NY, Dordrecht, Heidelberg: Springer.

Mikulincer, M., & Shaver, P. (2007). Relations between the attachment and caregiving systems. In M. Mikulincer & P. Shaver (Eds.), *Attachment in adulthood: Structure, dynamics and change* (pp. 347–362). New York, NY: Guilford Press.

Miller, A. (1990). *For your own good: Hidden cruelty in childrearing and the roots of violence* (H. Hannum & H. Hannum, Trans.). New York, NY: Farrar, Strauss, & Giroux. (Original work published 1983).

Miller, E. K., & Cohen, J. (2001). An integrative theory of prefrontal cortex function. *Annual Review of Neuroscience, 24*, 167–202. doi:10.1146/annurev.neuro.24.1.167

Mohandas, E. (2008). Neurobiology of spirituality. *Mens Sana Monographs, 6*(1), 63–80. doi:10.4103/0973-1229.33001

Mohney, G. (2017). Abstinence programs are ineffectual and stigmatizing, study finds. *Healthline*. Retrieved from www.healthline.com/health-news/abstinenceprograms-ineffectual -and-stigmatizing-study-finds#modal-close

Morin, J. (1995). *The erotic mind: Unlocking the inner sources of sexual passion and fulfillment*. New York, NY: HarperCollins.

Nasir, M., Xia, W., Xiao, B., Baucom, B., Narayanan, S. S., & Georgiou, P. G. (2015). Still Together?: The Role of Acoustic Features in Predicting Marital Outcome. In *Sixteenth Annual Conference of the International Speech Communication Association*.

Newberg, A. B. (2014). The neuroscientific study of spiritual practices. *Frontiers in Psychology, 5*(215). doi:10.3389/fpsyg.2014.00215

Novak, M. A., & Harlow, H. F. (1975). Social recovery of monkeys isolated for the first year of life: I. Rehabilitation and therapy. *Developmental Psychology, 11*(4), 453–465. Retrieved from http://dx.doi.org/10.1037/h0076661

Ornstein, P. (2016). *Girls and sex: Navigating the complicated new landscape*. New York, NY: Harper-Collins.

Pan, Y., Cheng, X., Zhang, Z., Li, X., & Hui, Y. (2017). Cooperation in lovers: An fNIRS-based hyperscanning study. *Human Brain Mapping, 38*(2), 831–841. doi:10.1002/hbm.23421

Panksepp, J. (1998). *Affective Neuroscience: The foundations of human and animal evolution*. New York, NY: Oxford University Press.

Panksepp, J. (2009). Brain emotional systems and qualities of mental life: From animal models of affect to implications for psychotherapeutics. In D. Fosha, D. J. Siegel, & M. Solomon (Eds.), *The healing power of emotion* (pp. 1–26). New York, NY: W. W. Norton.

Peciña, S., Smith, K. S., & Berridge, K. C. (2006). Hedonic hot spots in the brain. *The Neuroscientist, 12*(6), 500–511. doi:10.1177/1073858406293154

Perel, E. (2006). *Mating in captivity: Reconciling the erotic and the domestic*. New York, NY: Harper-Collins.

Perls, F. (1973). *The Gestalt approach & eye witness to therapy*. Palo Alto, CA: Science and Behavior Books.

Perls, F., Hefferline, R. F., & Goodman, P. (1951). *Gestalt therapy: Excitement and growth in the human personality*. New York, NY: Dell Publishing Co.

Perls, L. (1973). *Some aspects of Gestalt therapy*. Paper presented at the orthopyschiatric Association.

Perper, T. (1985). *Sex signals: The biology of love*. Philadelphia, PA: ISI Press.

Polster, E., & Polster, M. (1974). *Gestalt therapy integrated: Contours of theory & practice*. New York, NY: Vintage Books.

Porges, S. W. (2011). *The polyvagal theory: Neurophysiological foundations of emotions, attachment, communication, and self-regulation*. New York, NY: W. W. Norton.

Raising Children Network. (2017). Retrieved from http://raisingchildren.net.au/articles/brain_development_teenagers.html

Reich, W. (1961). *The function of the orgasm*. New York, NY: Farrar, Straus & Giroux.

Reich, W. (1980). *Character analysis* (3rd ed., V. Carfagno, Trans.). New York, NY: Farrar, Straus & Giroux.

Resnick, S. (1975). Gestalt therapy as a meditative practice. In J. O. Stevens (Ed.), *Gestalt Is*. Moab, UT: Real People Press.

Resnick, S. (1994). Sex and pleasure. In V. Bullough & B. Bullough (Eds.), *Human sexuality: An encyclopedia* (pp. 457–464). New York, NY: Garland.

Resnick, S. (1997). *The pleasure zone: Why we resist good feelings & how to let go and be happy*. Berkeley, CA: Conari.

Resnick, S. (2002). Sexual pleasure: The next frontier in the study of sexuality. *The SIECUS Report*, *30*(4), 6–11.

Resnick, S. (2004). Somatic-experiential sex therapy: A body-centered Gestalt approach to sexual concerns. *Gestalt Review, 8*(1), 40–64.

Resnick, S. (2012). *The heart of desire: Keys to the pleasures of love*. Hoboken, NJ: Wiley.

Resnick, S., Warmoth, A., & Selin, I. A. (2001). The humanistic psychology and positive psychology connection: Implications for psychotherapy. *Journal of Humanistic Psychology, 41*(1), 73–101. Retrieved from http://dx.doi.org/10.1177/0022167801411006

Richardson, J., & Schuster, M. A. (2004). *Everything you never wanted your kids to know about sex (but were afraid they'd ask): The secrets to surviving your child's sexual development*. New York, NY: Harmony Books.

Rosenthal, D., Moore, S., & Flynn, I. (1991). Adolescent self-efficacy, self-esteem and sexual risk-taking. *Journal of Community & Applied Social Psychology, 1*(2), 77–88. Retrieved from http://dx.doi.org/10.1002/casp.2450010203

Ryan, R. M., & Deci, E. L. (2001). On happiness and human potentials: A review of research on hedonic and eudaimonic well-being. *Annual Review of Psychology, 52*, 141–166. doi:10.1146/annurev.psych.52.1.141

Seligman, M. E. P., & Csikszentmihalyi, M. (2000). Positive psychology: An introduction. *American Psychologist, 55*, 5–14.

Schermer-Sellers, T. (2017). *Sex, god, & the conservative church: Erasing shame from sexual intimacy*. New York, NY: Routledge.

Schick, C. (2004). Interview with Charlotte Selver. *USA Body Psychotherapy Journal, 3*(1).

Schnarch, D. (1991). *Constructing the sexual crucible*. New York, NY: W. W. Norton.

Schore, A. N. (1994). *Affect regulation and the origin of the self: The neurobiology of emotional development*. Hillsdale, NJ: Eribaum.

Schore, A. N. (2003). *Affect regulation and the repair of the self: The neurobiology of emotional development*. Hillsdale, NJ: Eribaum.

Schore, A. N. (2012). *The science of the art of psychotherapy*. New York, NY: W. W. Norton.

Schore, A. N. (2014). The right brain is dominant in psychotherapy. *Psychotherapy, 51*(3), 388–397. Retrieved from http://dx.doi.org/10.1037/a0037083

Schore, J. R., & Schore, A. N. (2014). Regulation theory and affect regulation psychotherapy: A clinical primer. *Smith College Studies in Social Work, 84*(2–3), 178–195. Retrieved from https://doi.org/10.1080/00377317.2014.923719

Sherfey, M. J. (1966). *The nature & evolution of female sexuality*. NY: Random House.

Siegel, D. J. (2009). Mindful awareness, mindsight, and neural integration. *The Humanistic Psychologist, 37*(2), 137–158. doi:10.1080/08873260902892220

Singer, M. (2002). Childhood sexuality: An interpersonal-intrapsychic integration. *Contemporary Sexuality*, November, 36, 11.

Sprecher, S., & Cate, R. M. (2004). Sexual satisfaction and sexual expression as predictors of relationship satisfaction and stability. In J. H. Harvey, A. Wenzel, & S. Sprecher (Eds.), *The handbook of sexuality in close relationships* (pp. 235–256). London, UK: Psychology Press.

Stelmack, R. M., & Campbell, K. B. (1974). Extraversion and auditory sensitivity to high and low frequency. *Perceptual and Motor Skills, 38*(3. 1), 875–879. Retrieved from http://dx.doi.org/10.2466/pms.1974.38.3.875

Stolorow, R. D. (2002). Impasse, affectivity, and intersubjective systems. *Psychoanalytic Review, 89*(3), 329–337. Retrieved from https://doi.org/10.1521/prev.89.3.329.22075

Stone, A. (2014). Smell turns up in unexpected places. *The New York Times*. Retrieved from www.nytimes.com/2014/10/14/science/smell-turns-up-in-unexpected-places.html

Thouin-Savard, M. (In press). Erotic mindfulness: A core educational and therapeutic strategy in somatic sexology practices. *International Journal of Transpersonal Studies*.

Tracy, J. L., Shaver, P. R., Albino, A. W., & Cooper, M. L. (2003). Attachment styles and adolescent sexuality. In P. Florsheim (Ed.), *Adolescent romance and sexual behavior: Theory, research, and practical implications* (pp. 137–159). Mahwah, NJ: Erlbaum.

Trevarthen, C. (1993). The self born in intersubjectivity: The psychology of an infant communicating. In U. Neisser (Ed.), *The perceived self: Ecological and interpersonal sources of self-knowledge.* New York, NY: Cambridge University Press.

Tronick, E. Z. (1989). Emotions and emotional communication in infants. *American Psychologist, 44*(2), 112–119.

Tronick, E. Z., Als, H., Adamson, L., Wise, S., & Brazelton, T. B. (1978). The infant's response to entrapment between contradictory messages in face-to-face interaction. *American Academy of Child & Adolescent Psychiatry, 17*(1), 1–13. Retrieved from https://doi.org/10.1016/S0002-7138(09)62273-1

Vasilenko, S. A., Kugler, K. C., & Lanza, S. T. (2015). Latent classes of adolescent sexual and romantic relationship experiences: Implications for adult sexual health and relationship outcomes. *Journal of Sex Research, 53*(7), 742–753. Retrieved from https://doi.org/10.1080/00224499.2015.1065952

Vaughn, B. E., & Bost, K. K. (1999). Attachment and temperament: Redundant, independent, or interacting influences on interpersonal adaptation and personality development? In J. Cassidy & P. R. Shaver (Eds.), *Handbook of attachment: Theory, research, and clinical applications* (pp. 198–225). New York, NY: Guilford Press.

Vohs, K. D., Catanese, K. R., & Baumeister, R. F., (2004). Sex in "his" vs. "her" relationships. In J. H. Harvey, A. Wenzel, & S. Sprecher (Eds.), *The handbook of sexuality in close relationships.* Mahwah, NJ: Lawrence Erlbaum Associates (pp. 461–467).

Weber, L. V., Al-Refae, K., Wolk, G., Bonatz, G., Altmüller, J., Becker, C., . . . Hatt, H. (2016). Expression and functionality of TRPV1 in breast cancer cells. *Breast Cancer: Targets and Therapy, 8*, 243. doi:10.2147/BCTT.S121610

Wheeler, G. (1997). The tasks of intimacy: Reflections of a Gestalt approach to working with couples. In G. Wheeler & S. Backman (Eds.), *On intimate ground.* San Francisco, CA: Jossey-Bass.

Wheeler, G., & Axelsson, L. (2015). *Gestalt therapy.* Washington, DC: American Psychological Association.

Witkin, M. H. (1993). Sex therapy: A holistic approach. In B. Wolman & J. Money (Eds.), *Handbook of human sexuality.* Northvale, NJ: Jason Aronson Inc.

Yontef, G. (2009). The relational attitude in Gestalt theory and practice. In L. Jacobs & R. Hycner (Eds.), *Relational approaches in Gestalt therapy.* Santa Cruz, CA: Gestalt Press.

Zinker, J. (1977). *Creative process in Gestalt therapy.* New York, NY: Vintage Books.

Index